Votes, Vetoes, and the Political Economy of International Trade Agreements

Votes, Vetoes, and the Political Economy of International Trade Agreements

Edward D. Mansfield and Helen V. Milner

PRINCETON UNIVERSITY PRESS

PRINCETON AND OXFORD

Published by Princeton University Press, 41 William Street, Princeton, New Jersey 08540
In the United Kingdom: Princeton University Press, 6 Oxford Street, Woodstock, Oxfordshire
OX20 1TW

press.princeton.edu

Library of Congress Cataloging-in-Publication Data

Mansfield, Edward D., 1962–
    Votes, vetoes, and the political economy of international trade agreements / Edward D.
Mansfield and Helen V. Milner.
        p. cm.
    Includes bibliographical references and index.
    ISBN 978-0-691-13529-8 (hardcover : alk. paper)—ISBN 978-0-691-13530-4 (pbk. : alk. paper)
1. Commercial treaties. 2. International trade. I. Milner, Helen V., 1958– II. Title.
    HF1721.M36 2012
    382'.9—dc23

                                                                        2011040447

British Library Cataloging-in-Publication Data is available

This book has been composed in Minion Pro

Printed on acid-free paper. ∞

Printed in the United States of America

10 9 8 7 6 5 4 3 2 1

Contents

List of Figures and Tables

Preface and Acknowledgments

SINCE THE CONCLUSION OF WORLD WAR II, there has been a proliferation of international trade agreements. Social scientists have expressed substantial interest in the sources of this development. Many economists have argued that the roots of these agreements lie in the promise they hold for improving the welfare of signatories. Other researchers posit that trade agreements are a response to global political conditions. The role of domestic politics, however, has received short shrift in the literature on this topic. In this book, we argue that domestic politics provides a crucial impetus to the decision by governments to enter trade pacts. Of particular importance in this regard are the regime type and the number of "veto players" that exist in each country. Democracies are especially likely to enter trade agreements, and such agreements become increasingly unlikely as the number of "veto players" within prospective members increases, for reasons that we explain in the coming pages.

This book has been a long time in the making. In the 1990s, we had been working separately on the domestic sources of international cooperation (Milner 1997; Milner and Rosendorff 1996 and 1997) and the political economy of regionalism and preferential trade agreements (PTAs) (Mansfield 1993 and 1998). We joined forces in an effort to analyze how domestic politics affects cooperation on international trade. In the many years spent working on this topic, we have accumulated a large number of debts, but we are particularly grateful to two individuals. Some of our initial work on the political economy of trade was conducted with B. Peter Rosendorff (Mansfield, Milner, and Rosendorff 2000 and 2002). Later we wrote a set of papers covering some of the issues addressed in this book with Jon Pevehouse (Mansfield, Milner, and Pevehouse 2007 and 2008). Both Peter and Jon are wonderful collaborators, enormously talented researchers, and good friends. We are grateful for their many contributions to this book.

We also owe a large debt of gratitude to a remarkable group of individuals who helped us conduct the research included in this study. Raymond Hicks worked tirelessly to compile the database of PTA ratification dates that we use. He, David Francis, and Rumi Morishima also helped us to conduct much of the data analysis in this book. More recently, Torben Behmer and Sarah Salwen helped us to edit the book manuscript, and Jason McMann provided research assistance. We thank all of them profusely.

We are also indebted to a large number of scholars who commented on all or parts of this book. In September 2009, we held a book conference at which Joanne Gowa, Robert Keohane, Lisa Martin, Ronald Rogowski, Peter Rosendorff, Kenneth Scheve, Jack Snyder, and Michael Tomz gave us many excellent comments and suggestions. Indeed, they furnished us with so many that it took over a year to revise the manuscript and even then we were able to address only a fraction of the terrific ideas that surfaced during that event. We are deeply thankful that this highly distinguished group was willing to furnish their time and expertise. This book is surely much improved because of their insights.

Further, we have benefited from many other individuals who commented on all or part of the book over the past decade. We thank many of the fellows at Princeton University's Niehaus Center for Globalization and Governance who endured reading parts of the book: Terry Chapman, Gökçe Göktepe, Susan Hyde, Stephen Kaplan, Basak Kus, Adam Luedtke, Heather McKibben, Andreea Mihalache, Krzysztof Pelc, Christina Schneider, and T. Camber Warren. In addition, Leonardo Baccini, David Baldwin, Christina Davis, Henrik Horn, Mareike Kleine, Marc Meredith, Rumi Morishima, Ben Shepard, Dustin Tingley, Johannes Urpelainen, and Kate Weiss offered us many helpful suggestions. We also received useful feedback at a conference held by the World Trade Organization (WTO) in November 2010, at a 2009 conference held at the Stanford Law School, and at a seminar at the University of California, San Diego in 2009.

This study could not have been completed without the support of the University of Pennsylvania and Princeton University. We are especially grateful to University of Pennsylvania's Christopher H. Browne Center for International Politics and to Princeton's Niehaus Center for financial and logistical assistance. Pat Trinity at the Niehaus Center deserves special thanks for her strong administrative support.

Princeton University Press editor Chuck Myers offered us encouragement and thoughtful advice over the many years it has taken to complete this book. We thank him for his editorial expertise, patience, and good humor.

Portions of the book have appeared elsewhere and we are grateful to the publishers of these earlier articles for allowing us to use them here. In particular, a portion of chapter 1 appeared in "The New Wave of Regionalism," *International Organization* (53) 3 (Summer 1999), 589–627. A portion of chapter 4 appeared in "Regime Type, Veto Points, and Preferential Trading Arrangements," *Stanford Journal of International Law*, (46) 2 (June 2010), 219–42.

Our greatest debts are to our families. Mansfield thanks Charlotte Mansfield, Katherine Mansfield, and Andréa Castro. They have been a source of love, support, and perspective. Equally, they have been remarkably gracious when work on this book has crowded out other tasks. I am especially grateful to Charlotte for her persistent queries about the book's progress and her unflagging encouragement when I inevitably responded that it was going slower than planned.

Milner thanks David Baldwin, without whom this book could not have been written. He provided the space and intellectual nourishment to allow me to finish this many-year project. I owe him a deep debt of thanks. Having been chair of the department when most of this was written meant that I had little time for anything else, and David made sure that everything was taken care of so I could find the time.

Commonly Used Abbreviations

AEC	African Economic Community
ANC	African National Congress
ASEAN	Association of Southeast Asian Nations
BITs	Bilateral Investment Treaties
CACM	Central American Common Market
CAEU	Council of Arab Economic Unity
CET	Common External Tariff
CIS	Commonwealth of Independent States
CM	Common Market
CMEA	Council of Mutual Economic Assistance
COMESA	Common Market for Eastern and Southern Africa
COW	Correlates of War
CU	Customs Union
DSM	Dispute Settlement Mechanism
EAC	East African Community
EC	European Community
ECOWAS	Economic Community of West African States
ECSC	European Coal and Steel Community
EEC	European Economic Community
EFTA	European Free Trade Agreement
EIA	Economic Integration Agreement
EU	European Union
FTA	Free Trade Area
GAFTA	Greater Arab Free Trade Area
GATT	General Agreement on Tariffs and Trade
ILFTA	Indo-Lanka Free Trade Agreement
IMF	International Monetary Fund
LAIA	Latin American Integration Association
Mercosur	Common Market of the Southern Cone
MFN	Most-Favored Nation
MTN	Multilateral Trade Negotiation
NAFTA	North American Free Trade Agreement
OECD	Organisation for Economic Cooperation and Development
PA	Preferential Agreement
PTA	Preferential Trade Agreement
RTA	Regional Trade Agreement
SACU	Southern African Customs Union

SADC   South African Development Community
SAPTA   South Asian Preferential Trade Agreement
SPARTECA   South Pacific Regional Trade and Economic Cooperation
                  Agreement
WTO   World Trade Organization

CHAPTER 1

Introduction

INTERNATIONAL TRADE AGREEMENTS have played an important and growing role in the global political economy. Among the most important agreements of this sort are preferential trade agreements (PTAs), a set of institutions that are designed to foster economic integration among member-states by improving and stabilizing each member's access to other participants' markets. All PTAs require members to mutually adjust their trade policies, granting each member preferential access to the others' markets. As such, they are one of the most prominent forms of international cooperation. This book addresses why and when countries join these trade agreements and how they design them.

PTAs have proliferated rapidly. Scores of these institutions have formed over the past half-century and almost every country currently participates in at least one. By 2010, according to the World Trade Organization (WTO), roughly four hundred PTAs had been signed, covering more than half of total world trade. The European Union (EU) is the most widely studied PTA, but Europe is not the only region marked by such agreements. The North American Free Trade Agreement (NAFTA) has helped to promote economic integration among the United States, Canada, and Mexico. In South America, Mercosur—an agreement involving Argentina, Brazil, Paraguay, and Uruguay, with four associate members and Venezuela in the process of acceding—plays an important role in integrating the economies of the Southern Cone. African nations have also formed various PTAs, and the South African Development Community (SADC) is currently one of the most important trade accords. It involves fifteen African nations, including South Africa, the continent's economic powerhouse. Asia is the last frontier for PTAs. Since 2000, many Asian countries have formed and joined trade agreements, though countries in this region have been much slower to sign PTAs. In addition, PTAs regulate many types of trade and many aspects of international economic relations. They often affect trade in manufactures, agriculture, and services, as well as foreign investment, labor rights, and environmental practices. Some PTAs regulate more sectors than the WTO (Horn et al. 2010). Indeed, various analysts speculate that if the Doha Round of global trade negotiations convened by the WTO fails, PTAs could become the dominant method of regulating international economic relations (e.g., Baldwin 2011). This book focuses on why and when governments elect to enter trade agreements.

Gaining a fuller understanding of international trade agreements is important because trade is crucial to the global economy and contributes heavily to many national economies. For the largest 110 countries in the world, overseas trade (i.e., the sum of exports and imports) amounted to 65 percent of total income in 1975, a figure that grew to almost 90 percent in 2005 (World Bank 2011). In 2008, furthermore, world exports amounted to roughly $20 trillion, accounting for close to a third of global output. International trade has generally grown faster than world output since the 1950s as well (World Trade Organization 2008). PTAs cover well over half of all world trade, a trend that shows no signs of abating. Trade flows have also been tightly linked to global capital flows, as exporters and multinationals develop global production ties linked to their trade. Trade has been an important engine of the world economy, and institutions like PTAs that affect both the volume and direction of trade flows merit attention.

Despite the importance of PTAs to the international trading system, we lack an adequate understanding of why and when governments choose to enter these institutions. Some countries have rushed to join many of these arrangements, whereas others have joined very few of them. Moreover, states have entered them at different points in time. The purpose of this book is to improve our understanding of the political economy of PTA formation. In so doing, this study will also contribute to the larger literature on the sources of international cooperation. We focus on how domestic political factors influence international coordination. While also examining the role of international forces, we argue that certain domestic political factors exert a strong impact on trade cooperation, which previous studies of such agreements have overlooked. We focus attention on a country's regime type and the constraints on its chief executive as central to the demand for and design of PTAs.

Trade and international trade agreements often stimulate domestic interest and opposition. In part this is because trade is a large and critically important element of many countries' economies. As Ronald Rogowski (1989) has pointed out, changes in trade flows can have a profound effect on domestic political coalitions. Others have noted that heightened exposure to international trade can have important effects on individuals' political beliefs, as well as on the political institutions they support (Cameron 1978; Katzenstein 1978; Rodrik 1998; Scheve and Slaughter 2001).

Trade agreements also have political implications. Autocratic governments often eschew trade agreements since they constrain the government's ability to dole out rents (from protectionist trade policies) and because of the domestic fissures they can open (Bueno de Mesquita et al. 2003). Democracies, as we explain further in this book, have a far greater incentive to conclude trade agreements. The Dominican Republic, for example, negotiated no PTAs before it became democratic in 1978; since then it has signed about ten trade agreements. South Korea joined one PTA before it became democratic around 1988; it has subsequently entered more than seven agreements. Taiwan signed no agreements before becoming democratic in 1992, and then signed six of them.

Trade agreements are often sources of political contestation; in some cases they have prompted significant domestic turmoil. In 2003, for instance, South Korea experienced daily protests against its proposed free trade agreement (FTA) with Chile. A few years later, large and sustained protests in South Korea delayed its proposed trade agreement with the United States (Park 2009, 457). In Swaziland, the government was shaken by large protests during 2011 when its revenues from the Southern African Customs Union (SACU) were cut. These revenues accounted for over 60 percent of its government budget (Bearak 2011; Cloete 2011). The domestic benefits of trade agreements may also attract political support. President Clinton's support for NAFTA and President Obama's support for the Korean, Panamanian, and Colombian trade agreements are cases where the domestic political and economic advantages of such accords motivated leaders to press for ratification.

In democracies, struggles over ratification are often epic battles between political parties and their sympathizers. Such a fight erupted in Canada over NAFTA, pitting the Progressive Conservative Party against the Liberals and Left Democrats. In Mexico, the major political parties—the Partido Revolucionario Institucional (PRI), Partido Acción Nacional (PAN), and Partido de la Revolución Democrática (PRD)—argued over whether to enter NAFTA. Costa Rica experienced a pitched battle over the United States-Dominican Republic-Central America Free Trade Agreement (CAFTA) between its supporters in the Partido Liberación Nacional (PLN) and its opponents in the Partido Acción Ciudadana (PAC) (Hocking and McGuire 1999; ACAN-EFE 2006; de la Cruz 2006). In the United States, votes on trade agreements have been among the most hotly contested and narrowly decided. The ratification of CAFTA in 2005 was decided by a single vote in the House of Representatives. And as one commentator summed up the NAFTA experience in the United States, Canada, and Mexico, "what perhaps stands out in all three countries is how hard-fought the free trade [agreement] vote was, how entrenched the industrial and labor opposition was, and how great a political leadership was necessary [to conclude the agreements]" (Doran 1999, xii). As these examples illustrate and as we explain in more detail throughout this book, domestic politics and international trade agreements are often tightly linked.

PTAs have not been universally lauded and their economic impacts have been a subject of fierce debate. Some observers fear that these arrangements have adverse economic consequences and have eroded the multilateral system that has guided international economic relations during the post–World War II era. Others argue that such institutions are stepping-stones to greater multilateral openness and stability. This debate has stimulated a large body of literature on the economic and political implications of PTAs.[1] Surprisingly little research, however, has analyzed the factors giving rise to these agreements.

---

[1] See Freund and Ornelas (2010) for a recent overview of this debate.

Much of the scholarship on PTAs, especially the vast majority conducted by economists, does not adequately explain the origins of preferential agreements. These agreements discriminate against imports from third parties, while economic theory emphasizes that free trade is generally the optimal strategy for each country and that an open, nondiscriminatory multilateral trading system is optimal as well. PTAs contrast with the multilateral trade regime established after World War II—undergirded by the General Agreement on Tariffs and Trade (GATT) and more recently by the WTO—which has promoted open overseas commerce.[2] In the view of many observers, the stability of this regime has reduced the incentives for states to form trade agreements. As such, economic research has furnished few clear answers about why PTAs now abound. In contrast, we emphasize the *political* costs and benefits of PTAs and show how politics has driven their proliferation. Governments may decide to conclude trade agreements in part because they provide domestic political benefits. Leaders trade off the constraining aspect of trade agreements in order to improve their domestic political fortunes.[3]

To explain why leaders would opt to sign a trade accord, which by definition circumscribes their policy-making ability, we focus on the political benefits that leaders can derive from these agreements. Heads of government aim to remain in power and favor policies that help them do so. The calculations of chief executives also involve the domestic political costs of such agreements, which are not limited to the constraints placed on foreign economic policy. Rational leaders calculate both the associated costs and benefits before choosing a policy, as well as the relative merits of alternative policies. Our central hypotheses are that democratic countries are more likely to enter PTAs than nondemocratic regimes and that as the number of groups within a country that can block policy change—so-called "veto players"—rises, the likelihood of that state entering a PTA is reduced.[4] More generally, we argue that domestic politics affects both why and when states have cooperated to form PTAs. We theorize about these two claims in more detail in the next chapter. We also extend the logic of these arguments to develop a number of auxiliary hypotheses about the nature of PTAs that countries sign and the impact of other domestic political factors.

---

[2] There is a debate on this point. Rose (2004) argues GATT/WTO has had no impact on trade; Gowa and Kim (2005) argue it has increased trade for the developed countries in the agreement; and Goldstein et al. (2007) claim it increased trade for members if they had institutional standing.

[3] We use the terms government, leader, head of government, and chief executive interchangeably. We assume that governments sign trade agreements, not countries per se.

[4] Veto players are those individuals or groups that occupy an institutional position such that they can block any policy change from the status quo. In a simple game, a veto player is one that belongs to all winning coalitions. Veto players are strategic in our setting; that is why they are agents, not veto points (Tsebelis 2002). This concept is addressed at greater length in chapter 2.

In the remainder of this chapter, we begin by defining PTAs, noting the different types and their economic and political effects, and discussing their importance. Afterward we describe some patterns in PTA formation over time and across various geographical regions. Then we summarize our argument about the domestic sources of PTAs. Next we place our study in the context of the larger economic questions it concerns and the theoretical debates on which it touches, and conclude by describing our plan for the rest of the book.

What Are PTAs and Why Are They Important?

PTAs are not only prolific, they are also important. PTAs are international agreements that aim to promote economic integration among member-states by improving and stabilizing the access that each member has to the other participants' markets. All of these arrangements require members to mutually adjust their trade policies, granting each member preferential access to the others' markets. PTAs can be bilateral or multilateral, but they differ in key respects from the WTO. In the current multilateral system, any market access agreements negotiated by two or more members must be extended to all members of the WTO; this most-favored nation status makes trade nondiscriminatory. Hence, whereas the centerpiece of the multilateral trade regime is the most-favored nation (MFN) treatment accorded to all participants, PTAs are discriminatory since their benefits only accrue to member-states. On the other hand, PTAs may cover many more economic sectors and may regulate many more economic policies than the WTO.

There are five different types of PTAs (Pomfret 1988; Anderson and Blackhurst 1993; Bhagwati 1993; de Melo and Panagariya 1993a; Bhagwati and Panagariya 1996a):

- First, what we refer to as a preferential agreement (PA) grants each participant preferential access to particular segments of the other members' markets. Trade barriers on certain products are lowered by each member and these concessions are not extended to third parties. The initial Association of Southeast Asian Nations (ASEAN) agreement involving Indonesia, Malaysia, Philippines, Singapore, and Thailand in 1977 was such an accord. It was upgraded to an FTA in 1992.
- Second, a free trade area (FTA) is marked by the reduction or elimination of trade barriers on most (if not all) products within the arrangement. Among the most prominent FTAs are NAFTA and both ASEAN (since 1992) and the SADC (since 2000).
- Third, customs unions (CUs) are arrangements in which members eliminate trade barriers on other participants' goods and impose a common external tariff (CET) on imports from third parties.
- Fourth, a common market (CM) is a CU that is augmented by similar product regulations and the free flow of factors of production among members.

- Fifth, an economic union is a common market whereby members also coordinate fiscal and monetary policies.

As an example, Western European countries have participated in each of the three latter types of PTAs over the past half-century. In 1957, the Treaty of Rome bound the six original members of the European Coal and Steel Community (ECSC) into a customs union. Since then, there has been a progressive broadening of the membership and the issue areas that it covers. After 1985, the EEC became a common market with the conclusion of the Single European Act. The Maastricht Treaty of 1992 led to its evolution from a common market to the EU, an economic union covering many issue areas in addition to trade and including seventeen members in a monetary union.

Different types of PTAs are designed to achieve varying degrees of integration, with PAs being the least integrative and economic unions being the most integrative. Initially, we will treat all trade arrangements as a single group since the argument we advance in this book is focused primarily on why states join a PTA rather than on the particular type that they enter. Equally, most of the extant empirical research on PTAs treats them as a group. Afterward, we will briefly address why states choose to enter a particular type of arrangement, an important issue that has received little empirical attention to date. We also analyze aspects of the design of PTAs. Using our theory, we examine whether the choice between PTAs that include formal mechanisms to adjudicate disputes and help enforce agreements and those that do not is affected by domestic political factors. Increasingly, such dispute settlement mechanisms (DSMs) have been embedded in these agreements, and we seek to explore this important aspect of PTA design.[5]

Gaining a fuller understanding of the conditions under which governments join PTAs is likely to contribute to the study of international cooperation, a central topic in the field of international relations. All PTAs involve cooperation by the contracting parties. International cooperation is marked by mutual policy adjustment among nation-states (Keohane 1984, 51–52). Policy adjustment of this sort is intended to achieve a particular set of goals that will benefit the associated countries, although these benefits need not actually be realized or distributed in any particular way for state actions to constitute cooperation (Milner 1997a, 7–8). PTAs meet this definition since they involve reciprocal trade barrier reductions among the contracting parties that are intended to promote foreign commerce and economic integration within the arrangement.

---

[5] Recent research has focused on other important aspects of PTAs (Bagwell and Mavroidis 2011). Horn et al. (2010), for instance, examine the number and depth of regulatory domains covered in PTAs but not in the WTO. Prusa and Teh (2011) examine escape clause measures (e.g., antidumping, countervailing duties, and safeguards) in PTAs and how they differ from one another and from the WTO.

Economic Effects of PTAs

Social scientists have expressed a lively interest in PTAs for over a century, largely due to a belief that these agreements influence important aspects of international relations. The bulk of research conducted on the effects of PTAs has focused on their economic welfare implications. PTAs have a two-sided quality, liberalizing commerce among members, while discriminating against third parties. As we noted earlier, this quality is what distinguishes PTAs from the multilateral trading system and the WTO, which is based on the principle of reciprocity embodied in the MFN status of member-states. Since such arrangements rarely eliminate external trade barriers, economists consider them inferior to those that liberalize trade worldwide. Just how inferior PTAs are hinges largely on whether they are trade creating or trade diverting: that is, on whether trade barrier reductions within an arrangement will shift the production of traded goods from less efficient producers outside the grouping to more efficient producers within it, or whether such reductions will shift the production of such goods from more efficient suppliers outside the arrangement to less efficient suppliers within it (Viner 1950).

Over the past few decades, economists have tried to determine whether PTAs are trade creating or trade diverting. There is consensus that the preferential arrangements forged during the nineteenth century tended to be trade creating and that those established between World War I and II tended to be trade diverting. However, there is a striking lack of consensus on this score about the PTAs developed since World War II. As an important empirical study on this topic concluded, PTAs "can, depending on the circumstances, be associated with either more or less general liberalization" (Frankel and Wei 1998, 216). Recent research has not made the case any clearer. Some studies, such as John Romalis's (2007) analysis of NAFTA and Won Chang and Alan Winters's (2002) assessment of Mercosur, find evidence of trade diversion. Other studies, however, find strong evidence that contemporary PTAs are marked by trade creation (Baier and Bergstrand 2004; Magee 2008; Freund 2011). Furthermore, in the most recent review of the empirical research on PTAs, Caroline Freund and Emanuel Ornelas (2010, 160) conclude that "trade creation, not trade diversion, is the norm."

Theoretical work on this topic has also failed to arrive at a consensus about whether PTAs promote or undermine welfare. Gene Grossman and Elhanan Helpman (1995, 687), for instance, argue that since a trade agreement requires the assent of various governments, it will most likely occur when "the agreement affords enhanced protection rather than reduced protection to most sectors." In the same vein, Pravin Krishna (1998) finds that trade-diverting PTAs are easier to form from a domestic political standpoint than trade-creating arrangements. For both Grossman and Helpman (1995) and Krishna (1998), the relative ease of forming preferential arrangements that degrade national welfare stems from the role played by interest groups. In contrast, other studies conclude that political leaders will only sign such agreements if doing so generates greater domestic political benefits than costs. Ornelas (2005), for example, shows that because PTAs destroy rents for key interest groups, rational politicians will only sign PTAs that generate large enough welfare gains for society as a whole to compensate for the reduced contributions that these groups will provide to the government as a result of the decrease in rents. Martin Richardson (1994) and Kyle Bagwell and Robert Staiger (2001) also observe that FTAs tend to weaken protectionist pressures against nonmembers and thus may be welfare enhancing. Economic theory, then, does not provide clear expectations about the welfare consequences of PTAs.[6]

Taken as a group, economic studies have reinforced Jacob Viner's (1950) conclusion that the welfare implications of trade agreements are ambiguous (Gunter 1989, 16–20; Baldwin and Venables 1995, 1605–13). In addition, recent research suggests that the preference margins gained by most countries in these agreements have been very small, especially for members of the GATT/WTO. That is, the difference between the trade barriers that PTA members offer to their fellow participants relative to nonmembers tends to be quite modest (World Trade Organization 2011). In light of these findings, it is difficult to sustain the argument that states join PTAs for economic reasons alone. Later we will revisit these mixed economic effects as they relate to the domestic political benefits and costs of PTAs.

Political and Security Effects of PTAs

In addition to their economic impact, PTAs may affect political-military relations among countries. Over a century ago, for example, Wilfred Pareto argued that "customs unions and other systems of closer commercial relations [could serve] as means to the improvement of political relations and the maintenance of peace" (quoted in Machlup 1977, 143). At the conclusion of World War I,

---

[6] In addition to creating or diverting trade, PTAs can affect the welfare of states by influencing their terms of trade and their capacity to realize economies of scale. Forming a PTA typically improves members' terms of trade vis-á-vis the rest of the world, since the arrangement almost always wields more market power than any constituent country. At the same time, however, attempts by a PTA to exploit its market power may backfire if other such arrangements exist, since the blocs may become enmeshed in a trade war that harms everyone (Krugman 1991, 16). A trade agreement can also influence the welfare of members by allowing firms located in member-states to realize economies of scale due to their preferential access to a larger market (Cooper and Massell 1965a and 1965b; Johnson 1965; Bhagwati 1968). This motivation contributed to the spate of PTAs established by less developed countries throughout the 1960s, although few such arrangements were successful from an economic standpoint. More recent studies addressing the welfare effects of PTAs have examined whether the proliferation of these arrangements will accelerate or inhibit multilateral trade liberalization, an issue that Bhagwati (1993 and 2008) refers to as "the dynamic time-path question" and that Baldwin (2008) refers to as part of "big think regionalism."

John Maynard Keynes (1919, 249) echoed this view, speculating that "[a] Free Trade Union, comprising the whole of Central, Eastern, and South-Eastern Europe, Siberia, Turkey, and (I should hope) the United Kingdom, Egypt and India, might do as much for the peace and prosperity of the world as the League of Nations itself." Since World War II, scholars have continued to advance the argument that PTAs dampen hostilities between participants, and policy makers have established various preferential groupings in an effort to stimulate peace as well as prosperity (Nye 1971; Fernández and Portes 1998; Schiff and Winters 1998).

A number of empirical studies have concluded that PTAs do in fact inhibit political-military hostilities (Nye 1971; Mansfield et al. 1999; Mansfield and Pevehouse 2000; Bearce 2003). Despite the ambiguous welfare implications of PTAs, most states enter them expecting to derive at least some economic benefits. Sometimes these expected benefits are realized; sometimes they are not. Regardless, conflict between member-states can scuttle these anticipated benefits by damaging economic relations between participants and the arrangement itself. States may avoid conflict then if they fear its effects on their economic gains from greater openness. PTAs also inhibit antagonism by establishing a forum for bargaining and negotiation among members, thereby facilitating the resolution of interstate tensions prior to the outbreak of open hostilities (Nye 1971, 109). Furthermore, trade agreements facilitate the construction of focal points that forestall conflicts by shaping states' expectations about what constitutes acceptable behavior and by identifying deviations from such behavior (Garrett and Weingast 1993).

Finally, recent research also suggests that PTAs can be useful in fostering cooperation in other issue areas. Nuno Limão (2005), for example, demonstrates that trade agreements can be used to improve environmental policy coordination. Emilie Hafner-Burton (2009) concludes that PTAs often promote human rights enforcement. And Tim Büthe and Helen Milner (2008) and Badi Baltagi et al. (2008) show that PTAs can induce greater foreign investment in developing and transition countries, perhaps accelerating their economic development. Such arrangements, then, affect a variety of outcomes in world politics.

International relations would be altered if these agreements did not exist. Trade and investment among nations might be depressed and flow in different directions; patterns of conflict might change; and policy covering areas like human rights, intellectual property, and the environment might look very different in the absence of trade agreements. Trade agreements are important components of the global political economy and they have been for some time.

PTAs in Historical Perspective

We focus on explaining PTA formation since World War II. The vast bulk of contemporary research on PTAs centers on this time period and we lack the data necessary to systematically address the determinants of trade agreements in earlier eras. However, it is important to recognize that PTAs are not just recent phenomena. Countries have formed them at various points over the past two centuries (Mansfield and Milner 1999). To place the post–World War II proliferation of these arrangements into historical perspective, we now turn to a brief description of these episodes.

The initial phase occurred during the second half of the nineteenth century and was largely a European phenomenon (Pollard 1974; Kindleberger 1975; Lazer 1999).[7] Throughout this era, intra-European trade both rose dramatically and constituted a vast portion of global commerce (Pollard 1974, 42–52 and 62–66). Besides the well-known German Zollverein, the Austrian states established a customs union in 1850, as did Switzerland in 1848, Denmark in 1853, and Italy in the 1860s (Pahre 2008, 318–19). In addition, various groups of nation-states forged customs unions, including Sweden and Norway and Moldavia and Wallachia (Pollard 1974, 118; Irwin 1993, 92).

The development of a broad network of bilateral commercial agreements also marked this era. Precipitated by the Anglo-French commercial treaty of 1860, they were linked by unconditional MFN clauses and created the bedrock of the international economic system until the late nineteenth-century depression (Kenwood and Lougheed 1971; Pollard 1974; Irwin 1993; Lazer 1999; Pahre 2008). Furthermore, the desire by states outside this commercial network to gain greater access to the markets of participants stimulated its rapid spread. As of the first decade of the twentieth century, Great Britain had concluded bilateral agreements with forty-six states, Germany had done so with thirty countries, and France with more than twenty states (Irwin 1993, 97). These arrangements contributed heavily to the unprecedented growth of European integration and to the relatively open international commercial system that characterized the latter half of the nineteenth century, underpinning what Douglas Irwin (1993, 97) refers to as an era of "progressive bilateralism."[8]

---

[7] For a somewhat different characterization, see Pahre (2008), who argues that there were various episodes of preferential trade agreements during the nineteenth century. Note that PTAs were not confined solely to Europe during this era. Prior to 1880, for example, India, China, and Great Britain comprised a "tightly-knit trading bloc." Afterward, Japan's economic development and its increasing political power led to marked changes in intra-Asian trade patterns. Kenwood and Lougheed (1971, 94–95) report that "Asia replaced Europe and the United States as the main source of Japanese imports, supplying almost one-half of these needs by 1913. By that date Asia had also become Japan's leading regional export market."

[8] Some recent research contests this view of the trade agreements in the nineteenth century. Accominotti and Flandreau (2008, 175), for example, maintain that "the empirical evidence reported here suggests that nineteenth-century bilateralism did not give any boost to international trade whose expansion actually started losing momentum after 1860. Thus, the evidence leans toward the age-old wisdom emphasized long ago by the classics, that if the goal is liberalization, then treaties are pointless." Their research supports our view that economic benefits do not seem to be the major factor driving countries to sign trade agreements.

Domestic politics played a role in the formation of many of these PTAs (Nye 1991; Irwin 1993; Pahre 2008). Trade policy was intensely political during this era and frequently aroused intense domestic debate. Autocratic leaders often used protectionism to seal domestic alliances that solidified their continued rule. The "marriage of iron and rye" in Germany is one of the most famous instances of this tack (Schonhardt-Bailey 1998). The 1860 Anglo-French Treaty of Commerce, which many believe "served as the catalyst for virtually all the major trade treaties in 19th century Europe," was also a hotly contested political affair in both countries, but especially in France where Napoleon III and the legislature disagreed on the course of trade policy (Nye 1991, 474; Lampe 2009). Robert Pahre (2008) also shows that domestic political institutions affected nineteenth-century trade relations. He finds that more democratic states in Europe were particularly likely to cooperate on trade and sign trade treaties (Pahre 2008, 228). Moreover, he concludes that the ratification of trade treaties depended heavily on domestic institutions and divided government (Pahre 2008, ch. 9). In sum, then, domestic politics played a key role in many of the trade agreements formed during the nineteenth century.

World War I disrupted the growth of trade agreements. But soon after the war's conclusion, numerous PTAs were signed, most of which had a decidedly more discriminatory cast than earlier ones. The agreements formed between World War I and II tended to be highly preferential. Some were created to consolidate the empires of major powers, including the customs union France created with members of its empire in 1928 and the Commonwealth system of preferences established by Great Britain in 1932 (Pollard 1974, 145). Most, however, were formed among sovereign states. For example, Hungary, Romania, Yugoslavia, and Bulgaria each negotiated tariff preferences on their agricultural trade with various European countries. The Rome Agreement of 1934 led to the establishment of a PTA involving Italy, Austria, and Hungary. Belgium, Denmark, Finland, Luxembourg, the Netherlands, Norway, and Sweden concluded a series of economic agreements throughout the 1930s. Germany also initiated various bilateral trade blocs during this era. Outside of Europe, the United States forged almost two dozen bilateral commercial agreements during the mid-1930s, many of which involved Latin American countries.[9]

Longstanding and unresolved debates exist about whether these PTAs deepened the economic depression of the interwar period and contributed to political tensions culminating in World War II (Condliffe 1940, esp. ch. 8–9; Kindleberger 1973; Hirschman 1980 [1945]; Oye 1992). Contrasting this era with that prior to World War I, Irwin (1993, 91) presents the conventional view:

---

[9] On the commercial arrangements discussed in this paragraph, see Condliffe (1940, ch. 8–9), Hirschman (1980 [1945]), Kenwood and Lougheed (1971, 211–19), and Pollard (1974, 147–49). While our focus is on trade agreements, this era was also marked by the existence of at least five currency regions. For an analysis of the political economy of currency regions, see Cohen (1997).

In the 19th century, a network of treaties containing the most favoured nation (MFN) clause spurred major tariff reductions in Europe and around the world[, ushering] in a harmonious period of multilateral free trade that compares favorably with . . . the recent GATT era. In the interwar period, by contrast, discriminatory trade blocs and protectionist bilateral agreements contributed to the severe contraction of world trade that accompanied the Great Depression.[10]

The latter group of PTAs is often associated with the pursuit of beggar-thy-neighbor policies, protectionism, depression, and political conflict. Kerry Chase (2005, ch. 4) provides an interesting account of how domestic politics in the major imperial powers of the time helped build these exclusive trading blocs. These two historical episodes thus suggest that PTAs can have very different consequences; they underline the view that the economic gains from PTAs may be positive, negative, or nonexistent, and hence not determinative of the demand for such arrangements.

Since World War II, states have continued to negotiate trade agreements, despite the existence of a multilateral economic framework. To help illustrate the contemporary growth of PTAs, figure 1.1 shows the frequency with which countries have joined these agreements since 1950, as well as the total number of PTAs in the world; figure 1.2 illustrates the number of countries in each region entering a PTA during this era.

Clearly, the incidence of PTA formation and the frequency with which states have entered such arrangements has waxed and waned. Few were established during the 1950s, then a surge in trade agreements occurred in the 1960s and the first part of the 1970s, after which the incidence of PTA creation leveled off. But there was an explosive rise in these agreements and the number of states joining them during the 1990s; and by the end of the twentieth century, more than 50 percent of all world commerce was conducted within these agreements (Serra et al. 1997, 8, figure 2; Freund and Ornelas 2010, 140). The rush to form such arrangements continued during the first decade of the twenty-first century. Indeed, PTAs have become so pervasive that Mongolia is currently the only WTO member that does not belong to at least one, and the average WTO member now has agreements with more than twelve countries (World Trade Organization 2011, 56, figure B.1b). As figure 1.2 shows, there is also substantial variation across geographical regions in the extent to which states participate in PTAs. In Western Europe, Africa, and Latin America, countries have entered PTAs with considerable regularity. In East Asia and the Middle East, by contrast, these agreements have been much less pervasive, although—led by China—East Asian countries have demonstrated an increasing interest in

---

[10] He notes, however, that these generalizations are somewhat inaccurate, as do Eichengreen and Frankel (1995). But both studies confirm a difference between the effects of PTAs in the nineteenth century, the interwar period, and the present; and both view PTAs in the interwar period as most malign.

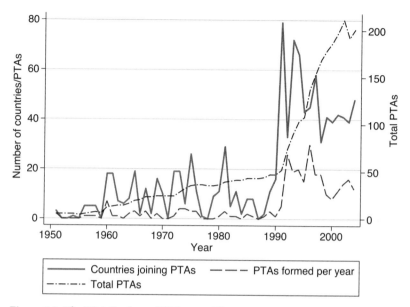

Figure 1.1: The Distribution of PTAs over Time, 1951–2004

entering these institutions over the past decade (Pomfret 2007). In later chapters, we will address the regional variations in PTAs.

Our brief historical overview indicates that PTAs have been enduring features of the international political economy and that domestic politics has been an important element in their formation. A substantial amount of research has been conducted on the economic and political effects of PTAs. Very little work, by contrast, has been conducted on the sources of these agreements.[11] Furthermore, most of the work conducted on this topic has focused on either the economic or the international factors shaping PTAs. In contrast, this book offers one of the first analyses of the domestic political determinants of PTA formation.

---

[11] It is important to distinguish our focus on PTAs from a focus on economic regionalism. Regionalism is generally defined as heightened economic integration among geographically proximate countries or, relatedly, a process whereby economic flows grow more rapidly among a given group of states (in the same geographical region) than between these and other states (Mansfield and Solingen 2010). Heightened integration within a region, however, need not stem from the economic policy cooperation among countries on which our study is focused (Fishlow and Haggard 1992; Yarbrough and Yarbrough 1997, 160 fn. 1). Furthermore, regionalism implies that the states involved are located in the same region. Many PTAs (for example, the United States's arrangements with Israel and Jordan, or South Korea's arrangements with Chile and New Zealand) are not regional in any conventional sense of the term. Regionalism and PTAs are different phenomena, and our focus is on the latter.

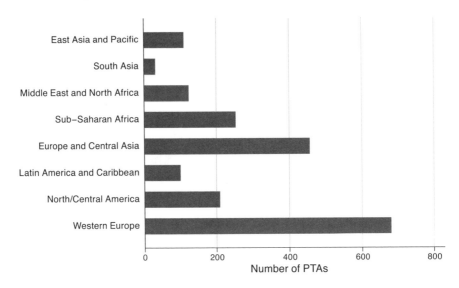

Figure 1.2: Total Number of PTAs per Geographical Region, 1951–2004

THE EFFECTS OF DOMESTIC POLITICS ON PTAS: THE ARGUMENT IN BRIEF

Our central argument is that trade agreements are often motivated by domestic political conditions. We seek to explain why leaders choose to enter these agreements. Such agreements are costly for political leaders since they constrain a chief executive's ability to set policy. Hence, for a leader to rationally choose to enter a PTA, he or she must calculate that membership will provide benefits that outweigh these costs. In contrast to most of the literature on PTAs, which emphasizes their economic benefits and costs, we argue that a country's domestic politics has an important influence on whether and when it elects to sign a trade agreement. It also affects the design of the agreement itself.

In chapter 2, we develop a rationalist theory to explain why governments negotiate PTAs. We argue that political leaders focus on how trade agreements can reassure the public and domestic groups about their decision making, but that they also worry about the domestic costs involved in ratifying agreements. Balancing these two forces is central to a decision maker's calculations regarding whether to sign a PTA. In particular, a country's regime type and its institutional veto players—that is, those groups that can block policy change—are crucial in this regard. Both factors have been analyzed in recent work on trade policy, but very little research has been conducted on whether regime type and veto players influence the formation of PTAs.[12] Regime type and veto players are two distinct elements of a country's domestic political institutions. Regime type is linked to the degree of political—especially, electoral—competition, while veto players affect the checks and balances on the executive branch. We maintain that democratic countries are more likely to join a preferential arrangement than nondemocratic states. Equally, as the number of veto players increases, the likelihood of joining a PTA declines. From this general argument about the factors influencing why and when political leaders choose to enter PTAs, we also derive a variety of auxiliary hypotheses that help to further probe the underlying logic of our claims.

Regime Type

Our first argument is that democracies have greater reason to enter PTAs than other countries. The notion of democracy that we employ here is Schumpeterian (Schumpeter 1976 [1942]) and therefore stresses domestic political institutions. The existence of competitive elections in which leaders can be replaced is the sine qua non for democracy, according to this widely used definition. It focuses attention on the features of regimes that make elections possible, free, and fair. Many regimes have elections, but not all such contests are competitive ones where incumbents face the prospect of being removed from office. Autocracies, for example, frequently hold elections, but they are much less likely to lead to leadership turnover than democratic elections. Instead, autocrats must maintain the allegiance of small, select groups within the country, often including the military, labor unions, key members of the ruling party, or owners of the means of production. The greater political competition for office in democracies, we argue, motivates leaders to sign international trade agreements.

Leaders in various types of polities are caught between the pressures of special interest groups and the preferences of voters. Some special interests press for policies—such as protectionist trade policies—that adversely affect the economy. Heads of government may want to satisfy these interest groups in exchange for benefits like campaign contributions. But giving in to all interest group demands would have very harmful economic consequences and could imperil their hold on office. Leaders, however, face a domestic political problem. They have a hard time convincing the public that they will not accede to special interest demands. When elections take place in times of adverse economic circumstances, voters may blame incumbents for economic problems and turn them out of office. As such, chief executives need to find ways to reassure the public and other domestic groups that they are not overly compliant with respect to the demands of protectionist groups. Heads of government

---

[12] For an exception that addresses the effects of regime type on trade agreements in the nineteenth century, see Pahre (2008).

would prefer to remain in office and do less for special interest groups if they could convince voters of their actual behavior.

PTAs provide such a reassurance mechanism. They allow leaders to commit to a lower level of protectionism than chief executives might otherwise desire, and to signal voters that leaders will not allow trade policy to be determined solely by special interests. Voters, if reassured that leaders are generally abiding by the terms of the international agreement, thus have reason to believe heads of government who claim that their policies did not cause tough economic times. In turn, these leaders are more likely to remain in office since voters will choose to reelect them even during economic downturns. The more political competition that exists, the more leaders have to worry about being ejected from office and the greater the costs generated by their inability to reassure the public. Hence, we argue that democratic governments, which encounter greater political competition in general, should be more likely to sign trade agreements since they face larger costs from not doing so.

For autocracies, the calculations differ. Interest group pressures for protectionism in autocracies vest leaders of these countries with an incentive to resist entering PTAs that reduce the rents they can provide to supporters. Equally, leaders do not face as great a cost since electoral competition is less likely to determine their fate. Consequently, autocrats have less incentive to enter into trade agreements than their democratic counterparts. This argument, which we develop in chapter 2, provides the microfoundations for understanding leaders' (differential) domestic motivations for negotiating trade agreements.

Veto Players

A rational leader deciding to enter a trade agreement focuses not only on the benefits of doing so but also on the associated costs. A central domestic political cost of signing a PTA involves the ratification process. Our second argument is that the number of players that can block policy change because of their institutional position affects the transaction costs that governments bear when ratifying a PTA. These costs are greater in countries marked by a large number of veto players, thereby reducing the incentives of leaders to negotiate and ratify PTAs. Political institutions can then provide both inducements and obstacles to international cooperation.

Veto players have the ability to block policy change; their assent is necessary to alter existing policies (Tsebelis 1995 and 2002, 2). We focus on veto players, rather than veto points, since we assume that these groups are active, strategic participants in the policy process, especially the ratification of international agreements. They calculate their interests and, because of their institutional positions, can block policies that they oppose. Conceptually, regime type and veto players are distinct and we treat them as such. Veto players exist in all types of regimes. Even in nondemocratic countries, domestic politics is rarely a pure hierarchy with a unitary decision maker and no constraints on leaders (Bueno de Mesquita et al. 2003; Gandhi 2008; Weeks 2008). Domestic groups with varying preferences that have veto power often compete for influence over policy, and even dictators depend on them in making policy and retaining office. Democratic regimes are more likely to have veto players than nondemocratic regimes, although the number of such players varies considerably even among democracies

In most countries, the executive sets the agenda in foreign affairs and has the power to initiate foreign economic policy. However, veto players must ratify policy choices made by the executive, such as joining a trade agreement. Formally, the head of government in a democracy—prime minister, president, chancellor, or premier—is often required by the national constitution to obtain the approval of the legislature for international agreements, including PTAs. He or she will therefore need to anticipate the legislature's (or any other veto player's) reaction to the proposed arrangement and ensure it is domestically acceptable.

Ratification can also be less formal. In dictatorships, shifts in foreign economic policy often require the support of groups like the military or local leaders; implicitly these groups have ratified a trade agreement when they have the ability to veto it and choose not to. Informal ratification also occurs in democracies. If a leader needs to change a domestic law, norm, or practice in order to implement a PTA, even if no formal vote on the arrangement itself is required, a legislative vote on any necessary domestic change becomes a vote on the agreement.

Because of this ratification constraint, veto players affect the formation of PTAs. As the number of veto players increases, so does the likelihood that at least one such player will have a constituency that is adversely affected by the PTA and therefore will block its ratification. To ratify an agreement when many veto players exist is costly for political leaders. They either have to modify the agreement to fit the preferences of the veto groups or to bribe the veto groups into accepting the agreement. These means of securing ratification pose transaction costs for leaders. And the greater these transaction costs, the less likely leaders are to enter into trade agreements and the more difficult it will be to secure ratification.

Domestic Politics and Trade Agreements: Auxiliary Hypotheses

The claims that we outlined in the previous section about regime type and veto players are developed in greater detail in chapter 2, where we also develop seven novel hypotheses that follow from our argument and that allow us to probe some of the causal mechanisms underlying this argument. These hypotheses explore in more detail the logic of the main claims and some puzzles that arise from them.

First, our argument implies that a government should realize an increase in political support as a result of signing a PTA. More specifically, since PTAs help leaders overcome domestic political problems, leaders who sign them should have a longer tenure in office than those who do not sign such agreements. Second, partisanship should affect the likelihood of a government signing and ratifying a PTA. Left-wing governments should be more likely to join a trade agreement because they have a greater need to reassure the public that they will not engage in excessive protectionism than centrist or right-wing governments. Third, underlying our argument about the propensity of democracies to sign PTAs is that democratic leaders need an external mechanism to convince voters that they have not mismanaged the economy. Entering a PTA to create such a mechanism, however, is likely to be much more effective in countries that depend heavily on foreign commerce. Hence, we examine whether democracies that are heavily trade dependent are more likely to enter PTAs than other democratic regimes. Fourth, whereas we expect that nondemocratic regimes will sign fewer PTAs than democracies, the former regimes nonetheless do join various trade arrangements. Nondemocratic regimes exhibit considerable variation in the extent of domestic political competition and we expect that more competitive nondemocracies are more likely to accede to PTAs than less competitive regimes.

Fifth, we mentioned earlier that different types of preferential arrangements are designed to achieve different degrees of economic integration among members, with PAs being the least and economic unions being the most integrative. It follows from our argument that democracies should seek PTAs that aim to achieve deeper integration. Further, leaders can choose to include institutional features in PTAs to enforce trade integration. Chief among these are DSMs, which furnish member-states with the means to legally settle disputes over the agreement. Leaders who have a greater need to reassure the public about their economic activities have greater reason to include a DSM in trade agreements; as such, democratic countries are more likely to enter PTAs that include DSMs than autocratic ones.

Sixth, the institutional design of a PTA is likely to be affected by the number of veto players in a country, as well as its regime type. More integrative arrangements have more pronounced distributional consequences. Equally, the inclusion of a DSM bolsters a trade arrangement's enforcement capacity. As the number of veto players rises, there is a growing likelihood that at least one such player will be adversely affected by greater integration and enforcement within the arrangement, reducing the likelihood that a country marked by a large number of veto players will enter a highly integrative arrangement or one with a DSM. Seventh, veto players not only affect whether a country enters a PTA, they also influence the length of time that it takes to ratify such an arrangement. In countries where the number of veto players increases between the signing and the ratification of a PTA, the length of time needed to ratify the arrangement should grow.

Using a variety of new datasets, in chapter 5, we elaborate on and examine empirically these auxiliary hypotheses. Our analysis of these novel hypotheses should help to build confidence in our main claims about the important role of domestic politics in international trade cooperation.

Our focus on domestic political considerations in the calculations of governments stands in stark contrast to most existing work on the formation of trade agreements, in general, and PTAs, in particular. For the most part, such work has taken one of three tacks. First, some economic studies have argued that states enter trade agreements in order to generate welfare gains. Clearly, states sometimes form PTAs for economic reasons. However, we argue that they do so for political reasons as well and that economic analyses of trade agreements often ignore these political factors. Second, some studies emphasize that international political factors stimulate PTA formation. We do not dispute this claim and we analyze many of these factors in the empirical portions of the book. However, studies cast at the international (or systemic) level of analysis usually give short shrift to domestic politics. We argue that domestic factors are also important for the purpose of explaining PTAs. Indeed, unlike almost all previous empirical analyses of PTA formation, we combine a systemic investigation of PTAs in chapter 3 with a country-level focus in chapters 4 and 5. Furthermore, in order to conduct these tests, we have compiled the most comprehensive dataset on reciprocal trade agreements formed since World War II. Third, various studies of PTAs have focused on the effects of domestic politics, but almost all of them have stressed the role played by interest groups. We agree that such groups may be influential; however, these studies generally ignore the role played by political leaders within domestic institutions. We view the interaction between these institutions and domestic trade policy preferences as important.

THE BROADER THEORETICAL CONTEXT

Our analysis of the domestic sources of PTA formation bears on a host of important theoretical issues in the fields of international relations and political economy. For example, it contributes to certain avenues of research on the political economy of trade policy. Much of the contemporary research on trade policy relies on an open economy politics (OEP) approach. As David Lake (2009, 221) points out, one of the two main questions that OEP deals with is "how, when, and why do countries choose to open themselves to transborder flows of goods and services, capital, and people? In other words, what are the political determinants of what we now call globalization?" The issue at the core of our study centers on this question. Why do countries decide to open their economies internationally, even if this opening is only partial? Historically and politically, such decisions to open up are rare and thus are worthy of attention.

OEP models tend to involve three logical steps in addressing this question (Lake 2009, 225). They begin at the microlevel, seeking to identify the policy preferences of the individuals, sectors, or factors of production within a country. Taking economic models as their baseline, they usually assume that these agents are most concerned with maximizing income and that an underlying economic model provides information linking policy choice to income distribution and hence setting forth their policy preferences. The second step outlines how domestic political institutions serve as the means by which all of these preferences are aggregated and how the government makes its policy choice at the end of the day. The third step introduces bargaining among states and the role of international institutions in setting the outcome at the global level. For OEP models, then, "interests, institutions, and international bargaining explain the choice of policies by countries and the outcomes experienced by the world economy.... OEP proceeds towards an explanation in a linear, unidirectional fashion" (Lake 2009, 230). The argument in this book falls within this paradigm but also pushes it in new directions.

There are three primary differences between OEP models and our approach. First, our focus is less on the derivation of domestic preferences than is typical in OEP models. Instead, we emphasize how political institutions shape leaders' calculations about foreign economic policy. Second, we focus less on international bargaining than on the role of international trade institutions in affecting domestic politics. Our aim is to address how political leaders view the role of trade agreements in terms of their domestic political situation. Third, we argue that leaders sign trade agreements because they yield domestic political benefits. PTAs can reshape the domestic political landscape. As Lake (2009, 237–38) asserts,

> if international institutions really matter, they will alter the interests and possibly institutions within states as well. This feedback from the international political economy to the domestic arena is now almost entirely ignored in OEP, but need not be. Indeed, in a way fully consistent with the core assumptions of the paradigm, international institutions may actually create an important endogenous dynamic with important effects on politics.

We show that such a dynamic movement between domestic and international institutions is likely in the case of PTAs. They can help political leaders in their domestic political struggles and thus affect domestic politics, while also being a product of domestic political institutions. Thus, this book is located within the tradition of the OEP models but links international institutions much more closely to domestic politics.

Our study presents a rationalist model of international cooperation. It locates the decision to join a PTA in leaders' political calculations about its effects. It therefore falls within the large literature on rationalist models of cooperation and international institutions (e.g., Krasner 1983; Keohane 1984; Goldstein et al. 2001; Koremenos et al. 2004). Unlike much of this literature, however, we link the role of international institutions back to domestic politics. We also focus on leaders' motivations for signing an international agreement.

Further, we contribute to the research on the design of international institutions (Koremenos et al. 2004; Hawkins et al. 2006). We ask what motivates leaders to agree to join different types of PTAs and what makes them include dispute settlement mechanisms. While PTAs all have the same primary function—that is, reciprocal trade barrier reduction—some go much further in this direction than others. We try to explain this diversity of form in terms of variations in the domestic institutional environment. We thus relate domestic politics to international cooperation and the diversity of forms it can take.

Like much recent research in the fields of international relations and comparative politics, we focus attention on domestic institutions (e.g., Shepsle 1979 and 1989; North and Weingast 1989; Acemoglu et al. 2001; Bueno de Mesquita et al. 2003). In the comparative politics field, the role of democracy has been especially important in understanding economic growth and development (North and Weingast 1989; Barro 1996; Acemoglu et al. 2001; Keefer 2004; Aghion et al. 2007). In international politics, there is a large literature on the "democratic peace" (Doyle 1983a and 1983b; Russett and Oneal 2001; Mansfield and Snyder 2005), the alliance behavior of democracies (Gaubatz 1996; Weart 1998), and whether democracies tend to win the wars they start (Lake 1992; Reiter and Stam 2002). Work on the international political economy has analyzed whether democracies trade more and are less protectionist than other countries (Mansfield et al. 2000 and 2002; Milner and Kubota 2005; Eichengreen and Leblang 2008; Milner and Mukherjee 2009). The importance of democracy for international relations and comparative politics is still debated, but many observers have concluded that democracies are distinctive in various ways. Our argument advances the main claims of this research program.

A large body of recent research on both comparative politics and international relations has also emphasized the role of veto players (Tsebelis 1995 and 2002; Henisz 2000 and 2002; Hallerberg 2002; Keefer and Stasavage 2003; Henisz and Mansfield 2006; Mansfield et al. 2007). Many of these studies have found that veto players affect a wide variety of important economic outcomes, such as economic growth, investment, and trade policy. Nonetheless, the impact of veto players remains the subject of fierce debate. We enter this debate by offering one of the first assessments of how this institutional feature affects PTA formation.

ORGANIZATION OF THE BOOK

The rest of this book is organized as follows. Chapter 2 lays out our argument and the theory underlying it. We develop in detail our argument about the domestic political costs and benefits of trade agreements and explain why democracies are more likely to form PTAs and highly integrative arrangements than nondemocracies. Furthermore, we explain why PTAs are less likely to be established by countries that have a large number of veto players, which are in turn particularly likely to inhibit the formation of arrangements that aim to promote more extensive integration.

Chapters 3, 4, and 5 contain the empirical portion of our analysis. Much of the empirical work on the political economy of PTAs has been cast at the international or systemic level of analysis. In chapter 3, we introduce and test various arguments about the impact of the distribution of power and the spread of democracy in the international system on the formation of PTAs. These systemic arguments about PTA formation are important because we need to account for the key international factors affecting PTAs once we turn to our analysis of domestic political factors in chapters 4 and 5. Our analysis shows that certain systemic factors have contributed heavily to global patterns of commercial agreements: hegemony, the spread of democracy, and strategic interaction among both states and PTAs have been especially influential in this regard.

In chapter 4, we turn to a test of our argument about the effects of regime type and veto players on the formation of PTAs. Here we focus on the country-level decisions to join and ratify a PTA. Our new dataset provides ratification dates on all PTAs between 1951 and 2004, and allows us to examine the domestic and international forces that lead to a country's decision to sign and ratify an agreement. In chapter 5, we examine the auxiliary hypotheses that flow from our main argument. We analyze the effects of PTA membership on a leader's political survival, the role of partisanship, the interaction of democracy with a country's dependence on trade, the depth of integration that a PTA aims to achieve, the effects of veto players on the length of time between the signing and ratification of a PTA, and the impact of political competition on whether autocracies sign PTAs. Chapter 6 summarizes the key findings and discusses the implications of our results for the study of international relations and international trade. There we return to many of the major themes we outlined in this chapter.

International trade agreements are undoubtedly important elements of the international political economy; world politics would look quite different without the EU, Mercosur, or NAFTA, for example. These agreements have had a wide range of political and economic effects, from reducing conflict to increasing foreign investment and helping enforce human rights across the globe. Gaining a better sense of why governments enter these agreements is likely to promote a fuller understanding of PTAs, the sources of international cooperation, and the evolution of the international political economy.

CHAPTER 2

A Political Economy Theory
of International Trade Agreements

IN THIS CHAPTER, we present a theory of the domestic political conditions that lead countries to enter into formal trade agreements. More specifically, we aim to explain the establishment of PTAs, institutions in which member-states reciprocally lower their trade barriers on each other's products and thereby grant each member preferential market access. As we discussed in chapter 1, our focus is on why and when countries have chosen to enter such agreements, understanding that there is substantial variability in the spread of PTAs over time and the countries that join them. Why have some countries joined many PTAs, while others have joined very few, and what explains the timing of PTA formation? In this chapter, we first present a rationalist theory of domestic politics to explain the pattern of PTAs. We then develop seven auxiliary hypotheses that follow from the logic of our model to further explore the model's implications.

Trade agreements are products of international negotiations. In order to take effect, however, legislatures and other veto groups in the contracting states must approve an agreement, or at least not block its passage and implementation (Putnam 1988; Milner 1997a). For an agreement to occur, governments and certain domestic groups have to find the accord preferable to the lack of one. To be rational instruments, agreements must provide net benefits to some domestic groups in all of the participating countries. Equally, the governments involved must decide that the benefits from concluding the agreement will exceed the associated costs. It is on these costs and benefits that we focus in analyzing the conditions under which rational political leaders will enter a PTA.

The costs and benefits of joining a trade agreement could be economic, political, or both. As we noted in chapter 1, economists have spent much energy debating the welfare consequences of PTAs. Whether they promote the economic welfare of states—let alone of the world economy—is still much debated. Existing studies have reached mixed conclusions about whether PTA members realize net economic gains. Many such studies also find that PTAs impose costs on third parties. Thus, it seems unlikely that governments are motivated to sign these agreements for purely economic reasons. Instead, we argue that governments sign PTAs for domestic political reasons.[1]

---

[1] Pahre (2008) proposes a model that begins at the domestic level, as we do. But his domestic political model is different since it focuses solely on political competition between exporters and import-competing firms.

More specifically, we maintain that these agreements can help leaders by increasing their political support. Leaders cannot credibly promise to ignore special interest pleading for trade protection, which creates a major domestic problem for heads of state. We begin by explaining the nature of this problem and then demonstrate how its severity relates to the extent of political competition. The upshot, we argue, is that democratic chief executives have a greater incentive to enter PTAs than their nondemocratic counterparts.

We also argue that leaders face transaction costs when making a trade agreement. The domestic ratification process contributes heavily to the magnitude of these costs. As the number of veto players expands, domestic ratification of an international agreement becomes more difficult. These two different domestic political factors—the nature of the regime and the number of veto players— play a significant role in determining whether countries are willing and able to form a PTA. In contrast to many other studies, therefore, we emphasize how domestic politics can shape international cooperation.

A POLITICAL ECONOMY THEORY OF PTAs

Why do political leaders enter PTAs? We claim that they do so because joining a preferential grouping yields domestic political benefits for heads of state that are difficult to obtain through unilateral policy measures. PTAs are a form of international cooperation since the participating countries mutually adjust their trade barriers. These adjustments require agreement both among countries and among actors within them. The demand for international cooperation is heightened when states are unable to solve or manage a problem through unilateral action alone. For example, Kyle Bagwell and Robert Staiger (2002) have shown that when countries face the prospect of international terms-of-trade externalities, the optimal solution is an agreement where all parties make market access concessions.[2] Unilateral reactions to this problem are likely to precipitate a trade war that adversely affects all of the countries. Further, as Giovanni Maggi and Andrés Rodríguez-Clare (1998 and 2007) argue, trade agreements can also have domestic political benefits by helping to bolster the credibility of a chief executive's commitment to trade liberalization and assisting the leader in avoiding capture by interest groups.

Negotiating a trade agreement is not without costs, however. Governments incur transaction costs, including search and information costs, bargaining

---

[2] A country's terms of trade refer to the ratio of its average export price to its average import price. Terms of trade are said to improve when this ratio increases and to worsen when it decreases. A country that has a large market can affect its terms of trade by increasing its tariffs; this leaves it better off but other countries worse off, creating an externality. If all countries do this, no one gains an advantage and everyone loses.

costs (associated with crafting a contract acceptable to both domestic and international actors), and the costs of policing and enforcing the agreement once it is in place. These costs can be significant and their magnitude is one reason that countries often opt for unilateral rather than multilateral solutions to international problems. Governments, then, must balance the gains from a trade agreement with the transaction costs incurred from forging it.

A rational government will only cooperate if the expected benefits provided by the agreement exceed the costs of negotiating and ratifying it. This cooperation is a voluntary exchange, which should be Pareto-improving in the sense that at least one party to the transaction is made better off and no party is made worse off (than its next best alternative) by the transaction. But the benefits and costs we explore are political, rather than economic.

Like some recent research on the political economy of trade agreements, we emphasize the domestic costs that leaders face if they lack a credible commitment over trade policy. It is useful to engage in a brief review of these models, since they serve as a point of departure for our analysis. Maggi and Rodríguez-Clare (1998 and 2007) have developed a series of models of trade agreements that incorporate domestic politics. Governments face a time inconsistency problem that makes them vulnerable to interest group pressures for protection. As Aaron Tornell (1991, 6) notes, "[a] common assumption made in these arguments is that government authorities can credibly precommit to end protection in the future. This is a very strong assumption . . . [given that] government authorities maximize a welfare function or they react to political forces. . . . If these authorities grant protection in the present, it is unlikely that they will not grant it in the future." Building from this idea, Maggi and Rodríguez-Clare (1998) show that even in the absence of terms-of-trade externalities, domestic politics may lead governments to form trade agreements in order to provide credible commitments to interest groups. They also find that even with terms-of-trade externalities, governments face a time inconsistency problem (Maggi and Rodríguez-Clare 2007). Many interest groups want protection. Governments find it difficult to resist protecting them, but protection causes investment distortions, which harm the government politically by reducing efficiency and growth. Governments then use trade agreements to make commitments that are credible and prevent interest groups from demanding greater barriers in the future.

Robert Staiger and Guido Tabellini (1999) use a similar model and provide evidence that international trade agreements actually do enhance government credibility vis-à-vis the private sector. Staiger and Tabellini argue that governments face production distortions due to time inconsistency problems surrounding trade policy. Groups benefiting from protection will expand too much and harm the economy because governments cannot commit to avoid protecting them. Staiger and Tabellini show, moreover, that international trade agreements provide more credibility for governments than do domestic institutions.

Commitments made in both the GATT/WTO and PTAs bind leaders and enable them to avoid making excessive concessions to interest groups.

Devashish Mitra (2002) builds on the analysis conducted by Maggi and Rodríguez-Clare (1998), but demonstrates that the commitment problem for politicians is more general than they posit. The demand for a precommitment to a free trade agreement does not have to be driven by the possibility of capital misallocation alone, as Maggi and Rodríguez-Clare (1998) argue, or by the possibility of organizational costs arising in the expectation of protection. Demand for such an agreement can occur when governments or interest groups face resource costs prior to lobbying because of the actions taken in the expectation of successful lobbying. Mitra shows that the inability of governments to commit unilaterally to resist protectionist pressures by interest groups creates substantial costs for governments. Under certain conditions, these costs can drive governments to seek international trade agreements.

Our argument about the role of domestic politics is similar to that advanced by Maggi and Rodríguez-Clare (1998 and 2007), Staiger and Tabellini (1999), and Mitra (2002). In our case, governments face a time inconsistency problem vis-à-vis the public and free trade interest groups. The latter are those economic groups that gain from trade liberalization, including exporters and importers or multinational firms with global production operations (Milner 1988; Gilligan 1997; Chase 2005). Without the ability to reassure the public and these domestic groups, governments run the risk of being blamed for adverse economic conditions by the public and free trade interest groups that may erroneously assume that these conditions have arisen because leaders gave in to protectionist demands or engaged in rent-seeking. Governments face the possibility that the public and free trade interest groups will try to oust them from office even when they have not given in to protectionist interests. That contingency creates a domestic political incentive for heads of government to sign trade agreements since such agreements can provide a visible mechanism of reassurance.

In some ways, our argument is just the reverse side of the claims laid out by Maggi and Rodríguez-Clare, Staiger and Tabellini, and Mitra. They focus on protectionist interest groups and the misallocated spending or production by them as a result of a government's lack of credible commitment. We focus on the reaction of the public and free trade interest groups to the possibility of the government giving in to protectionist interest groups. One could think of the public and free trade interest groups in our model as punishing the government for the likely capital misallocation posited by Maggi and Rodríguez-Clare or the production distortions posited by Staiger and Tabellini, and the attendant drag on economic growth resulting from the government's inability to avoid conceding to demands made by protectionist special interests.

Trade agreements can enhance the utility of both governments and the public. They can convey information to the public and free trade interest groups about the nature and activities of leaders. Such information can increase political support for leaders, helping them retain office. The public and interest groups differ in their preferences about trade policy and free trade is not a majority preference. Rather, some positive level of protectionism is acceptable to most groups. Governments balance the benefits of increased social welfare from trade liberalization with the rents gained from protection for special interest groups (Grossman and Helpman 1994). Rents for governments rise with the level of protection. Although leaders may not desire as much protection as their special interest groups demand, they are tempted by the rents that accrue from giving protection.

The argument we present here is a more general and less formal version of the argument we made in a prior study (Mansfield et al. 2002). In that article, leaders are assumed to be purely rent-seeking, while we relax that assumption in this book. Leaders vary in their preferences for social welfare and rents. This assumption is very common and follows the well-known Grossman-Helpman models. The assumption underlying our earlier study made the results of our formal model less reliant on the leaders' preferences and made the PTA equilibrium more difficult to induce. But the assumption about leaders' preferences that we rely on in this book is more realistic and makes the PTA equilibrium easier to derive. In addition, we assume that there is moral hazard as voters do not know the precise trade policy chosen by the government and must extract a signal about the policy from the overall economic situation, as in Mansfield et al. (2002). But we also add some adverse selection problems; namely, the public does not know exactly what type of leader exists and how susceptible he or she is to interest group influence. Consequently, leaders can vary and voters can not only sanction leaders through elections but can also try to select better types, which may be a more robust and feasible strategy (Fearon 1999; Besley and Preston 2007). Adverse selection is more realistic than pure moral hazard since leaders differ in their preferences and competence. Partisanship is one form of difference, as we discuss later.

Here we also address the possibility that interest groups can play a role in advocating protection or trade liberalization through their lobbying over a PTA. While not formally part of our model, we suggest that societies are composed of two sets of interest groups: free trade groups that support PTAs and protectionist groups that oppose them. We do not present a formal model in this book, but other social scientists have developed ones that are similar to our argument showing that voters can constrain leaders and leaders can be left better off as political competition increases. A model that includes such adverse selection along with elections and interest groups is developed by James Snyder and Michael Ting (2008). They show that adding a second interest group with opposing preferences to a society having only a single group can benefit both leaders and voters. Leaders are more likely to get reelected and voters are more likely to get their most preferred policies when a second interest group competes for influence over policy. In our case, PTAs tend to mobilize interest groups that oppose protection, like exporters, importers, and multinational corporations with global production networks (Gilligan 1997; Chase 2005). Negotiating a PTA, then, may activate a countervailing interest group that opposes protectionism and thus allows leaders to choose a policy that is ultimately better for them and for voters, as Snyder and Ting's model suggests. Hence, the argument here is more complex but perhaps more realistic than in our earlier study (Mansfield et al. 2002).

Interest groups are therefore important and do not have uniform preferences. Not all special interests desire protection. Exporters and multinational firms with global trading activities are likely to prefer low trade barriers at home and abroad (Milner 1988 and 1992; Chase 2005; Manger 2009). Indeed, we assume that there are free trade interest groups that oppose protectionist demands and that therefore have preferences closer to the public at large.

Governments tend to prefer higher trade barriers than the median member of the public and some free trade interest groups. These groups do not gain from the rents created by protectionism, as do their political leaders. This tension between members of the public and leaders—with parts of the public attempting to restrain an extractive leader—is centrally important. If the government's ideal level of trade barriers was less than that of the median member of society, the political problem would be different. No longer would the public be concerned with restraining the rent-seeking impulses of its leaders; instead, it would encourage leaders to choose higher trade barriers. If the median member of the public is highly protectionist, and even more so than leaders, the decision to establish trade agreements is itself puzzling. One then has to explain why leaders would negotiate agreements to adopt policies that are opposed not only by many special interest groups (for example, import-competing groups), but also by a majority of the populace. Furthermore, one would have to explain why governments are more likely to sign these agreements in democracies than in autocracies, even though the public dislikes them and democratic governments are more responsive to public interests than their autocratic counterparts.

Some arguments about the establishment of PTAs do focus on the role played by interest groups (Manger 2009). However, the puzzle generated by such arguments is why interest groups pushing for such agreements dominate protectionist groups and why leaders ignore the majority of public opinion. In our theory, the median member of the public and some free trade interest groups induce leaders to contemplate PTAs, while protectionist groups may oppose such efforts. To the extent that protectionist groups are represented by veto players in government, as we discuss later, leaders will pay costs for negotiating trade agreements. Only when the benefits to leaders from the extra political support they derive from the public and free trade interest groups exceeds the costs of this opposition will leaders sign agreements.

Leaders may prefer different levels of protection, based on the weights that they assign to the benefits of rents versus social welfare (Gawande et al. 2009). Promoting social welfare is important to them because it generates political support among the public and free trade interest groups that helps lengthen their stay in office. The public generally cannot be certain what balance between rents and social welfare a government truly desires. It does not know the government's exact preferences; nor does the public know the exact trade policy chosen by the government in the absence of an agreement. There is thus both a moral hazard and an adverse selection problem for the public. The public needs some kind of reassurance about the motives and actions of the government.

The public also has heterogeneous preferences about trade policy: some individuals prefer high levels of protection whereas others prefer freer trade. The median member of the public, who commands the attention of leaders, prefers a positive level of trade barriers but cannot directly control or monitor trade policy. Since trade barriers create rents for interest groups, office-holders may seek to raise barriers beyond the level preferred by the median member of society to extract these rents. The public, which does not gain from these rents and probably loses because of them, does not know the extent of government rent-seeking since citizens do not know their leaders' exact trade preferences or policies. Governments would like to limit the amount of protection they furnish since it hurts the economy in the long run and thus lowers their reelection prospects.

But the government cannot credibly reassure the public that it will not overprotect when such protection is demanded by special interests. As others have noted (Maggi and Rodríguez-Clare 1998 and 2007; Mitra 2002), governments face a time inconsistency problem vis-à-vis interest groups. They would like to be able to resist protectionist demands, but when such demands arise, governments are usually better off giving in to each group that presses for protection. The public and free trade interest groups know this and are harmed by government rent-seeking. They can threaten action to lower the incumbent government's probability of retaining office. But they also face an informational problem. Members of the public may not know the preferences of or the exact trade policy chosen by the government, and thus they cannot distinguish perfectly between adverse exogenous economic shocks and the extractive policies of leaders. An economic downturn could be caused by either highly protectionist policies or an exogenous shock, such as a global recession or an international crisis. Both events, for example, might increase the price that the public pays for goods and services, and thus dampen the public's political support for the government.

Leaders, in turn, would like to find a way to demonstrate to their public that poor economic performance is not the result of their extractive policies, thereby reducing the domestic political costs that they face. While they could choose to unilaterally lower trade barriers, doing so is time inconsistent. Leaders can reduce barriers, but they and the public know that future special interest demands for protection may well be met. So heads of government must find other ways to reassure the public that they will not engage in excessive protectionism.

One way of doing so is by entering into an international trade agreement. An agreement is both a visible commitment to restrict protectionism and an institutional reassurance to convey to the public and free trade interest groups that a relatively open trade policy has been adopted. The agreement commits participating countries to a level of trade barriers below each government's ideal unilateral level and it serves as a monitoring mechanism. Other member-states can use aspects of the trade institution (such as the dispute settlement mechanism included in various trade agreements) to signal to each participating government's society if its trade barriers rise above the agreed upon level. The commercial agreement is public and therefore provides information that society and free trade interest groups can use to more closely monitor their chief executive. As Susanne Lohmann (2003, 100) observes about institutions, including those institutions that shape trade, "[c]reating an institution draws a line in the sand that focuses the expectations of an audience: voters, wage-setters, financial markets, other policy-makers. The line in the sand is a public focal point that allows hundreds, thousands, or even millions of people to coordinate their beliefs about the trigger-punishment strategies that will be executed in the event of an institutional defection." The monitoring that an international trade agreement provides can help political leaders overcome their reassurance problem.

Thus, a government benefits from entering into a trade agreement because its political support should remain relatively robust even when the economy experiences a downturn beyond the leader's control and the government has not violated the agreement. Absent the agreement, the government faces greater difficulty retaining office since it cannot credibly reassure voters and free trade interest groups that the downturn was beyond its control. These political benefits are what help motivate leaders to sign trade agreements.

EXAMINING THE ASSUMPTIONS UNDERLYING THE THEORY

Our argument raises several important issues concerning interest groups' and the public's knowledge about and attitudes toward trade agreements, the ability of domestic and international groups to monitor trade agreements, and the difference between multilateral and preferential trade agreements. The argument we propose makes assumptions about each of these issues; consequently, it is useful to briefly address why these assumptions are reasonable.

Our argument relies on the median member of the public not being strongly protectionist. We assume that the median member of society does not oppose trade barriers completely, but that she or he also supports trade enough so that leaders want to pursue trade agreements. PTAs rarely eliminate all barriers to trade; more typically they lower many and open the economy with respect to overseas commerce. But does the public desire such exposure to the international economy? Public opinion surveys covering international trade have only recently been conducted outside the United States. The Pew Research Center Global Attitudes Survey examined attitudes toward trade in a large number of countries in 2002, 2007, and 2008.[3] In all of these cases, an overwhelming majority of respondents felt that trade was good for their country. In Africa, data on eleven countries, including the largest—Nigeria and South Africa—show that on average over 80 percent of the public favored trade. In Latin America, eight countries were surveyed and there the results were similar. On average 80 percent of the public supported trade (Pew Research Center 2002). Latinobarometro surveys done in the early 2000s show that attitudes toward free trade agreements were generally positive; on average over 50 percent of the public in most of the countries favored the agreements (Lagos 1996, 2003, 2004, 2006, 2007). In Eastern and Western Europe, surveys show similar levels of public support for trade. In roughly eleven countries in this region in 1988, over 60 percent of the public on average supported free trade compared to trade restrictions (Reif and Melich 1988). Other surveys in the 2000s also demonstrate public support for trade. A variety of Pew polls in 2002, 2003, 2007, and 2008 show that trade is seen as a positive factor for a majority of the public in ten European countries (Pew Research Center 2002, 2003, 2007, 2008). In sum, public opinion polls in Europe, Latin America, and Africa provide support for the claim that the median member of the public views trade favorably, providing some justification for our assumption that the public tends to be more supportive of open trade than of protectionism.

Another claim we make is that some members of the public and certain interest groups are aware of the trade agreements their government has signed and generally view such accords favorably. Public opinion data suggests that, in many countries, there is a public awareness of and a favorable attitude about international trade accords. For example, Afrobarometer (Africa et al. 2003/2004) conducted a survey in 2003–2004 about mass attitudes toward the three main African PTAs: SADC, Economic Community of West African States (ECOWAS), and East African Community (EAC). A large majority of the public in fourteen out of fifteen African countries felt that these trade agreements were beneficial. In addition, a survey conducted in 1995 revealed that 44 percent of U.S. respondents and 74 percent of Canadians respondents had heard quite a bit or a lot about the North American Free Trade Agreement (NAFTA), whereas only 15 percent of the U.S. respondents and 3 percent of the Canadian ones had heard nothing. Equally, 31 percent thought it would benefit the United

---

[3] They generally asked a question such as "what do you think about the growing trade and business ties between your country and other countries—do you think it is a very good thing, somewhat good, somewhat bad or a very bad thing for our country?" Sometimes they used the phrase greater economic trade and sometimes they asked about the impact on the respondent's family.

States and 22 percent thought it would not; 65 percent of Canadians thought it would benefit Canada and only 32 percent thought otherwise (ISSP Research Group 1995). In Western Europe, the 1995 International Social Survey Programme (ISSP) generated similar findings about public attitudes toward the EU. A large majority of those surveyed had heard quite a bit or a lot about the EU, and most respondents felt that being a member benefited his or her country. Eastern European respondents knew less about the EU than their Western European counterparts, but they too exhibited considerable support for it. The 2003 ISSP indicated that both knowledge about and support for the EU were continuing to increase in Eastern Europe. The 2003 ISSP also indicated that 43 percent of Uruguayan respondents knew quite a lot or a lot about Mercosur, whereas only 13 percent knew nothing. Fully two thirds of the Uruguayan public thought this PTA yielded benefits for the country and 83 percent would vote for it in a referendum (ISSP Research Group 2003). More generally, Latin American survey data shows that large majorities support economic integration there (Lagos 1997, 1998, 2001, 2002, 2005, 2008; Baker 2008). Though this overview of public opinion data can hardly be considered conclusive, it does suggest that there is considerable awareness of and support for various PTAs.

Do the public or interest groups know anything—and can they learn anything—about their government's behavior as a PTA member? Reporting on the behavior of signatories is a key function of many commercial agreements, although it is frequently overlooked. The EU issues public summaries of the extent to which countries are adopting and implementing its directives (Martin 2000, ch. 7). NAFTA's dispute settlement mechanism serves a similar purpose: countries can be publicly accused of violating their international commitments and forced to undergo a long, open process of defending their behavior. Members of society and free trade interest groups do not actually read these documents. Rather they are more likely to hear about complaints regarding their government's violations of a trade agreement than they are to learn about changes in domestic trade policy. Such international accusations of bad behavior are more newsworthy than are unilateral changes in trade policy, as many countries (such as Mexico and Canada during the negotiations over NAFTA) have realized.

Indeed, the institutions set up by trade agreements can help transmit information to domestic groups about governments' behavior about which they would otherwise remain ignorant. The legalized dispute processes, for instance, often associated with international institutions, such as the WTO's DSM, play an important role in transmitting information about the policies of member governments to previously uninformed subnational actors, such as the voting public. Many important U.S. trade policies, like antidumping and countervailing duties, receive very little media coverage until other WTO members choose to challenge them under the WTO's DSM. One recent study shows that a WTO challenge can result in significantly increased media coverage for even the most obscure trade policies. The policy of "zeroing," for example, received virtually no media coverage until it became the subject of a WTO dispute, after which it received much more coverage, even landing on the pages of *The New York Times* and *The Washington Post* (Chaudoin 2012).[4]

Furthermore, it is not just trade institutions that can act as monitors. Xinyuan Dai (2007, 56), for instance, has shown that even weak international institutions tend to produce groups that monitor and help enforce them. As she notes, "export-oriented and import-competing firms are often in a convenient position to detect both the effect and source of noncompliance by trading partner countries. The fact that victims of noncompliance can serve as low cost monitors . . . leads to a particular form of decentralized monitoring: private producers detect noncompliance and their governments bring it to the" dispute settlement mechanism of the trade agreement.

Foreign partners can and do report violations, and domestic groups that benefit from the trade agreement frequently inform the public about deviations from it. Foreign partners have reason to sound an alarm when another country cheats. Often this will induce export-oriented groups at home to further publicize the government's behavior since they do not want the foreign partner to retaliate and jeopardize their access to overseas markets. In 2009, for example, Mexico charged the United States with violating the trucking agreement in NAFTA. Moreover, it sanctioned the United States for this longtime violation by imposing duties on about ninety U.S. products, representing about US$2.4 billion in exports from forty states. Opposition to this protectionist action was strong in the United States as well. As the Economist Intelligence Unit (2011, section 6) reported, "[v]arious sectors of the US business community and entities such as the US Chamber of Commerce want the [Mexican] trucking ban lifted, seeing it as an impediment to free commerce and damaging to US exporters." Export interests in the United States responded by launching a campaign to convince Congress to make the policy adjustments needed to address this violation (Hitt et al. 2009). The affected U.S. groups publicly accused the government of giving in to protectionist demands. As one account reported,

> [b]usiness interests ranging from Pennsylvania-based Hershey Co. to the USA Rice Federation are urging the White House to permit qualified Mexican truckers to drive on U.S. roads. Exporters affected by the tariffs say the government is causing economic damage by catering to unions that are more concerned with protecting jobs than improving safety. "This is the Obama administration trying to appease the Teamsters union without taking into account the effect it's going to have," said John Crossland, chairman of the California Association of Winegrape Growers [one of the affected export groups] (Conkey 2009, A3).

---

[4] Zeroing refers to a method for calculating antidumping duties; critics claim it tends to overestimate the duty assessed relative to the actual dumping performed.

Pressure by export interests and groups opposing this protectionist measure eventually reduced opposition to its settlement. "DeFazio [Democratic Congressman from Oregon and a major opponent of the Mexican trucking agreement] conceded that the Mexican retaliatory tariffs have convinced some House members who otherwise would have opposed opening up the border to support a trucking solution, since a solution would remove the higher tariffs facing exporters from their districts" (*Inside U.S. Trade* 2011, 5). American public attention was drawn to the protectionist actions of the United States by the NAFTA agreement; the DSM procedure activated export and other free trade interests to lobby the government for a change in the protectionist policy. In March 2011, Presidents Obama and Calderón signed an agreement to end the dispute, opening up the American market to Mexican trucking (Williamson 2011).

Similarly, in 2002 President George W. Bush imposed trade barriers on steel products in contradiction to the WTO agreements. The EU announced this violation and targeted U.S. export interests, which launched a campaign to eliminate these trade barriers. At the time, it was noted that "U.S. trade partners are angrier than Mr. Bush's foreign policy advisers expected. And users of steel are more vociferous than his business advisers anticipated, prompting the administration to carve exceptions to the tariffs" (King Jr. 2002, A1).

In each of these episodes, the U.S. public was informed about deviations from trade agreements as a result of the actions of foreign governments and domestic export groups. In the U.S.-EU steel episode, the EU retaliated against U.S. trade barriers by targeting goods produced in electorally sensitive states for the Bush administration. As *The Wall Street Journal* (Winestock and King Jr. 2002, A2) reported,

> [t]he EU is preparing a list of U.S. imported products valued at $2.1 billion annually that could be hit with heavy tariffs. Among the items on the list: Harley-Davidson motorcycles, Tropicana orange juice, and textiles and steel products. Many of the targeted industries are concentrated in states such as Florida, Wisconsin, Pennsylvania and West Virginia, which Mr. Bush battled for in his narrow election victory in 2000. These states figure prominently in the White House's effort to retain control of the House of Representatives in the fall elections.

Consequently, this trade dispute gained widespread publicity in these states and became the subject of national media attention as well. The loss of public support due to violating a trade agreement can keep leaders from giving in to protectionist demands.

In addition, opposition parties can help to inform the public about the government's behavior. As Kenneth Schultz (2001, 80) points out,

> [s]tudies of public opinion show that people are highly responsive to the cues they receive from elites. . . . Unity of opinion at the elite level tends to generate a similar

unity at the mass level. As a result when the opposition supports the government . . . , the latter enjoys a certain amount of political cover. . . . On the other hand, when the opposition opposes the government, it tends to polarize public opinion. . . . Thus, if large segments of the electorate are likely to follow the opposition party . . . , this strategy can generate a political payoff for the opposition and increase the political risks for the government.

In countries marked by genuine electoral competition, the opposition usually wants to discredit the government and the incumbent party. One way to do so is by charging that the government has been captured by special interests and has neglected the national interest. In bad economic times, this charge is likely to carry more weight since the government will have difficulty demonstrating that the downturn was not due to its rent-seeking. If, however, the government has signed and abided by a PTA, the opposition's argument will be harder to establish. As a result, the opposition may not advance this claim in the first place. If it does so, the government can respond that its hands were tied through a trade agreement that restricted its ability to protect special interests. Hence, it is not responsible for the adverse economic circumstances and should be reelected.

To voters, this argument by the government should be more convincing than if the government had not signed a PTA or if it signed and then violated a PTA. Without a trade agreement or in the face of one that the government has violated, the opposition's claims may be taken more seriously and the government may pay an electoral price for the economic malaise. In sum, members of the public and free trade interest groups—that is, exporters, importers, or multinational corporations—can learn about their government's behavior from the country's trading partners or trade institutions. International accusations of bad behavior are more newsworthy than unilateral changes in trade policy, and hence international trade agreements can provide greater reassurance than do politician's promises made solely in the context of domestic policy.

Our argument also emphasizes how international agreements can help leaders reduce the potential for lost political support by reassuring the public in advance about their intentions. But does society care about whether its government has signed and abided by PTAs? Publicly exposed cheating on trade agreements can generate domestic "audience costs" for political leaders, increasing the penalties they face for violating the accord (Fearon 1994; Lohmann 2003; Tomz 2007). This cost helps create a credible commitment. Recent public opinion research, for example, suggests that voters value trade agreements and believe they are needed to support an open trading system, implying that leaders may pay a political price for violating the rules of such institutions (Herrmann et al. 2001).

Further, Fiona McGillivray and Alastair Smith (2008) show that the public wants the government to target leaders of countries that cheat on international agreements, and that being named as a cheater has negative consequences for a country's leader. Such domestic punishment for cheating may deter it from engaging in such actions in the first place. Furthermore, the costs associated with cheating tend to be higher in democracies than in other regimes because the political survival of democratic leaders hinges on the outcome of competitive elections. Hence, democratic governments are at a greater disadvantage if they violate an international agreement. International economic cooperation can help democratic governments boost their chances of reelection, thereby providing a strong inducement for them to pursue PTAs.

Finally, it is useful to consider why leaders would choose a PTA rather than—or in addition to, as is usually the case now—joining the multilateral trade regime. Membership in the GATT/WTO may well provide a credible commitment mechanism for some countries (Maggi 1999). For many countries, however, it is much less likely to do so. One reason is that PTAs are often more binding agreements than the GATT/WTO. Most developing countries in the multilateral regime have had very high bound tariffs or have often been subject to special and differential treatment that allowed them to continue protecting their economies (Michalopoulos 2000; Özden and Reinhardt 2005). Many developing countries thus do not participate fully in the reciprocity that is central to the GATT/WTO.[5] In contrast, in most PTAs developing countries have to bargain for reciprocal trade barrier reductions. In all of the PTAs that we analyze, reciprocity is a defining feature. Consequently, for many of them, PTAs impose more stringent trade barrier reductions than the WTO. Furthermore, in many PTAs the difference between bound and applied tariff rates is much smaller than in the WTO (Hale 2009). This implies that countries often face greater constraints over their trade policy in PTAs than they do in the WTO setting.

A second reason is that PTAs are often better monitored and enforced than the WTO, especially with respect to the activities of smaller trading states. PTAs are frequently signed with one's neighbors or one's major trading partners and these countries have strong incentives to monitor the agreement.[6]

---

[5] As Michalopoulos (2000, 3–4) notes,

[t]oday developing countries probably account for over two thirds of the 135 Members of the World Trade Organization; and the WTO agreements contain a very extensive set of provisions addressing the rights and obligations of developing and least developed countries. . . . Developing countries sought to emphasise the uniqueness of their development problems and challenges and the need to be treated differently and more favourably in the GATT, in part by being permitted not to liberalise their own trade and in part by being extended preferential access to developed country markets.

[6] In our empirical analysis, we show that trade agreements are more likely to arise between relative equals than between pairs of countries marked by highly asymmetric power relations. This again suggests that monitoring and enforcement might be more likely within PTAs since relatively equal partners can more credibly threaten to punish one another.

This local monitoring may be more effective than multilateral monitoring for these countries. In sum, for the largest trading countries in the world, the WTO may function as a strong credible commitment device and one that restrains terms-of-trade competition. But for many states it may help their leaders less than a PTA.

In this section, we have explored several key assumptions in our argument. Our goal has been to increase confidence in the argument by providing evidence that these assumptions are reasonable, although it is important to recognize that they need not be completely realistic to be useful (Friedman 1953). Our argument suggests that international cooperation can help political leaders increase their chances of remaining in power, thereby providing a strong reason for them to pursue such agreements. By making an agreement, the executive trades some of her policy-setting discretion for the greater certainty that she will remain in office. The leader may benefit from the agreement because it reassures the public and reduces the prospects of being punished by voters and free trade interest groups, especially when economic downturns occur. These political benefits induce leaders to sign PTAs.

AN ALTERNATIVE ARGUMENT ABOUT PTAS AND DOMESTIC POLITICS: THE ROLE OF INTEREST GROUPS

To better understand our claims, it is useful to describe the main alternative argument about how domestic politics shapes the decision to enter PTAs. In general, research on the domestic political sources of these international agreements has been scant. In contrast to our focus, however, most extant research cast at the domestic level of analysis has centered on the effects of interest groups. In this view, the gains that certain interest groups expect from a trade agreement are the motivation for the agreement itself. These domestic groups pressure the government to realize the international accord in order to advance their interests.

Some of the earliest work in this vein was conducted by neofunctionalists (Deutsch et al. 1957; Haas 1958; Nye 1971). They saw the development of economic relations among countries as creating groups that gained from further ties, and thus the creation of pressure groups that pushed their governments to pursue further economic integration. As Joseph Nye (1988, 239) points out, "[w]hat these studies had in common was a focus on the ways in which increased transactions and contacts changed attitudes and transnational coalition opportunities, and the ways in which institutions helped to foster such interaction." Lately, there has been a revival of interest in neofunctionalism; some of that scholarship addresses whether PTAs form among countries with extensive economic ties as an institutional means to ensure that these ties will not be disrupted in the future (Sandholtz and Stone-Sweet 1998; Stone-Sweet et al. 2001).

These studies, many of which center on the EU, emphasize that domestic social groups that gain from a trade agreement constitute the main source of demand for economic integration agreements.

Most of the contemporary research on interest groups and PTAs, however, is not neofunctionalist. Instead, various studies have analyzed the incentives for different industries to lobby for or against the establishment of these arrangements. Andrew Moravcsik (1998, 473), for example, concludes that

> the most persistent and powerful source of varying national preferences concerning [European] integration over the past four decades has been economic, in particular commercial, interests . . . which locates the source of European integration in the explosion of world trade after World War II. In response . . . , governments tended to be heavily influenced by the commercial interests of domestic producer groups, interests that reflected respective positions in the global market.

Some interest groups have an incentive to press for trade agreements, and preferential ones often generate greater benefits for these groups than a multilateral one.

As we noted earlier, PTAs discriminate against third parties. Industries that could ward off competitors located in nonmember countries, if they were covered by a PTA, have an obvious reason to press for its establishment. So do export-oriented sectors that would benefit from preferential access to overseas markets. Michael Gilligan (1997), for instance, argues that export-oriented firms have a strong incentive to lobby for reciprocal trade agreements because they will realize the lion's share of the benefits stemming from reciprocal (but not unilateral or multilateral) trade liberalization. In the same vein, Helen Milner (1997b) and Kerry Chase (2003 and 2005) claim that exporters are particularly likely to support the formation of PTAs if they operate in industries characterized by economies of scale, since PTAs will both protect them from foreign competition and offer them access to a larger market, thereby allowing them to realize significant reductions in per-unit production costs. A number of scholars further attribute interest in PTAs to the pressure of multinational corporations, which have global trading and production networks that induce them to seek to protect their networks through PTAs (Solis 2003; Manger 2005 and 2009). These studies thus identify large, multinational firms in the major trading countries as a prime source of political pressure for PTAs. Demands by these types of actors should be a primary force for initiating a trade agreement.

Another set of studies on the role of interest groups has argued that the redistributive effects of PTAs within countries are likely to influence the political support for and opposition to these arrangements. Public officials must strike a balance between promoting a country's aggregate economic welfare and accommodating interest groups whose support is needed to retain office. Gene Grossman and Elhanan Helpman (1995) argue that whether a country chooses to enter a PTA is determined by how much influence different interest groups exert and how much the government is concerned about the median voter's welfare. They demonstrate that the political viability of a PTA often depends on the amount of discrimination it yields. Agreements that are trade diverting will benefit special interests, while creating costs borne by the populace at large. If these groups have more political clout than other segments of society, then a PTA that is trade diverting stands a better chance of being established than one that is trade creating.

In the same vein, Pravin Krishna (1998) shows that governments are more likely to form preferential arrangements if they are trade diverting, since such arrangements create rents for interest groups that have considerable political clout.[7] As noted above, Maggi and Rodríguez-Clare (1998 and 2007) have developed models of trade agreements, including PTAs, which emphasize the role of interest groups. In these models, the government extends trade protection to industries in exchange for their political contributions and support. Finally, Etel Solingen (2008) argues that the origins of PTAs are sometimes best explained by the nature and preferences of the dominant internal coalitions in member-states. Both economists and political scientists then have identified interest groups as a major impetus for international trade agreements, especially preferential ones.

In these studies, the gains that some interest groups expect from such agreements motivate them to lobby governments to pursue PTA membership. The more that the agreement diverts trade, the more of these gains they can capture. Hence, if PTAs are driven by interest groups, they are likely to be trade diverting and to degrade the economic welfare of both the country itself and the rest of the world. Governments nonetheless supply such agreements because of the political contributions and support they can generate from these interest groups, which can compensate for any loss they suffer from the adverse impact of trade diversion. As a recent review of the regional trade agreement (RTA) literature points out, "[i]f governments were simply interested in national welfare in their countries, there would be no reason for concern: Only trade-creating, welfare-improving RTAs would come into force. But governments also have other motivations and are in particular influenced by special interest groups. . . . Governments influenced by special interest groups will seek primarily trade-diverting RTAs" (Freund and Ornelas 2010, 142).

Thus, if interest group arguments are correct, PTAs should be largely trade diverting. But the empirical literature strongly suggests that "trade diversion is not a major concern, although in some agreements and sectors it may matter"

---

[7] Ornelas (2005, 1476–77), however, concludes that "[a]nticipating these effects, and recognizing that lower rents imply lower contributions, a politically motivated government will adopt only FTAs that raise national welfare enough to compensate for the lower rents—that is, those that are sufficiently trade-creating." Richardson (1994) and Bagwell and Staiger (1999) also argue that FTAs tend to weaken protectionist pressure groups in member-states.

(Freund and Ornelas 2010, 144). The bulk of empirical evidence is therefore inconsistent with the thrust of interest group arguments about PTAs. Indeed, Baier and Bergstrand (2004 and 2007) show that trade creation is the modal outcome of these agreements and that states form PTAs when there are gains to be realized from trade liberalization. Our argument suggests not only which governments are likely to enter trade agreements, but also why they might prefer to join trade-creating arrangements.

Although interest groups can play a role in shaping PTAs, they are not the focus of our study for three reasons. First, because trade policy has distributional consequences, certain domestic coalitions will favor freer trade and others will favor protectionism (Rogowski 1987 and 1989; Milner 1988; Hiscox 2002). The composition and power of these distributional coalitions differ across countries, since states vary with respect to their comparative advantage and factor endowments. In a cross-national context, however, it is extremely hard to determine how to identify and empirically specify the structure of interest groups in each country. There are no existing measures that delineate the distribution of interest groups across countries or over time.

Second, as we explained in chapter 1 and as we discuss in greater detail below, one of our central arguments concerns the effects of veto players on PTA formation. Like many existing studies of veto players, we assume that interest groups affect trade policy indirectly. On the one hand, these groups shape the preferences of the executive, since he or she worries about retaining office and thus requires their support. The executive negotiates with interest groups over the choice of whether to proceed with a PTA and over its terms prior to engaging in international negotiations. Thus, the executive's position already reflects the influence of those interest groups that are important to the executive.

In addition, interest groups affect policy indirectly through their influence on the preferences of veto players. Trade policy creates distributional winners and losers, and thus generates incentives for interest groups to organize and press for their policy preferences. One way these pressures become manifest is through political parties and their platforms. There is a long tradition of associating parties with the trade policy preferences of different interest groups (Rogowski 1989; Milner and Judkins 2004). Preferences over trade policy often structure political cleavages that are represented in party systems. Hence, we expect interest groups to operate through parties, and leaders of such parties constitute the executive and legislature. In our model of veto players, the structure of the legislature and its partisan composition are key elements. We therefore indirectly account for interest groups through their impact on the preferences of the chief executive and political parties.

Third, arguments about the effects of interest groups on trade agreements suggest that these groups—and not the government—are the primary drivers of PTAs. But it is not clear that interest groups play much of a role in the decision to form a PTA. In fact, heads of government often decide to enter a PTA, regardless of interest group preferences. Consider the situation Napoleon III faced on the eve of the 1860 Anglo-French commercial arrangement. Anxious to liberalize trade with Great Britain, he encountered a French legislature and various salient domestic groups that were highly protectionist. But while the legislature had considerable control over unilateral trade policy, the Constitution of 1851 permitted the emperor to sign international treaties without this body's approval. Napoleon therefore was able to skirt well-organized protectionist interests by concluding a PTA (Kindleberger 1975, 39–40; Irwin 1993, 96). Moreover, this is not an isolated case. Douglas Irwin (1993, 116 fn. 7) notes that, during this era, "[c]ommercial agreements in the form of foreign treaties proved useful in circumventing protectionist interests in the legislature throughout Europe." It is the decision of leaders to enter these agreements that often needs explanation, and this is the focus of our argument.

Similarly, governments that propose a program of liberal economic reforms and encounter (or expect to encounter) domestic opposition may enter a PTA to bind themselves to these changes (Summers 1991; de Melo et al. 1993; Haggard 1997; Whalley 1998). Mexico's decision to enter NAFTA, for example, is frequently discussed in such terms (Tornell and Esquivel 1997, 54; Whalley 1998, 71–72). For a state that is interested in making liberal economic reforms, the attractiveness of locking in such changes through an external mechanism, like joining a PTA, is likely to grow if influential segments of society oppose reforms and if domestic institutions render policy makers especially susceptible to societal pressures. Our model of domestic politics builds on this idea of domestic "lock in," but it elaborates some conditions under which these agreements are politically profitable for the government.

These claims form the main alternative domestic political argument about PTAs. The domestic interest group argument cannot be directly examined in our quantitative analysis. But we do consider some of its implications in our short case studies below. And, as we noted, we do take interest groups into account indirectly through our analysis of veto players.

REGIME TYPE, DOMESTIC POLITICAL COSTS, AND PTAS

Our argument helps to explain why leaders might want to enter PTAs. But the domestic political costs and benefits that we emphasize are difficult to measure and test directly. Therefore, we develop a testable hypothesis about the conditions under which these costs and benefits are more likely to arise, influencing the incentives for joining a PTA.

The extent of the domestic political costs generated by a leader's inability to resist engaging in excessive rent-seeking varies according to a country's regime type. While autocracies have difficulty reassuring the public about their intentions, there is less need for them to do so since they are not regularly confronted by voters and interest groups who can easily remove them from office. Democratic leaders, by contrast, are confronted with more substantial reassurance problems. Domestic political competition can generate political costs that leaders seek to mitigate through international cooperation, including PTAs.

Our analysis of regime type emphasizes the role of elections. It shows how international cooperation in trade is affected by the control that the public and interest groups exert over political leaders, a factor that varies in important ways between democracies and autocracies. Fundamental to all democracies is the regular occurrence of fair and competitive elections (Dahl 1971, 1–5; Schumpeter 1976 [1942], 269). As G. Bingham Powell (2000, 4) observes, "[t]here is a widespread consensus that the presence of competitive elections, more than any other feature, identifies a contemporary nation-state as a democratic political system." Schumpeter (1976 [1942]) points out that such elections vest the public with control over government leaders that is absent in nondemocratic polities. Free and fair elections have the greatest influence on the behavior of democratic leaders if the public and interest groups care about the policy choices made by leaders.

Both democracies and autocracies can and do hold elections (e.g., Gandhi and Przeworski 2007). What differs across regimes is the degree to which these contests affect the executive's fate. The more democratic a country, the more important elections are in determining whether the incumbent leader retains office. If the election's outcome is binding on the executive, the regime is democratic. If, on the other hand, the executive retains office irrespective of the voters' decision, the regime is autocratic. We expect a continuum of possibilities for the role of elections and hence for the type of regime: the degree to which the election controls the fate of the executive ranges from low to high. We therefore view regime type as a continuous variable that depends on the competitiveness of the electoral system.

Differences in the degree of electoral competition in political systems affect the optimal foreign economic strategy of political leaders. Some international trade agreements stem from the economic gains that leaders expect to derive from cooperation. Equally important but far more poorly understood, however, are the *political gains* that motivate leaders to cooperate on trade. The degree of electoral competition affects leaders' domestic political incentives. As the fate of a government becomes more dependent on free and fair elections, its leaders derive increasing gains from PTAs, prompting public officials to engage in greater cooperation with other countries on commercial issues. Hence, the probability of a country concluding a trade agreement rises as its domestic institutions grow more democratic. In our analysis, the greater electoral constraints faced by democratic heads of government influences them to be more cooperative internationally than their nondemocratic counterparts. The reassurance that PTAs provide to societal groups in democracies helps alleviate the concern that some voters and free trade interest groups have about governments yielding too much to protectionist demands.

PTAs can help both governments and voters. Trade agreements can convey information to voters and free trade interest groups about the nature and activities of leaders; and such information can increase political support for leaders, helping them retain office. Governments generally want to remain in power. In countries marked by genuine electoral competition, they will be highly motivated to take actions that maintain or increase their political support. But governments face a time inconsistency problem. They would prefer to resist protectionist demands, but when these arise they are usually better off giving in to each group that requests protection. Voters and free trade interest groups know this and are harmed by excessive government rent-seeking. They, in turn, can threaten action to lower the incumbent's probability of retaining office. That is, they can threaten to sanction incumbents and to select new leaders.

But voters and free trade interest groups also face an informational problem. They may not know the preferences of or the exact trade policy chosen by the government, thereby hampering their ability to distinguish between adverse exogenous economic shocks and the extractive policies of leaders. An economic downturn could be caused or exacerbated by highly protectionist policies or by an exogenous shock such as a global recession or economic crisis. Both events, for example, might increase the price that the public pays for goods and services, and thus dampen the public's support for the government.

In a democracy, voters may, as a result of this informational problem, reduce their support for the incumbent leader during economic downturns, even if that leader has not engaged in excessive rent-seeking. This prospect creates a cost for the government. Voters may turn against the government even though it did not cave in to protectionist interests, and there is little way for the government to change voters' behavior. That is, the median voter may decide to punish the incumbent and support the challenger in response to bad economic times. Voters may not know much about trade policy, but they do know something about overall economic conditions. The public may not display much interest in or knowledge of policy issues, but economic performance is typically of great concern (e.g., Fiorina 1981; Kiewiet 1983; Lewis-Beck 1988; Fair 2009). When the economy sours, voters will be more likely to reject incumbents and this is the dynamic upon which our argument relies. Voters take many factors into consideration, but the state of the economy is an important criterion, as leaders recognize (Kramer 1971; Fair 1978; Fiorina 1981; Ferejohn 1986).[8]

Leaders would like to find a way to indicate that poor economic performance is not the result of their extractive policies, thereby reducing the likelihood that

---

[8] Fair (2009) shows that the economy influences both presidential and legislative elections; the economic factors he concentrates on are the growth rate and inflation rate. Trade policy can affect both of these aggregates; protectionism may slow growth and increase inflation.

they will lose power.[9] While they could choose to unilaterally lower trade barriers, this choice is time inconsistent. Entering into a trade agreement with another country, however, may provide a means to convince skeptical publics and interest groups, especially in democracies. An agreement represents a commitment to maintain a relatively open trade regime and is a device to reassure voters and free trade interest groups that a relatively liberal trade policy has been adopted. The public gains from lower levels of protection and from the reassurance and monitoring that the agreement provides. Leaders gain from the greater political support they may command with an agreement because of its monitoring and reassurance vis-à-vis domestic groups.

Of course, in democracies the public has many sources of information. On the one hand, it is possible that the public may not need a PTA to furnish information about the behavior of governments. On the other hand, however, these additional sources of information may not be terribly relevant for international issues like trade. The public is likely to derive more reassurance from an international agreement than from the information provided by domestic sources since many such sources are linked to the groups desiring protection and hence are biased in one way or another. PTAs could also furnish biased information, but this strikes us as less likely to occur. Moreover, any bias displayed by a PTA is likely to be different from that displayed by domestic sources, which creates an incentive for the public to pay attention to both types of information.

It is important to recognize that we are not arguing that democratic leaders have a greater preference for free trade than leaders in other regimes. Instead, democratic leaders are more likely to join PTAs than other governments because electoral competition creates an incentive for them to do so. PTAs solve an informational problem that hurts the head of government. Participating in a trade agreement reassures the public and interest groups favoring trade that executives will refrain from overprotecting special interests and thereby enhances the leader's political support.

Autocrats, however, do not face this cost. In general, they are less vulnerable to special interest pressures than democratic leaders. Even in cases where they are susceptible to such pressure, the public cannot sanction autocrats in the same way that they can punish democratic leaders. Furthermore, it is less likely that the public in an autocracy understands whether the government has signed and is abiding by an agreement, since autocracies lack many of the institutions—such as a free press and robust opposition parties—that provide information to the public in democracies. Because autocrats have less reason to worry about reelection, there is less need for them to solve this informational

---

[9] Even if the public's preferences for protection rise in bad economic times, our results still hold. As long as the median voter is slightly less protectionist than the executive, the public will still be concerned about the executive relinquishing too much to protectionist demands (Mansfield et al. 2002).

problem by concluding commercial agreements. With little electoral competition, autocrats are less likely to be removed from office than democratic leaders and do not have to worry as much about how economic conditions are going to affect their survival. They thus have fewer incentives to commit their country to a lower level of trade barriers in exchange for the informational advantages that an agreement could bring them. As McGillivray and Smith (2008, 54) point out,

> [w]hen the cost of replacing leaders is high [as in an autocracy], the citizens do not replace leaders in poor [international] standing. . . . When the cost of replacing leaders is low [as in a democracy], citizens replace leaders who are caught cheating [on international agreements]. By doing so, citizens ensure continued cooperation. . . . This desire to avoid cheating allows leaders to commit to maintain a level of commitment that the citizens themselves could not maintain.

Violating an international agreement does not carry the same costs for an autocrat as it does for a democratic government. Hence, it provides less reassurance.

Although we expect democratic leaders to enter PTAs at a more rapid clip than autocracies, it is clear that the latter regimes sometimes sign trade agreements. Our model does not bear directly on why autocracies do so, but it suggests that the extent of political competition within these states might affect their likelihood of joining a PTA. Furthermore, it suggests that autocracies are generally less likely to sign these agreements for domestic political reasons than are democracies. Instead, autocrats may be driven more by factors such as economic benefits of PTA membership or international political advantages. Moreover, the PTAs that autocracies enter are likely to aim for more shallow integration, with less trade barrier reduction. Finally, such PTAs might also be much more likely to fail (due to cheating) since autocracies would not pay as great a domestic political price for their collapse as would a democracy. Our model therefore generates some expectations about why autocracies might sign trade agreements; and especially some expectations about how they would differ from those signed by democracies. We elaborate on these later in this chapter and test some of these ideas in chapter 5.

Two Cases of Democracy and PTA Formation: SADC and Mercosur

Below we present two brief case studies of PTAs from different parts of the world that illustrate our argument. In both cases, the preferential grouping was established in the wake of a democratic transition in at least one member-state. In both cases, the decision to enter the grouping was made by political leaders who faced little interest group pressure, but substantial concerns about elections and political competition. We also present some evidence that the public had knowledge of the PTAs and had a positive opinion of them, suggesting that trade agreements might be a popular tool for political leaders.

South Africa and the SADC

South Africa's decision to join the SADC illustrates our argument about how democracy promotes PTA membership. It also shows the differences between our argument about domestic politics and those that rely more heavily on interest groups. Between 1990 and 1994, South Africa underwent a democratic transition as apartheid ended and the African National Congress (ANC), the main anti-apartheid party, competed in its first elections. As we describe in chapters 3, 4, and 5, we rely primarily on the Polity Project's 21-point index of regime type in this book, which ranges from 1 for the most autocratic countries to 21 for the most democratic states (Marshall and Jaggers 2005). South Africa's score rose gradually from 15 in 1989 to a high of 20 in 1994 and beyond. While it held competitive elections before 1994, the franchise and political rights were restricted to the white minority. Democratization in South Africa led to a widening of the franchise and extension of political rights to the entire population.

The SADC is one of the most important PTAs in the developing world. It is composed of a diverse group of fifteen countries with a total of more than 200 million inhabitants. Intraregional trade as a percent of total trade more than doubled during the 1990s for SADC countries, reaching 20 percent in 1997; and South Africa was the major beneficiary of this growth (De la Rocha 2003, 7). For South Africa, which is by far the biggest SADC member, foreign trade accounted for about 50 percent of its gross domestic product (GDP) by the turn of the twenty-first century. The formation of a PTA that promoted trade in the region was therefore in South Africa's interests.

Many observers have noted that this democratic transition was necessary for the South African government to join SADC, as well as a revised Southern African Customs Union (SACU)[10] and the African Economic Community (AEC) (e.g., Hentz 2005, 31; Gibb 2007). As Adam Habib and Vishnu Padayachee (2000, 245) mention, South Africa's democratic transition thrust new groups onto the political stage, which created "the possibility for significant changes in the economic policies." The South African government joined SADC in 1994, soon after its inaugural democratic election. In August 1996, SADC members approved a free trade area, which entered into force in 2000.[11] Democratization

---

[10] While the original SACU was signed many years earlier (1910), it was essentially a nonmutual PTA until recently, when it was renegotiated. "Post-apartheid South Africa prioritised 'democratisation', both domestically and throughout Africa, and the new 2004 SACU Agreement reflects this fundamental re-orientation of policy in South Africa. The 1910 and 1969 SACU Agreements were profoundly undemocratic, enabling Pretoria to determine tariffs and excise rates unilaterally for the whole SACU region" (Gibb 2007, 429–30). It signed the AEC agreement in 1997 and finally ratified it in 2001.

[11] South Africa ratified the FTA in 1999 and began implementing the FTA agreement in 2000. After a nearly ten-year phase-in, the full FTA was launched in 2008. Further moves include the establishment of a customs union by 2010, a common market by 2015, a monetary union by 2016, and a single currency and regional central bank by 2018 (SADC Barometer 2003). One reason for the delay between signing and ratification was due to domestic politics in South Africa. The

was an impetus for the ANC government to join this and a number of other PTAs, significantly lowering its trade barriers.[12]

Why, however, was the new ANC government interested in joining these PTAs? The new ANC government was the prime mover in the trade negotiations. Interest groups, largely because they were associated with the previous apartheid regime, were of little influence in this case. The decision to join was linked to an overall economic policy strategy that the ANC government decided upon.

Domestic political factors were especially important. This government faced a novel set of constraints and problems after the 1994 elections. It confronted a set of social actors who had been newly empowered by democracy and the elections. Even though it was elected by a large margin, fissures within the ANC and competition between it and other groups led to heightened political competition within South Africa. Further, the ANC faced the possibility that bad economic times could reduce or even eliminate its majority, especially if such circumstances split the ANC and precipitated the formation of a new party.

The end of apartheid resulted in the incorporation of the black population into the political system, extending them the franchise and political rights. The long struggle to end apartheid had consolidated black political support behind one party, the ANC, which represented a very broad and diverse set of interests. During the first years after apartheid, the ANC aimed to remain unified and prevent splinter parties from forming. The government won elections handily in the 1990s (and beyond) and it faced limited competition from the parties representing white voters. Its main source of political competition was internal. Differences in economic policy preferences among its various constituent groups were a central concern for the party, especially at the time of the first election in 1994. As one commentator noted at the time, "[e]conomic policy has the potential to split the ANC and to place great strain on its alliance with

---

clothing and textile industries, which opposed the SADC PTA, were influential veto players in South Africa's debate over ratification of the Protocol (Hentz 2005, 35). The unions and businesses in South Africa had two worries. The first was that eliminating tariffs within the SADC while allowing external tariffs to vary across SADC members would mean that the products of non-SADC members would enter the arrangement through the SADC country with the lowest external tariff (Sharpe 1998). A second concern was that the free trade area would lead to job losses in South Africa (Dludlu 1999), especially as businesses moved to the Southern African countries with the lowest labor costs (Hentz 2008, 505). In response to these concerns and with the help of the clothing and textile industries (Hentz 2005, 506), the South African government had to insert more protection of the clothing and textile industries into the SADC agreement, especially in the rules of origin. This also illustrates our argument about domestic veto players.

[12] "Between 1990–96, the average economy-wide tariff fell from 28 to 10 per cent, while the average manufacturing tariff dropped was reduced from 30 to 16 per cent. . . . The maximum tariff rate was cut to 61 per cent (40 per cent if 'sensitive' industries are excluded), the number of tariff lines was cut by a third, and the number of separate tariff 'bands' or rates cut from 200 to 49" (Lewis 2002, 347).

the South African Communist Party (SACP) and the Congress of South African Trade Unions (COSATU)" (Nattrass 1994, 343).

Left-wing factions in the ANC wanted nationalization of much of the economy combined with a vast redistribution of wealth. Parts of the ANC's left wing also advocated protectionism as a way to restructure the economy and pursue a state-run industrial policy, especially in the nationalized sector. But centrists in the ANC opposed this tack, viewing it as a costly tax on consumers who were mainly the poor black voters making up the ANC's chief constituency (Nattrass 1994, 354). This faction advocated reducing trade barriers as a way to prevent "the exploitation of South African consumers" (Nattrass 1994, 354–55). Centrists in the ANC also proposed liberalizing trade and forming PTAs due to their concerns over political competition within the party and a desire to maintain power. The centrists worried "that over-rapid redistribution would guarantee economic collapse, and thus guarantee also an ANC government forfeiting chances of re-election. [Thus,] over the course of 1991, the ANC's national leadership started projecting more moderate, business-friendly policies," including trade liberalization (Nattrass 1994, 351). By 1996, it unveiled the "Growth, Employment, and Redistribution" (GEAR) program, "a neo-liberal strategy designed to make South Africa a destination for foreign investment and a competitive global trading state" (Tieku 2004, 253). Crucial to this program was the belief that economic growth and stability would be needed to promote political and social stability (Evans 1999, 627). Economic liberalization would be necessary for political reasons and trade liberalization, including the formation of PTAs, was part of this larger strategy.

Throughout the 1990s, South Africa signed a series of PTAs, including SADC in 1994 and the AEC in 1997. It also joined the GATT/WTO. SADC committed South Africa to trade barrier reductions. It was opposed by big business in South Africa, especially by the textile, apparel, footwear, and furniture industries that were likely to face import competition as a result of such reductions (Hentz 2005, 43). Lowering trade barriers in industries without comparative advantage would mean more import competition. The ANC, however, had little political incentive to protect big business. Nor was it interested in protecting low skill industries.

On the contrary, the ANC leadership was committed to opening up these sectors. As David Lewis, Kabelo Reed, and Ethel Teljeur (2004, 160) point out,

[t]here is a certain common irony in the ANC's support for trade reform and competition policy. Both derive strongly from the ANC's anti-capitalist roots, or, at least, from its distance from domestic business interests. The relatively easy passage through the ANC and, particularly, its union allies, of trade reform has much to do with the exclusion of the ANC from the ranks of national capital, combined with the strongly held view that tariff protection amounted to little more than a feeding trough for white-owned business.

Interest groups then seem to have played little role in the ANC government's decision to join SADC. Instead, this decision was part of a political strategy for the government.

The ANC's strategy of lowering trade barriers by signing the SADC had at least some roots in South Africa's domestic political conditions. The government needed to reassure parts of the public about its support for trade liberalization to help stimulate economic growth and hence promote political support. It needed to demonstrate that it was not the handmaiden of protectionist interests and would not sacrifice the general welfare to special interests. Reinventing South Africa as a "global trading state" was the ANC government's goal for a set of domestic and international reasons (Evans 1999, 627). By signing the PTA, it avoided potential costs associated with the public's suspicion of its economic policies. The ANC government knew that the costs of reneging on a liberal trade policy would be much higher with an international agreement in place.

Further, the government recognized that industries in partner countries would be all too ready to monitor and complain about any violations of the agreement by South African businesses. South Africa is the economic leader in southern Africa; its gross domestic product is nine times larger than the other southern African nations combined (Lewis et al. 1999, 4).[13] It has also run large trade surpluses with its southern African neighbors. As a result, South Africa's partners in trade agreements are very sensitive to its dominance and to any sign that it is not living up to its obligations (Hentz 2005).

To address this concern, the agreement set up various institutions designed to monitor trade policy. The SADC Tribunal, for instance, hears disputes among the member-states, and the SADC Trade, Industry, and Investment Review provides annual audits of members' trade policies as well as other aspects of the agreement.[14] During the phase-in to the SADC FTA, a new mechanism of monitoring was set up to allow private sector groups to join the monitoring process.[15]

---

[13] "In 2003 approximately 90 per cent of SACU's GNP was produced in South Africa. The corresponding figures for SADC and COMESA are 66 per cent and 61 per cent, respectively. South Africa's real GNP is approximately three times larger than the combined GNP of the other 13 SADC states and in 2004 South Africa accounted for approximately 25 per cent of total African GNP" (Gibb 2007, 431–32).

[14] "Annexe [sic] VI of the SADC Trade Protocol provides for a trade dispute settlement mechanism, thereby underscoring and enforcing the point that it is a rules-based regional trading system" (SADC Barometer 2003, 10).

[15] "To monitor the implementation of the FTA, a Trade Monitoring and Compliance Mechanism has been set up by SADC. This body will ensure that SADC member states implement agreed programmes and provide a facility for resolving problems on a day-to-day basis. Its effectiveness, says SADC, depends on the full and active participation of the business community, which must take the lead in identifying problems related to cross-border trade." See Erasmus (2008) available at http://www.mediaclubsouthafrica.com/index.php?option=com_content&view=article&id=633:sadc-free-trade-area-180808&catid=45:economy_news&Itemid=55. (Last accessed July 27, 2011.)

Membership in the SADC helped solve an informational problem for the newly democratic South African government by helping reassure the public that its policies would promote the general welfare rather than enriching special interests pleading for protection. Data on public attitudes toward the SADC in South Africa also provides some support for this claim. The *Afrobarometer: Round II Survey of South Africa* in 2002 shows that about 50 percent of the public had heard of SADC. Of those individuals who had heard of SADC, close to 70 percent thought it was performing well.[16] As one discussion of SADC observes, PTAs like this one "can help address concerns over policy credibility by locking in domestically implemented trade liberalization and functioning as an agency of restraint" (Khandelwal 2003, 19).

Clearly, there are various reasons why South Africa opted to enter the SADC. Some of these owe little to domestic politics, including an interest in rewarding its regional neighbors for supporting the ANC when it was in exile during apartheid, attempting to stem the flow of illegal labor from these countries to South Africa, and its interest in bolstering its power base in the region.[17] Nonetheless, the South African case also illustrates how political competition in a democracy can induce governments to adopt PTAs that reassure their publics about their intentions and thus help them gain public support.

Argentina and Brazil in Mercosur

Argentina's and Brazil's decision to create Mercosur (i.e., the Common Market of the Southern Cone) in combination with Uruguay and Paraguay further illustrates our argument about the effects of democracy on PTA membership. Launched in 1991, Mercosur is one of the most robust PTAs in the developing world. Exports among Mercosur's member-states rose dramatically during the first years of the agreement, from US$4.1 billion in 1990 to US$20.4 billion in 1998. Additionally, intra-Mercosur trade as a percentage of members' total trade increased from 8.3 percent in 1989 to 23.7 percent in 1997 (Kaltenthaler and Mora 2002, 91). The agreement also contributed to domestic political stability in the countries involved, as we explain below.

Mercosur was formed on the heels of transitions to democracy in Argentina (1983) and Brazil (1985), following several decades of authoritarian rule in both countries (Vanden and Prevost 2002, 374–76 and 407). Based on the Polity Project's 21-point index of regime type that we discuss further in chapters 3, 4, and 5 (Marshall and Jaggers 2005), Argentina's score rose from 3 to 19 in

---

[16] *Afrobarometer: Round II Survey of South Africa*, 2002. The question was: "Giving marks out of ten, where 0 is very badly and 10 is very well, how well do you think the following institutions do their jobs? Or haven't you heard enough about the institution to have an opinion? Southern African Development Community (SADC)." Of the total respondents, about 35 percent responded at 5 or above.

[17] We are grateful to B. Peter Rosendorff for this point.

1983, and Brazil's score increased from 8 to 18 in 1985, indicative of a clear shift to democracy in both countries. These regime changes were essential for the formation of Mercosur. Political leaders in Brazil and Argentina saw the trade agreement as part of an economic strategy that would help them politically. They initiated the agreement with little input from interest groups and with substantial concern for their domestic political situations.

The idea of forming a PTA in the Southern Cone was hatched by Argentina's and Brazil's newly elected presidents—Raúl Alfonsín in Argentina (1983–1989) and José Sarney in Brazil (1985–1990), respectively—immediately after the transitions to democracy. Alfonsín and Sarney, however, did not achieve a common market. Instead, a meeting between their successors, Presidents Carlos Menem of Argentina and Fernando Collor de Mello of Brazil, in July 1990 culminated in the signing of the Act of Buenos Aires, which called for the creation of a common market by the end of 1994 (Gardini 2010, 91–92). Negotiations were expanded to include Paraguay and Uruguay in August 1990. Following a final round of negotiations in February 1991, all four countries signed the Treaty of Asunción, which formally established Mercosur. This PTA called for the free circulation of goods and services, the reduction of internal trade barriers, a common external tariff, and macroeconomic coordination (Gardini 2010, 95–96).

Alfonsín, Sarney, and their respective successors—Carlos Menem in Argentina and Fernando Collor de Mello in Brazil—viewed the trade agreement as a means to improve their countries' economies by facilitating economic stability, growth, and competitiveness, as well as deeper integration into the global economy (Manzetti 1993, 110; Oelsner 2003, 194 and 198–99; Perales 2003, 84–86; Gardini 2005, 417; 2007, 824). For these leaders, however, domestic political competition and electoral incentives also played key roles in the decision to establish Mercosur. Prior to the democratization process, autocratic leaders in both countries had made a number of attempts to develop trade agreements that promoted economic integration.

But those leaders were unable and unwilling to proceed very far. In Brazil, autocratic leaders were wedded politically to import-substituting industrialization (ISI) as a political strategy and it is unlikely their governments would have retained power with a sudden change to open trade (Kaltenthaler and Mora 2002, 73–75). Moreover, the macroeconomic crises both countries faced weakened their leadership politically and pushed them into more protectionist modes, which undermined any attempt at regional integration (Hirst 1988, 5–7; Kaltenthaler and Mora 2002, 73).

Democratization brought a dramatic change in both countries. The new political leaders had different political concerns and constituents. They were no longer beholden to the industries protected by ISI and they needed to generate economic stability and growth in order to survive politically. The initial decision to develop a PTA in the Southern Cone was political and had its roots in the desire for economic stability and growth to augment political support for both presidents. At its most basic level, democratization in Argentina and Brazil facilitated the popular political participation of individual voters whose electoral support would henceforth be necessary to ensure survival in office. Much of this electoral support depended on economic conditions. By 1990, the second generation of democratic leaders had watched the first generation fall from power because of serious economic setbacks; they became convinced that promoting regional economic integration would yield political fruit. At the same time, the legislature and organized domestic groups, such as business and labor, appear to have played little role in the actual integration process (Kaltenthaler and Mora 2002).[18]

A central problem for the new democratic governments in Argentina and Brazil was the lack of governmental credibility with respect to economic policy. Time and again, leaders had promised to keep inflation in check and avoid deficits, and they had usually given in to societal pressures when times turned difficult. As one study of Mercosur notes,

> [p]oliticians [in Brazil and Argentina] not only had to deal with a relatively unreceptive private sector, but also had a credibility problem that affected the implementation of their economic policy announcements. . . . In order to break the time inconsistency trap decision makers needed to establish the credibility of their commitments to reform. . . . By linking trade reform to an international bargain, leaders would be reinforcing the credibility of their commitments to economic openness. . . . The choice of a customs union over other forms of PTAs conforms to the commitment problem these governments were facing: the CET leads to stronger policy coordination among countries (Perales 2003, 94–95).

Political leaders understood that an international agreement would be a stronger signal for reassuring their publics than a simple domestic policy change and thus would have greater political benefits.

Both Menem and Collor were acutely aware that their future electoral success and chances for reelection would hinge upon their ability to produce economic stability and growth, as the failures of Sarney and Alfonsín had underlined.[19] Thus, despite the existence of single term limits, it is clear that concerns about domestic political support played a role in shaping executives' decision about Mercosur in Argentina and Brazil. As one pair of observers point out, "it was critical for Alfonsín and Sarney that their heterodox economic policies and state-directed integration process succeed in order to strengthen democratic

---

[18] The lesser role played by elected legislators in the decision on Mercosur compared to each country's executive is consistent with the high degree of "presidentialism" characterizing the political systems in both Argentina (Jones 1997, 259–62) and, to a somewhat lesser degree, Brazil (Mainwaring 1997, 55–56) at the time of integration. This was particularly apparent in the areas of economic policymaking and foreign policy (Perales 2003, 93; Gardini 2007, 822).

[19] This premise assumes that term limits would be altered, as they eventually were in the case of Argentina and Brazil.

rule and their domestic political position" (Kaltenthaler and Mora 2002, 85). Mercosur was seen as an economic means to a political goal. Democratic leaders in both countries wanted to use trade integration to bolster their domestic political positions.

It is also worth briefly considering the electoral incentives faced by legislators in Argentina and Brazil. The emphasis placed thus far on the salience of electoral constraints for incumbent executives is consistent with the observations of Latin America scholars, as well as nearly all scholars studying Mercosur, that Argentina and Brazil are both presidential political systems in which legislatures play a relatively weaker role (Jones 1997, 285; Mainwaring 1997, 55; Perales 2003, 93; Leiras and Soltz 2006, 25; Gardini 2010, 126–27). Nevertheless, characteristics of the political system that manifest themselves in each country's legislature may have exerted at least a marginal impact on the integration process, as entry into force of the Treaty of Asunción required ratification by both the Argentinean and Brazilian Congress (Gardini 2010, 114). In Argentina, high party discipline has historically encouraged legislators to vote along party lines, as was the case with ratification of the aforementioned trade accords under Alfonsín and Sarney (Jones 1997, 278–79). By contrast, in Brazil, the legislature has historically been characterized by much higher levels of party fragmentation, which made it more difficult for both Sarney and Collor to pass the trade agreement's legislation (Mainwaring 1997, 91–96).

Legislators also made it clear that their support for integration was driven to some extent by electoral concerns stemming from Argentina's and Brazil's recent transitions to democracy. For example, in Argentina, Unión Cívica Radical Congressman Federico Storani—the president and vice president of the Foreign Affairs Committee of the Chamber of Deputies from 1983 to 1989 and 1989 to 1991, respectively—notes that on the whole the Chamber of Deputies was both well-informed and in support of Alfonsín's push for regional economic integration. Moreover, Menem's Partido Justicialista was also largely in favor of the proposed integration project, with the exception of a small group of party members (Gardini 2010, 115–16). Given legislators' willingness to ratify the Treaty of Asunción, this lends added support to the argument that legislators viewed ratification of the integration accords as beneficial to their survival in office.

Patterns of legislative behavior in Brazil with regard to ratification of the integration accords were similar to those in Argentina. The ratification of the Buenos Aires Act and the Treaty of Asunción proceeded with relatively little controversy. The generally low profile of the Mercosur process among domestic groups and debates about constitutional reforms preoccupied legislators, thereby reducing the attention they paid to the trade agreement (Gardini 2010, 118–20). Some legislators in both Argentina and Brazil were more reticent to vote against ratification of the integration accords given Mercosur's key role in the broader economic agenda advanced by Menem and Collor and their predecessors. Others were actually eager to ratify the accords.

Both Menem and Collor were committed to trade liberalization via Mercosur as part of a broader neoliberal economic agenda intended to promote economic growth and stability and thus enhance their political support. Interest groups, as noted above, seemed to have played little role in the initiation and negotiation of Mercosur. Business was largely in favor of integration in the Southern Cone. Nonetheless, both Menem and Collor, as well as other political figures involved in negotiating the integration process, took pains to ensure that protectionist demands did not derail integration (Kaltenthaler and Mora 2002, 84; Perales 2003, 94–95).

Leaders in Brazil and Argentina, then, pursued the trade agreement as a means of bolstering their domestic political positions. Mercosur allowed the leaders to commit to trade liberalization and a broader market-oriented agenda that reassured society about their intentions. Mercosur's institutional structure and public opinion data (albeit limited in scope) further highlights the dynamics at play in the theory we propose. In particular, the institutionalization of Mercosur's DSM since the signing of the Treaty of Asunción helped ensure that domestic groups would be informed about trade violations and that they could monitor their chief executive's actions.

Equally, there existed a relatively high public awareness of Mercosur and strong preferences among a majority of Argentinean and Brazilian voters in favor of further integration. Latinobarometro surveys, for example, indicate that a large majority of individuals in Mercosur member-states had heard or read about the trade agreement. In 1995, 1996, 1997, 1998, and 2000, the Latinobarometro survey asked, "Have you read or heard anything about Mercosur?" In Argentina during those years, between 78 and 87 percent of respondents had heard or read about it; in Brazil, a substantial majority, between 53 and 70 percent, had done so (Lagos 1995, 1996, 1997, 1998, 2000).

Additional Latinobarometro survey evidence indicates that a large majority of individual voters were consistently in favor of Mercosur. In 1997, 1998, 2001, 2002, 2005, and 2008, the Latinobarometro asked, "Generally speaking, are you very in favor, quite in favor, slightly against, or very against the economic integration of the countries of Latin America?" In Argentina during those years, 78 to 90 percent of the respondents said they were very much or quite in favor of Mercosur; in Brazil, 67 to 86 percent said they favored it (Lagos 1997, 1998, 2001, 2002, 2005, 2008). These findings, in conjunction with domestic groups' willingness to rely on Mercosur's DSM to arbitrate disputes and the growing institutionalization of the DSM itself, suggest that domestic constituents were increasingly able to hold elected officials accountable for welfare-reducing violations of trade policy, such as those that might occur in support of demands made by domestic groups seeking protection.

Democratization and concerns over electoral competition played a key role in the decision to form Mercosur. Of course, this decision was shaped by a host of other factors as well. Both governments wanted to promote political-military cooperation; they believed that closer economic ties would reduce the prospect of political hostilities between Argentina and Brazil and would limit the military's ability to reassert itself in the domestic affairs of either country. They also believed that integration would contribute to regional economic stability and end repeated bouts of hyperinflation and economic mismanagement in the region. In addition, though, both Argentina's and Brazil's newly elected executives came into office with a heightened awareness of the need to ensure economic stability and growth in order to survive in office. The credibility of economic policy was also an issue, as previous governments had seemed to relent frequently to special interest pressures.

At the same time, political competition resulting from democratization rendered both executives and legislators more accountable to domestic constituents. Electoral shifts in party vote share and seat share, as well as the executives' ability to pass controversial economic legislation, depended on maintaining sufficiently high levels of popular support, which in turn was determined by voters' perceptions of the domestic economy. The fact that both presidents and their predecessors went to great lengths to exclude protection-seeking groups from the Mercosur negotiation process speaks to their attentiveness to the economic demands of the populace for economic growth and stability. Legislators' willingness to ratify the Treaty of Asunción, as well as the deepening institutionalization of Mercosur's DSM and the strength of public opinion in favor of economic integration, collectively lend support to our argument that signing a PTA is one way for governments facing political competition to reassure publics that they will promote the general welfare and resist the demands of special interests, thereby enhancing their political support.

Veto Players, Transaction Costs, and PTAs

In addition to regime type, a second element shaping a government's decision to enter a PTA is the extent of domestic transaction costs it faces in reaching an international agreement. Like most international agreements, PTAs do not have direct effects in signatory countries. In order for the arrangement to take hold, it has to be ratified by some set of domestic veto players (Yarbrough and Yarbrough 1992, 35).[20] Convincing these players to sign off on the agreement is as important as negotiating acceptable terms with the other signatory

---

[20] We focus on veto players instead of veto points, since we conceive of them as strategic actors in their own right. Veto players are not passive; they are part of the negotiation and ratification process and as such can affect both.

governments. One can think of transaction costs as reflecting the amount a government would need to bribe all veto players to accept the international agreement. The more veto players there are, the more costly the ratification, and the higher the transaction costs of cooperation.

The number of veto players is different from the degree of democracy in a country. All types of governments can have veto players. There are two important aspects of governance systems: (1) the extent of political—and especially electoral—competition, and (2) the degree to which leaders face checks and balances. Political leaders are constrained by competitive elections that can oust them from office and by institutions that influence the policy process. Veto players reflect different constraints on leaders, namely, the extent of checks and balances in a country's political institutions.

We argue that the number of veto players affects the ability of chief executives to enact their preferred policies. On average, democracies tend to have more veto players than other states. But veto players exist in all regime types. Even in dictatorships, groups with varying preferences often compete for influence over policy. More generally, veto players are usually embodied in institutions—such as legislatures, judiciaries, local governments in federal systems, and opposition parties—that can initiate, amend, and block policies proposed by the executive. The checks and balances that these institutions promote serve to increase political competition. However, political competition stemming from a large number of veto players is not a boon for international cooperation. Instead, this situation hampers international agreements by raising the domestic transaction costs for leaders.

Like domestic policy, trade policy is subject to the influence of domestic veto players. Such groups must ratify the policy choices made by the executive. Veto players contain a combination of interests in institutional roles that give them the capacity to block policy. The focus on veto players allows us to incorporate interest groups in our analysis while directing attention to the most politically important groups. Interest groups, as we mentioned previously, are not the center of our attention. Modeling and empirically specifying the structure of interest groups across all countries and over time is beyond the scope of this study. Groups opposing and supporting trade liberalization exist in all countries, but their identity and relative influence will vary depending on the specific national context.

We follow existing models of veto players in assuming that interest groups affect trade policy indirectly (Henisz 2000; Henisz and Mansfield 2006; Kono 2006; Mansfield et al. 2007 and 2008). One way they do so is by shaping the preferences of the executive, since he or she requires their support to retain office. The executive's position *ex ante* reflects the influence of politically important interest groups. In addition to influencing the preferences of heads of state, interest groups have indirect effects through veto players. We expect interest groups to operate through political parties, and leaders of such parties constitute the executive, the legislature, and the opposition. Thus, interest groups are indirectly incorporated in our analysis via their impact on the preferences of the executive and parties.

Strategic interaction among veto players and the executive is central to the formation of PTAs. In many cases, there are groups in society that have both preferences that diverge from the head of government and the institutional capacity to block a preferential agreement or prevent its implementation. Veto players must ratify policy change, including the creation of a trade agreement. Formally, the head of government in a democracy is often required by the national constitution to obtain the approval of the legislature for international agreements, including PTAs. Hence, the chief executive must negotiate a preferential arrangement that is acceptable to a majority of the legislature, either a simple plurality or some supermajority depending on the issue area and the country. In the United States, for example, any treaty negotiated by the president must be approved by two-thirds of the Senate. That the executive must obtain legislative approval will affect how he or she negotiates. Bringing home an unratifiable PTA is likely to be costly—domestically and internationally—for the executive. He or she will therefore need to anticipate the legislature's (or any other veto player's) reaction to the proposed arrangement and ensure it is domestically acceptable.

Ratification can also be less formal. In dictatorships, shifts in foreign economic policy often require the support of groups like the military or local leaders; implicitly these groups have ratified an enacted trade agreement if they had the ability to veto it and chose not to (Gandhi and Przeworski 2007). Informal ratification also occurs in democracies. If a leader needs to change a domestic law, norm, or practice in order to implement a PTA, even if no formal vote on the arrangement itself is required, a legislative vote on any necessary domestic change becomes a vote on the agreement.

One might argue that leaders could simply craft a PTA in ways to purchase the acquiescence of veto players. That is, a government could build flexibility into an agreement so that its terms would be weakened where domestic groups oppose it; or the government could exclude from the agreement all sensitive sectors that affect veto players adversely. In this way, a government could negotiate any agreement so that its veto players did not oppose it. Research has suggested that governments do indeed respond to domestic political conditions when designing international agreements (Downs and Rocke 1995; Koremenos et al. 2001; Rosendorff and Milner 2001). However, there are constraints on such behavior. First, the government cannot expect to successfully negotiate whatever terms its domestic veto players desire, since foreign countries have to sign on to the agreement. They are likely to want exactly those concessions that the domestic veto players oppose most fiercely. Indeed, Jon Pevehouse (2007) shows that veto players influence the ratification of agreements, even after accounting for their effects on the form of the agreement itself.

Second, as the number of veto players grows, the demands of these groups for exclusions or flexibility must also rise, making it more difficult for the executive to find an acceptable agreement with its foreign partners. Hence, as the number of veto players increases, the transaction costs of an international agreement are likely to grow, and the possibility of establishing a PTA lessens. Even though the design, negotiation, and ratification of international agreements are not independent events, veto players are likely to have an impact because of the transaction costs they can impose on executives at the ratification stage.

Imagine that the government could offer something valuable to a veto player to change its ratification vote. This is the most direct measure of the transaction costs incurred by a government to secure the ratification of an agreement. If such bribery is allowed—that is, if a government could transfer some of its utility to the veto groups in order to buy their acquiescence—an increase in veto players still increases the transaction costs facing a chief executive. Acting rationally, the government will only transfer as much utility as it gets from the agreement relative to the reversion point or status quo, thereby limiting its ability to bribe. As more veto players are added, at best the government has to bribe no more groups if all the new veto players are free traders; but at worst (that is, if their preferences are protectionist relative to the government's) it will have to make ever larger bribes. At some point, it will not be able to transfer enough utility to make the bribe effective. Consequently, adding more veto players tends to result in paying more bribes (and never results in paying fewer bribes), reducing the probability that an executive can bribe all the veto players. An increasing number of veto players therefore raises the transaction costs a leader must pay for an agreement and acts as a brake on PTA formation.

Some Illustrations of the Effects of Veto Players on PTA Formation

We present several brief cases that illustrate how a large number of veto players can delay, derail, or complicate attempts to negotiate and ratify international trade agreements. We also present some evidence that a smaller number of veto players can facilitate PTA formation. A number of these cases are drawn from Asia, a region that has been slow to adopt PTAs. In part, the slow pace of PTA formation may stem from the lack of democracy in the region. As an increasing number of countries in the region have become democratic, the pace of PTA formation has picked up. However, for many of these countries, a major stumbling block to any trade agreement has been the agricultural sector. In combination with key legislators and parts of the government bureaucracy, agricultural groups have formed a potent veto player. Only as this player has weakened politically have various Asian countries signed trade agreements.

South Korea and the Korea-Chile FTA

Consider South Korea during the period from 1998 to 2003. As we discuss in chapter 4, we use a measure of veto players (Henisz 2000) that ranges from 0 to 1, with higher values corresponding to a larger number of veto players. During this period, the veto player score for South Korea fell from 0.46 to 0.39, as the opposition party, the National Congress for New Politics (NCNP), consolidated power. In 1997, the longtime ruling Grand National Party lost its first major election. For the first time, power shifted to another party. Kim Dae Jung of the NCNP was elected president and formed a government with a large coalition, including the United Liberal Democrats (ULD) party (Kim 2000). The Kim government began a program of economic reform, which included trade liberalization and a desire for trade agreements (Lee and Moon 2008; Park and Koo 2008). This development accords with our claim that democracy induces leaders to seek trade agreements (Park and Koo 2008, 36).

The problem for Kim was that numerous interest groups with extensive connections to political parties and the bureaucracy were hostile to such reforms, especially trade liberalization. The Kim government reorganized the bureaucracy to weaken the influence of these groups. In the trade arena, it created an Office for the Ministry of Trade (OMT) that was devoted solely to promoting trade liberalization and negotiating trade agreements. The government began actively pushing for bilateral trade agreements in 2000, entering into negotiations with Chile. When the 2000 parliamentary elections yielded a legislature with an even larger majority of seats for the governing coalition, thus reducing the number of veto players, the government increased the pace of international negotiations.

Nonetheless, certain veto players remained in place. Some of them opposed the Korea-Chile FTA and slowed progress on the negotiations for three years. Agricultural groups and import-competing industries were particularly influential, using political parties and parts of the state bureaucracy to delay the negotiations. As Seungjoo Park and Chung-in Koo (2008, 36–37) point out,

> [d]uring the negotiations with Chile, opposition to the OMT's initiative came from the Ministry of Agriculture and Forestry and farmers' organizations such as the Korean Farmers League and the Korean Women Farmers Association. . . . In addition, the OMT's mission to maneuver through bureaucratic and social opposition was challenged by rival institutions, such as the Ministry of Commerce, Industry and Energy and the Ministry of Finance and Economy.

After making concessions to the agricultural interests, an international agreement was reached in early 2003.

However, some veto players almost derailed the agreement's ratification. Youngshik Bong and Heon-Joo Jung (2005, 149) observe that "[t]he general voting for ratification was postponed three times (December 29, 2003,

January 8, 2004, and February 9, 2004) due to a series of organized efforts by lawmakers from rural districts of both ruling and opposition parties to defeat the bill. Meanwhile, the protest of farmers' unions spread nationwide and became increasingly violent." The FTA was ratified in 2004 through a compromise whereby the government agreed to legislation that provided compensation to declining industries and agriculture (Park and Koo 2008, 39–41). Key veto players stalled the negotiations over this FTA and threatened to derail its ratification. But in the end, a decline in veto players allowed the government to move forward on the agreement and the reduction in the number of players allowed the government to craft a compensation package to buy them off and rescue the FTA.

Japan and PTAs

Another interesting case of veto players affecting PTA formation involves Japan. Around 2000, Japan began pursuing a series of bilateral trade agreements. In part, this decision was an outgrowth of domestic political changes. In the mid-1990s, the long-ruling Liberal Democratic Party (LDP) was forced to form a coalition government for the first time as it faced the prospect of losing power. This change led to a substantial rise in Japanese veto players. The LDP subsequently regained a majority in the late 1990s, precipitating a drop in the number of veto players. But the party and the government were forced to adapt to the heightened domestic political competition.

Agricultural interests had been a key source of opposition to trade agreements. Traditionally, these groups had been allied with members of the LDP (called *norin zoku*) who represented rural districts; such districts were significantly overrepresented as a result of the electoral system (George 1991/1992; Mulgan 2005; Hayes 2008). As Hidetaka Yoshimatsu (2006, 488) points out, "[s]trong lobbying by agricultural groups represented by the Central Union of Agricultural Cooperatives (*zenchu*) was involved in urging the *norin zoku* to oppose the progress of FTA talks." A combination of the Japanese bureaucracy, in particular the Ministry of Agriculture, Forestry and Fisheries (MAFF), in addition to groups of LDP legislators and agricultural and import competing industrial interests, opposed the PTA negotiations (Yoshimatsu 2006). By the late 1990s, however, industrial groups—including large exporters and multinational corporations—began advocating for trade liberalization.

Furthermore, in the 1990s, electoral reforms were completed that diminished the power of the rural districts, and the LDP and its partner the New Komeito party began to represent urban voters and other interests to a greater degree (Thies 2002; Mulgan 2005).

> The Japanese business community through its peak umbrella organization— Keidanren—began to press the government in the late 1990s for a more activist trade policy. . . . This business demand was at odds with the protectionist posture

of the agricultural lobby. . . . Despite adverse demographic trends (with the ageing and shrinking of the farming population) and changes in electoral rules (since 1994 the shift to single-member districts and the reduction of over-representation of rural areas), the Japanese agricultural lobby continued to be a formidable political force. The agricultural *zoku* still dominated intra-party policy-making, and the agricultural bureaucracy worked zealously to maintain the system of protection and subsidization that it administers (Pekkanen et al. 2007, 959).

In 2002, the LDP selected a reformer, Junichiro Koizumi, to be prime minister. Pressed by urban and industrial groups, he launched a set of bilateral trade negotiations. This development coincided with changes in the policy position of the MAFF and some agricultural groups toward trade agreements. As Yoshimatsu (2006) notes, both expanding trade with Asia and agricultural exports led to a decline in opposition to trade negotiations with other countries within the ruling LDP and in the MAFF.

> Thus, the agricultural groups changed their basic stance on FTAs from general rejection to conditional acceptance through co-operation with farmers in East Asia. The shift in preferences in the supporting groups influenced the LDP's *norin zoku*. With the agricultural groups changing their posture towards FTAs from rejection to conditional approval based on co-operation, politicians no longer had to continue their adamant opposition (Yoshimatsu 2006, 495–96).

Because of a decline in the number of veto players in Japan and the erosion of some veto players' opposition to PTAs, the government was able to forge ahead with international negotiations. These negotiations culminated in a rash of PTAs with Singapore (2002), Mexico (2005), Malaysia (2006), the Philippines (2006), Chile (2007), Thailand (2007), Brunei (2007), Indonesia (2007), ASEAN (2008), and Vietnam (2008). The erosion of Japan's veto players helped set the stage for this wave of PTAs.

India and ILFTA

A third case of interest is India. A signatory of the South Asian Preferential Trade Agreement (SAPTA) in 1993, India ratified it in 1995. In the wake of a series of shaky coalition governments, the Congress Party formed a minority government in 1991. Led by Narasimha Rao, the coalition government became more stable and larger over time, generating a reduction in the number of veto players from 1993 to 1996. Rao was thus able to begin an economic reform program that included trade liberalization. Many interest groups long protected by India's ISI program opposed these changes.

In December 1998, India also signed the Indo-Lanka Free Trade Agreement (ILFTA) with Sri Lanka (Associated Press 1998; Reuters 1998; Weerakoon 2007, 243). This agreement was partially facilitated by a decline in veto players in India that year. The number of veto players in India shot up from 1996 to 1998 as elections reduced the control of the Congress government. In mid-1998, however, elections were held after the Congress government ran into trouble and its coalition collapsed. The Bharatiya Janata Party (BJP) made gains in these elections and was the largest party in the legislature, with 251 of 539 seats. After some wrangling, the BJP was able to form a majority alliance with the support of regional leaders. However, the BJP majority was tenuous and India remained marked by a fairly large number of veto players (Jalan 1999).

Partly as a result of these domestic political conditions, ratification of the ILFTA agreement took about two years. Despite strong support for the trade agreement by both the Indian and Sri Lankan governments, the ILFTA encountered significant problems entering 1999. One sticking point was how to treat trade in tea and rubber, which were key Sri Lankan exports. The agreement had proposed to cut tariffs by half on Sri Lankan goods that were not on India's excluded list. Indian producers of these goods, such as those in the southern state of Kerala and the northeastern state of Assam, strongly voiced their desire to have tea and rubber put on the excluded list (Hussein 1999; Reuters 1999a). In March, India yielded to this pressure and decided to place tea and rubber on the excluded list from the ILFTA (Jayasinghe 1999a; Reuters 1999b). Talks stalled throughout 1999, as veto groups in India refused to give ground (Jayasinghe 1999b; Reuters 1999b).

By November 1999, negotiations were put on hold as both countries—and both incumbent leaders—faced elections. The results augured well for the continuation of the ILFTA. Sri Lankan President Kumaratunga easily won reelection in December, while Prime Minister Vajpayee's BJP government widened its majority substantially as well, leading to a sizable drop in the number of veto players. Following extended negotiations on the Indian proposal for tea and garments tariffs, final details were hammered out by April 2000 (Reuters 2000). In July 2000, India ratified the ILFTA. The vote easily passed the BJP majority-controlled parliament, despite continued opposition by domestic tea producers (Bhattacharjee 2000).

Vajpayee and the BJP were able to secure ratification of the agreement in 2000 because of their much stronger position after the 1999 election. Indeed, the BJP had called early elections in 1999 and their coalition had won 297 out of 539 seats in the legislature. Though the BJP had to join with 24 regional parties to form a working majority, it was the largest national party with 182 seats of its own right (297 with allies). The National Congress party held 114 seats (136 with its allies) and was the second largest party. Congress's decline in seats (from 167 with its allies before 1999), moreover, weakened the party as a veto player, since it could no longer threaten the government with collapse by withdrawing its support. In addition, whereas Congress had a sizable legislative presence in tea-trading regions before 1999, its electoral losses of that year diminished its seats in these regions as well. Clearly, the ILFTA's ratification was not due solely to the decline of representation of these regions in the governing majority. But the decline of Congress's seats and the widening of BJP's majority coincided with a decline in the relative power of tea-exporting regions, while the BJP government itself was more secure in parliament. Extensive veto players in India made passage of trade agreements generally difficult. But the reduction of veto players in the governing majority after 1999 seems to have helped India ratify the ILFTA.

Taken together, these cases illustrate how a large and rising numbers of veto players can complicate the negotiation and ratification of trade agreements. Increases in veto players can also cause delays in ratifying PTAs. As the number of veto players shrinks, in contrast, governments have an easier time overcoming opposition to trade deals.

FURTHER EFFECTS OF DOMESTIC POLITICS ON INTERNATIONAL TRADE AGREEMENTS: AUXILIARY HYPOTHESES

Thus far, we have developed arguments about how regime type and veto players affect PTA formation, and these hypotheses will be tested in chapter 4. Other models of trade agreements, however, yield similar predictions but for different reasons than the ones we emphasize (e.g., Pahre 2008). To help assess whether the mechanisms that we concentrate on are in fact driving the effects of democracy and veto players, we also test seven auxiliary hypotheses in chapter 5 that are logical outgrowths of our arguments and the causal processes underlying them. Such auxiliary hypotheses are often seen as a sign of a progressive research program because they are made up of newly predicted phenomena that can be empirically tested (Lakatos 1978).

Leadership Duration and PTAs

One direct implication of our argument is that a leader's political support should be affected by signing a PTA. If PTAs help chief executives overcome domestic political problems, then leaders who sign them should enjoy a longer tenure than those who do not. The reassurance mechanism that PTAs provide should make leaders less vulnerable to being tossed out of office, especially in bad economic times. The public, or significant segments of it, should gain confidence that the bad times are not due to the leader's policies (i.e., to his or her pandering to special interests), but rather to exogenous shocks that are beyond the leader's control. This should make some voters and interest groups less likely to reject an incumbent and hence extend his or her time in office.

In testing this hypothesis, it is important to compare heads of state in similar regime types. That is, among leaders who face substantial levels of political competition and could be turned out of office, we anticipate that they should last longer in office if they make trade agreements. Thus, among democracies, the effect of PTAs on longevity should be strongest, *ceteris paribus*. This implication flows directly from our argument and hence helps distinguish our claims from those of others who argue that democracies are more likely to cooperate for other reasons.

Partisanship and PTAs

Another auxiliary hypothesis that derives from our argument concerns the impact of partisanship on PTAs. We assume that leaders vary in their emphasis on social welfare versus rent-seeking and that most of the public is unaware of their government leaders' true preferences. In addition, the public does not know the exact trade policy that has been chosen; they only observe economic conditions and then support or oppose their leader as a consequence. One clue that is visible to the public eye about their leader stems from his or her partisan affiliation. We anticipate that partisanship should affect the probability of signing and ratifying a trade agreement.

Left-wing governments should be more likely to sign and ratify such agreements since they have a greater need to provide reassurance on trade policy. Left-wing governments tend to be more apt to intervene in the economy, often in ways that provide protection. They are thus in greater need of a reassurance mechanism to convince the public that they are not excessively protectionist. Hence, a PTA can provide a more powerful reassurance mechanism for left-wing governments, as it insulates them from claims that they overprotected and should be removed from office. For right-wing or centrist governments, the need for a reassurance mechanism is less pressing since claims that such governments are overly protectionist are less likely to be believed by the public or interest groups.

Regime Type and Exposure to the International Economy

Our argument implies that domestic actors have some incentive to pay attention to the international economy. Certain segments of the public and various interest groups are reassured about leaders' behavior when leaders enter trade agreements. These societal actors therefore condition their political support to some extent on trade policy. In turn, leaders enter trade agreements to generate political support and forestall the possibility that they will be turned out of office because the public blames them for economic problems beyond their control.

However, this argument should apply with greatest force to countries marked by extensive exposure to trade. Leaders in highly trade-dependent countries should be more likely to turn to trade agreements to solve their political problems, while the public and interest groups should be more likely to pay attention to trade policy in these more trade-dependent nations. In situations where leaders face heightened political competition, this dynamic should be even stronger. Hence, we expect that more trade-dependent democracies will be more likely to sign PTAs than less open ones. For the most autocratic countries, we anticipate that trade dependence will have little if any effect since leaders will not have domestic political incentives to join PTAs. We will therefore address whether the interaction of regime type and trade dependence affects the odds of entering a PTA.

Autocracies, Political Competition, and PTAs

Although autocracies sign fewer PTAs than democracies, they nonetheless do participate in various preferential groupings. In another extension of our argument, we address whether variations in the degree of political competition among autocracies influence their prospects of signing trade accords. If autocrats in countries with more politically competitive systems are more likely to be forced from office than other autocrats, they are also more likely to see trade agreements as reassurance devices. While all autocracies are less politically competitive than democracies in the sense that their leaders face a lower probability of losing office (especially because of the median voter), some autocracies that face relatively high competition may feel the need to seek international agreements to provide domestic reassurance. This causal mechanism is similar to that in democracies. We expect, then, that more politically competitive autocracies will be more likely to sign PTAs than their less competitive counterparts.

Regime Type and the Levels of Economic Integration and Enforcement

As we explained in chapter 1, all PTAs attempt to promote economic integration by improving and stabilizing the mutual access that each member offers to the other participants' markets, but important differences exist among these arrangements. In a preferential arrangement (PA), member-states grant the other participants preferential access to selected segments of their market; in a free trade agreement (FTA), members mutually reduce or eliminate trade barriers on many (if not all) products; in a customs union (CU), members eliminate barriers to trade with other participants and erect a common external tariff (CET) vis-à-vis third parties; in a common market (CM), countries augment a customs union by implementing similar product regulations and by permitting the free flow of factors of production between members; and in an economic union, members participate in a common market and coordinate fiscal and monetary policies.

Different types of trade agreements thus aim to achieve different degrees of economic integration among members, with PAs being the least integrative and economic unions being the most. It follows from our argument that domestic political conditions should influence the form of arrangements that rational leaders propose. More specifically, these conditions should affect whether a leader chooses to enter a PTA that aims to achieve minimal or substantial economic integration among member-states. Leaders will rationally calculate the optimal depth of integration given their domestic political situation. The need for greater reassurance will lead to deeper agreements. As such, we expect democracies to seek PTAs that aim to achieve deeper integration among member-states.

In addition, leaders can choose to incorporate stronger mechanisms for enforcing trade integration into their agreements. DSMs provide parties to an agreement with the means to legally settle disagreements. Countries that desire to enforce the terms of an agreement are more likely to want such a mechanism. Hence, leaders rationally designing a trade accord are likely to include or exclude DSMs on the basis of their domestic political situation. Where leaders have greater need for a reassurance mechanism, they are more likely to include a DSM. Therefore, more democratic countries are on average more likely to include DSMs than autocratic ones.

Veto Players and the Levels of Economic Integration and Enforcement

The institutional form of a trade agreement can also be affected by the number of veto players in a country. As we have noted, PAs, FTAs, CUs, CMs, and economic unions require member-states to undertake policy changes designed to foster increasing levels of integration. In addition, the inclusion of DSMs creates an enforcement mechanism that makes the agreements stronger. Such policy changes have distributional implications. Consequently, the number of veto players will also have a strong influence on the type of integration arrangement that a government enters.

The magnitude of domestic change needed to comply with a trade agreement and the associated political costs borne by leaders depend on the extent of integration that the agreement aims to achieve. As the proposed degree of economic integration rises, so do the expected adjustment costs for domestic actors. As the number of veto players increases, so does the likelihood that adversely affected groups are represented by at least one veto player. These players are increasingly likely to resist policy change, as their key constituents bear higher costs stemming from that change.

Deeper economic integration and tougher enforcement are likely to spur increasing opposition to trade agreements among certain segments of society. Heightened integration and the presence of a DSM tend to reduce the decision-making power of certain veto players (such as domestic legislatures), increase the adjustment costs and the portion of society affected, and attenuate the ability of domestic groups to lobby the government. All of these effects will be resisted by veto players, and they will add to the transaction costs that governments must pay for ratification. As the proposed level of integration deepens or the likelihood of a DSM rises, the number of actors affected is likely to grow considerably. Arrangements that envision more extensive integration are likely to cover more goods and services—and therefore to affect more sectors and a larger segment of society—than other trade agreements. With the adoption of a CET, moreover, the prospect of a sector in a given member-state obtaining protection against imports from third parties declines as well. Similarly, moving from a PA or an FTA to a CU, a CM, or an economic union increases the variety of issues that are covered by the arrangement (from trade to finance and immigration, among others) and the odds that additional domestic groups will face sizeable adjustment costs. Thus, as the breadth of the issues covered by a proposed trade agreement rises, so too does the likelihood that a significant portion of society will anticipate being adversely affected and therefore oppose entering the arrangement.

Ratification Delay and Veto Players

Veto players can affect more than just the probability of entering a trade agreement and the agreement's proposed level of integration. They may also affect the amount of time it takes to conclude and implement the agreement. At the outset of international negotiations, leaders understand the extent of domestic veto players they face. They must anticipate the kind of agreement that such veto players would accept. But problems can arise when there is a change in the number of the veto players before domestic implementation of the international agreement occurs. We expect that in countries where the number of veto players increases from the date an international agreement is signed to when it is ratified at home, delay should grow longer. More veto players add transaction costs and cause executives to take added time to find ways to make the agreement more palatable to those groups. Delay in domestic ratification arises from the introduction of new and greater numbers of veto players after an international agreement has been reached.

Delay is an important and interesting issue in politics, and prior research has indicated that it can be caused by a wide variety of factors (Lesbirel 1987; Alesina and Drazen 1991; Cramton 1992; Drazen 1996; Martin and Vanberg 2003; Manow and Burkhart 2008). Lanny Martin and Georg Vanberg (2003), for instance, show that greater ideological distances between the parties and a larger number of parties produce more delay between the conclusion of an election and the formation of a government. S. Hayden Lesbirel (1987) reports that more local interest groups, and better organized ones, lead to more delay in starting public works projects desired by a national government. As our South Korea case above indicates, veto players are often capable of obstructing both the length of international negotiations and domestic ratification. We propose, then, that high and rising numbers of veto players are likely to lead to greater time (i.e., more delay) between signing and implementing trade agreements, holding other factors constant.

CONCLUSION

In this chapter, we have developed a domestic political argument to explain why and when states decide to enter PTAs. Political leaders face a cost from their inability to assure their publics and free trade interest groups that they will not give in too much to protectionist pressures. Because they lack a reassurance device, they may lose popularity or be thrown out of office when the economy turns downward, with the public suspecting that they have given in to special interest groups' protectionist demands. While elections rarely turn on trade policy, they do often depend on the state of the economy and on voters blaming leaders for bad times (Kramer 1971; Fair 1978 and 2009; Fiorina 1981; Ferejohn 1986).[21] As elections play a larger role in determining whether leaders retain office, these costs rise in importance.

The costs can be reduced by entering a PTA, which increases the likelihood that leaders will be exposed if they give in to protectionist interest groups. Hence, these agreements help the government resolve the public's concerns over special interest protection. We cannot measure the political benefits from trade agreements directly but we know that they vary with the degree of competitiveness of elections. The more democratic a country is, the more elections matter to leadership survival. Thus, the greater the incentives for leaders in such regimes to pursue international trade agreements.

To sign and ratify international trade agreements can be costly for political leaders. These domestic transaction costs reduce the probability that leaders will seek trade agreements and that they will be capable of finding agreements acceptable to both domestic and international parties. One set of domestic transaction costs stems from interest groups that have sufficient influence to be able to veto policy proposals. These veto players occupy institutional positions that give them the ability to block policy changes. We have argued that the greater the number of such veto players, the higher the transaction costs and the less likely states are to join and ratify PTAs.

Finally, we have advanced a set of auxiliary hypotheses that flow from our argument and allow us to test it more thoroughly. First, our argument implies that leaders who sign PTAs should enjoy a longer tenure in office than those who do not sign them. Second, we expect left-wing governments to be more likely to sign PTAs than right-wing and centrist ones. Leftist governments need the public reassurance that PTAs will provide more than do right-wing ones. Third, the interaction between trade dependence and regime type should affect PTA formation. More trade-dependent democracies should be more likely to adopt trade agreements as trade has a more significant bearing on economic

---

[21] Note there are cases of elections that did revolve heavily around trade policy: for example, the United Kingdom in 1846 and in 1923; Canada in 1988; Costa Rica in 2006; as well as various EU entry cases. See Brander (1991), Irwin (1996), Schonhardt-Bailey (2006), and Hicks et al. (2008).

outcomes of concern to the public and interest groups. Fourth, while democracies are expected to display a greater propensity for signing PTAs than other countries, nondemocracies have entered such arrangements as well. We have speculated that the more politically competitive a nondemocracy is, the more likely it is to sign a PTA. Fifth, we have argued that democracies are more likely to enter PTAs that aim to achieve deeper integration and that are marked by DSMs than other regimes. Sixth, we claim that greater numbers of veto players reduce the likelihood of states entering arrangements that attempt to promote deeper integration and those with DSMs. Finally, veto players should affect the ratification process. More veto players and rising numbers of them should lengthen the time from signature to ratification. These specific hypotheses flow directly from our argument and thus provide us with extra empirical leverage in examining it.

In the following chapter, we initiate our empirical analysis. To begin, we focus on the international factors that might explain PTAs and present a systemic model. Although our central argument is about the effects of domestic politics, various studies have emphasized the international influences on PTA formation. It is important to evaluate these claims and to account for key international factors when we test our claims about regime type and veto players (chapter 4). After analyzing these international influences in chapter 3, we test our claims in chapter 4. This is an unusual empirical strategy. Most studies of international political economy do not include both domestic and systemic factors, but doing so is necessary to both evaluate our argument and adequately examine various prominent alternative arguments.

Systemic Influences on PTA Formation

THE CENTRAL ARGUMENT of this study is that domestic politics shapes the decision to form a PTA. Before turning to an empirical analysis of this topic in chapter 4, however, we spend this chapter addressing the international influences on PTAs. We do so for various reasons. Systemic theories of international relations argue that it is necessary to understand the global context in which nation-states make decisions before we can consider how domestic politics shapes these decisions (e.g., Waltz 1979; Gilpin 1981; Keohane 1984; Jervis 1997). Without a prior analysis of systemic factors, as Robert Keohane (1984, 26) puts it, "unit-level [that is, country-level] analysis of world politics floats in an empirical and conceptual vacuum." As such, we need to account for the international influences on PTA formation when examining the effects of domestic politics in the following chapter. If international factors are related to both domestic politics and the establishment of trade agreements, failing to account for them risks generating misleading results. Systemic features can lead states to take particular actions in the global arena and thus might be responsible for what would otherwise be attributed to domestic forces. Equally, the international sources of PTA creation have generated considerable interest and a large literature. Yet few systematic empirical efforts have been made to assess which of these factors are most important or the strength of their effects. We will use a new and comprehensive dataset on PTAs to analyze how various features of the international system influence both the frequency of PTA formation throughout the system and the incidence of countries joining these arrangements.

As shown in figure 1.1 (in chapter 1), both the incidence of PTA formation and the frequency with which states have entered such arrangements have varied over time. After World War II, few agreements were established until the 1960s, at which time there was an uptick in the creation of PTAs that lasted until the mid-1970s. For the next fifteen years or so, relatively few PTAs were formed. During the 1990s, however, states flocked to join these agreements, a trend that has continued into the twenty-first century.

What factors can explain the varying rate of PTA formation and accession since World War II? We examine four systemic factors that previous studies have linked to these outcomes: hegemony, strategic interaction among both states and PTAs, the global business cycle, and changes in the global balance of power. We also address whether the number of democracies worldwide has affected PTA formation and accession. Finally, we consider the effects of features of the GATT/WTO on these outcomes.

INTERNATIONAL INFLUENCES ON PTA FORMATION

In this chapter, we address two aspects of PTA formation: (1) the rate at which PTAs are established globally, and (2) the rate at which states join PTAs. Since much contemporary research emphasizes the rising number of both commercial institutions and countries that are party to them, analyzing each rate is appropriate (de Melo and Panagariya 1993a; Fernández and Portes 1998). Furthermore, in chapters 4 and 5, we will examine the factors that lead pairs of states to enter the same PTA. Both the rate at which PTAs form and the rate at which states enter them are associated with PTA formation by country pairs.

Existing studies have identified at least four systemic factors that are especially likely to affect these outcomes: hegemony, strategic interaction among both states and PTAs, the global business cycle, and changes in the global balance of power. In addition, we also address whether the number of democracies in the global system has influenced PTA formation. This variable is linked to one of our chief theoretical concerns, as we outlined in chapter 2. Although our primary focus is on how regime type operates at the domestic level rather than on global patterns of democracy, it will be interesting to assess whether the various waves of democratization that have occurred since World War II have affected PTA formation (Huntington 1991). However, this chapter does not take up the effect of veto players (the other variable emphasized in our argument), since this factor is not readily operationalized systemically. The average number of veto players across countries throughout the global system, for instance, strikes us as very distant from a measure of how costly it is for a government to ratify a trade agreement.

Hegemony

One strand of research on the systemic influences on PTA formation has stressed the effects of hegemony. Various scholars argue that international economic stability is a collective good, and that suboptimal amounts of it will be provided without a stable hegemon (Kindleberger 1973; Gilpin 1975; Lake 1988). Preferential trade arrangements, in turn, may be outgrowths of the economic instability fostered by the absence or the decline of such a country (Kindleberger 1973; Gilpin 1975 and 1987; Krasner 1976). In this vein, many observers maintain that the current wave of PTAs was triggered by the U.S. decision to pursue such arrangements in the early 1980s, once its economic power waned and the Uruguay Round of GATT stalled (e.g., Pomfret 1988; Baldwin 1993; Bhagwati 1993; Krugman 1993; Bhagwati and Panagariya 1996b). Other leading economic powers responded in kind to ensure that they would not be placed at a competitive disadvantage, giving rise to a set of loose economic blocs in North America, Western Europe, and East Asia (e.g., Gilpin 1987, 88–90 and ch. 10).

For over two decades, economists and political scientists have debated whether PTA formation is influenced by hegemony; that is, by whether there exists a single country that is powerful enough and willing to manage the international system. Some have suggested that hegemony is largely unrelated to PTAs (e.g., McKeown 1991); others maintain that it has some modest effect on these arrangements (e.g., Oye 1992; Yarbrough and Yarbrough 1992); and still others place considerable emphasis on hegemony's influence, but disagree about the nature of its effect.

That the lack of a stable hegemon fosters the formation of PTAs is a long-standing argument among the latter group of scholars (Kindleberger 1973; Gilpin 1975 and 1987; Krasner 1976). Their premise is that these blocs are discriminatory and thus antithetical to the maintenance of an open multilateral trading system. Equally, establishing and maintaining an open system is a collective good that will be underprovided absent a stable hegemon.[1] By virtue of its size, a hegemon, like a privileged group, has incentives to provide collective goods regardless of the contributions made to them by other states.[2] Although researchers advancing this argument disagree about the nature of these incentives, they agree that hegemonic decline reduces this state's contribution to the stability of the multilateral economic system and promotes the formation of preferential commercial arrangements.

This is not the only reason why the erosion of hegemony might stimulate the proliferation of PTAs. Waning U.S. hegemony may have prompted the creation and expansion of PTAs by a set of leading economic powers that felt these arrangements would assist them in managing the global economy (Yarbrough and Yarbrough 1992). Drawing smaller states into preferential groupings with a relatively liberal cast toward third parties might reduce the capacity of these states to establish a series of more protectionist blocs, bind them to decisions about the system made by the leading powers, and contribute to the maintenance of an open global trading system.

Whereas these arguments suggest that stable hegemony inhibits the formation of PTAs, the opposite view has also been advanced. Underlying the latter position is the assumption that states have an incentive to maximize their income. Countries with sufficient market power therefore have reason to impose an optimal tariff. Since hegemons are likely to be vested with such power

---

[1] See, for example, Gilpin (1975 and 1987), Kindleberger (1973), and Baldwin (2008). See also Krasner (1976), who argues that hegemonic decline stimulates PTA formation, but does not emphasize the provision of collective goods in the international system.

[2] On privileged groups, see Olson (1965).

(Lake 1988; Gowa 1994), other states may band together in PTAs to offset it. PTAs have more market power than their constituent members; states prefer to limit their susceptibility to the imposition of an optimal tariff (since the tariff reduces their gains from trade); and states (or groups of states) can more easily deter and respond to the imposition of optimal protection as their market power rises (Krugman 1991 and 1993).[3]

Despite the widespread and heated debates over the effects of hegemony on the stability of the international economic system, few systematic empirical efforts to determine if hegemony influences the incidence of PTA formation exist (Mansfield and Reinhardt 2003). Various observers identify the erosion of U.S. leadership in the GATT and the WTO, and its waning commitment to multilateralism, as central sources of the contemporary growth of PTAs (e.g., Gilpin 1987; Krugman 1991 and 1993; Baldwin 1993; Bhagwati 1993 and 2008; Bhagwati and Panagariya 1996b). On the other hand, an earlier wave of PTAs began during the 1960s, a period widely regarded as the apex of U.S. hegemony (Gilpin 1975 and 1987; Krasner 1976). In light of the dearth of systematic evidence bearing on this issue and the interest expressed in it, an empirical analysis of the relationship between hegemony and the proliferation of PTAs seems important.

Related to hegemony is the issue of U.S. foreign policy. The rapid proliferation of PTAs over the past two decades is often attributed to the U.S. government's decision to pursue a series of these groupings in the 1980s, once its economic power declined and negotiations within the GATT stalled (Pomfret 1988; Bhagwati 1993 and 2008; Krugman 1993). Other leading states responded by forming PTAs of their own. In Baldwin's (1995; see also Gilpin 1987) opinion, this development combined with the completion of the Single Market in Western Europe to set off a "domino effect" that produced the latest wave of regionalism. Consequently, after conducting some initial tests, we will explore whether the behavior of the world's hegemon influenced systemic patterns of PTA formation and accession.

Strategic Interaction and International Diffusion

The role of diffusion in international politics has generated considerable interest. Recently, attention has focused on the diffusion of neoliberal economic reforms (e.g., Simmons et al. 2006). Preferential trade agreements are sometimes related to these reforms since they often stimulate trade-barrier reductions among member-states.

---

[3] Whether hegemons have imposed optimal tariffs has been the subject of some dispute. Note, however, that this hypothesis does not depend on whether they have actually done so, but rather on their capacity to do so.

Theoretical analyses of PTA formation often highlight strategic interdependence among both PTAs and countries. Particularly important in this regard is whether PTA formation and expansion are characterized by positive contagion. Many researchers have found that the creation of a PTA does indeed beget the development of additional PTAs and a country joining a PTA encourages other countries to do likewise (e.g., Pomfret 1988; Oye 1992; Yarbrough and Yarbrough 1992; de Melo and Panagariya 1993b, 5–6; Baldwin 1995; Fernández and Portes 1998; Baldwin and Jaimovich 2010). There are various explanations for this finding. A PTA's creation, for example, may prompt fears by countries located outside the commercial union that it will degrade their competitiveness, thereby leading them to form a rival bloc. So, too, a state joining a PTA may generate concern among its economic rivals (outside the bloc) that this state's preferential access to an expanded market will furnish it with a competitive advantage, thus inducing the rivals to join other PTAs to obtain similar benefits.

In the same vein, positive contagion in the rates of PTA formation or states' involvement in PTAs may be due to a demonstration effect: the appearance that a PTA is benefiting members can foster the creation of additional commercial unions by countries eager to realize similar gains (Pomfret 1988; Yarbrough and Yarbrough 1992). Further, as noted above, PTAs heighten members' market power and hence their bargaining power (Oye 1992; Fernández and Portes 1998). PTAs are likely to form in reaction to one another and states are likely to join PTAs in response, since the proliferation of these agreements erodes the bargaining power of states that remain outside.

In fact, preferential arrangements have formed in reaction to one another throughout history. During the nineteenth century, contagion stemmed from the interest that many countries expressed in obtaining MFN treatment. Obtaining such treatment involved becoming enmeshed in the web of bilateral trading arrangements that marked the international political economy (Irwin 1993; Lazer 1999; Pahre 2008). In the period between World Wars I and II, the tendency for PTAs to form in reaction to one another was an outgrowth of mercantilist policies and political rivalries among the major powers (Condliffe 1940; Buzan 1984; Eichengreen and Frankel 1995).

Since World War II, anecdotal evidence suggests that strategic interaction has continued to guide the establishment of PTAs. It has been argued, for example, that the European Free Trade Agreement (EFTA) was created in response to the European Economic Community (EEC); the latter also spurred the formation of various regional arrangements among less developed countries (LDCs) (Pomfret 1988, 161–78). Deepening European integration, it is claimed, contributed to the formation of NAFTA (Bhagwati 1991, 72; Fernández and Portes 1998) and NAFTA spurred preferential groupings in both the Western Hemisphere and the Asia-Pacific region (Baldwin 1995; Serra et al. 1997, 8–9). Also in accord with this view, many observers have pointed out that the recent spate of PTAs has led various developing countries to join commercial agreements to insure that their access to important foreign markets will not be curtailed (e.g., Bhagwati 1991, 72; de Melo and Panagariya 1993b; Perroni and Whalley 1996; Fernández and Portes 1998).

But while these illustrations are suggestive, very few empirical analyses address the extent to which PTAs' growth has been marked by positive contagion. This chapter's systemic focus obviously limits our ability to directly assess the extent to which strategic interdependence guides the formation and expansion of PTAs. Nonetheless, the following results will be among the first bearing on this topic and therefore should be of interest.

The Global Business Cycle

In addition to the international political factors discussed thus far, global economic factors also affect the formation of PTAs. Relatively little attention has been devoted to identifying the particular economic features that are most influential in this regard, but the global business cycle seems likely to be especially important. The nature of its effect on the establishment of PTAs, however, is likely to depend on whether preferential arrangements tend to dampen or heighten competitive pressures on import-competing firms.

Recessions may stimulate PTA formation by depressing the demand for goods and services, thereby squeezing firms' profits, reducing employment, and creating incentives for import-competing firms and other segments of society to press for protection (Mattli 1999). Joining a PTA—comprised of countries whose principal industries do not rival domestic industries—is one way a government can address these pressures while simultaneously benefiting export-oriented firms seeking greater market access in the face of depressed global demand. Doing so, rather than imposing unilateral trade barriers, affords parties to the GATT/WTO particular advantages. As Richard Pomfret (1988, 158) points out, "if a country intends to raise MFN tariffs or introduce import quotas, it is both contravening GATT and risking retaliation. A bilaterally negotiated discriminatory trade barrier is a way to sidestep GATT obligations without an open breach."

Alternatively, global recessions may depress the rate of PTA formation. Import-competing firms that expect intrabloc liberalization to heighten domestic import penetration are likely to resist a PTA's formation, especially during global recessions when downward pressure is already placed on profits. Further, global expansions tend to spur global trade, and some studies have concluded that rising commerce among a group of countries often fosters the establishment of a PTA to help insulate the flow of trade from future disruptions (e.g., Yarbrough and Yarbrough 1992). Clearly, these studies are not pitched at the systemic level of analysis, but they nonetheless imply that global economic expansions may increase the rates at which PTAs form and countries join them.

The Balance of Power and the End of the Cold War

The global balance of power also bears on the question of why countries sign PTAs. In the Cold War period, the world was divided into two camps, which were integrated through two alliance systems, the North Atlantic Treaty Organization (NATO) and the Warsaw Pact. Their economic systems differed sharply, with command economies in the East and market economies in the West. Trade agreements across these camps were unlikely; agreements were more likely within the Western camp. This bipolar structure has been identified as an influence on trade and trade agreements (Gowa 1994). The collapse of the Soviet Union and the end of this bipolar structure could have affected the propensity of countries to sign trade agreements.

The 1990s and the first few years of the twenty-first century witnessed a rapid rise in PTAs. This development was undoubtedly due to a combination of factors, but one of the most significant was the end of the Cold War. In 1949, the Soviet Union and its allies established the Council of Mutual Economic Assistance (CMEA). This PTA was intended to restructure trade away from the West and toward member-states, thereby promoting economic development and reducing any dependence on their Cold War adversaries (Holzman 1976, 51). The fall of the Berlin Wall in 1989 precipitated the CMEA's demise and prompted a rush by member-states to form arrangements with other countries, especially those in Western Europe. The trend was accelerated in 1991, when the Soviet Union's collapse created a sizable number of new countries seeking to conclude PTAs with each other and with European countries. In the following analyses, we therefore consider the effects of the Cold War's end on PTA formation and the rate at which states have entered these arrangements. Doing so is especially important because the conclusion of the Cold War also stimulated a wave of democratization in parts of what had been the Soviet orbit. While we expect such democratization to promote PTA formation, there are other reasons why the Cold War's end might have led states that were in this orbit to enter preferential arrangements. Consequently, it is useful to ensure that any observed effect of democracy is not being driven by this episode.

Alliances are a second and related feature of power relations that are likely to influence PTA formation. Open trade within a PTA generates efficiency gains and the growth of national income, which can be used to enhance member-states' political-military capacity. Countries can attend to these security externalities stemming from commerce by forming PTAs with their political-military allies, rather than with other states (Gowa and Mansfield 1993; Mansfield 1993; Gowa 1994). In PTAs composed of allies, the gains from liberalizing trade among members bolster the alliance's overall political-military capacity and the common security aims of members attenuate the political risks that states benefiting less from the arrangement might otherwise face from those benefiting more. In the same vein, adversaries have few political reasons to form a PTA and allies that establish one are unlikely to permit their adversaries to join, thus limiting the scope for the expansion of preferential arrangements. Either situation could undermine the security of members, since some participants are likely to derive greater economic benefits than others. It is no coincidence, for instance, that the preferential arrangements between the EC/EU and EFTA, on the one hand, and various states formerly in the Soviet orbit, on the other hand, were concluded only after the end of the Cold War and the Warsaw Pact's collapse.

Whereas we will examine the effects of the Cold War in this chapter, we will defer an analysis of alliances until chapter 4, when our focus will shift from the international system to country-pairs or dyads. As we explain in more detail below, our tack in the current chapter is to explain the number of PTAs that form per year and the number of states that join such arrangements annually. It is difficult to generate a theoretically meaningful measure of system-wide alliance activity that would be expected to affect these outcomes.

Democracy

One of our core arguments is that democracies are more likely to enter a PTA than nondemocracies. Democratic leaders have reason to enter PTAs because these institutions often provide information about the actions of member-states. Membership, in turn, reduces the likelihood that a leader will be turned out of office by voters who mistakenly hold him or her responsible for economic outcomes that were actually beyond his or her control. Autocrats have far less reason to safeguard against this contingency. While democracy is not a systemic factor, we can address whether the spread of democracy since World War II is linked to the spread of PTAs. Clearly, such tests are rather crude and we will examine this argument more directly and in greater depth in chapters 4 and 5. Nonetheless, this analysis will provide some initial evidence about whether there is a relationship between global patterns of democracy and PTA formation.

The Models and Estimation Procedures

To test these hypotheses, the following models are estimated:

(3.1) $Form\ PTA_t = \beta_0 + \beta_1\ Hegemony_{t\text{-}1} + \beta_2\ PTA_{t\text{-}1} + \beta_3 \Delta GWP_{t\text{-}1} + \beta_4\ Democracy_{t\text{-}1}$
$+ \beta_5\ Post\text{--}Cold\ War_t + \beta_6\ Number\ of\ Countries_{t\text{-}1} + \beta_7\ Form\ PTA_{t\text{-}1} + e_t$

(3.2) $Join\ PTA_t = \alpha_0 + \alpha_1\ Hegemony_{t\text{-}1} + \alpha_2\ Country\ PTA_{t\text{-}1} + \alpha_3\ \Delta GWP_{t\text{-}1}$
$+ \alpha_4\ Democracy_{t\text{-}1} + \alpha_5\ Post\text{--}Cold\ War_t + \alpha_6\ Number\ of\ Countries_{t\text{-}1}$
$+ \alpha_7\ Join\ PTA_{t\text{-}1} + z_t$

The Dependent Variables

Form PTA$_t$ is the number of PTAs formed from year t-1 to year t, and *Join PTA$_t$* is the number of countries joining a PTA from year t-1 to year t. The primary source of data for these variables is the list of PTAs notified to the GATT under Article XXIV and the Enabling Clause (reported in World Trade Organization [2009]). Since the WTO only lists PTAs formed by its members and those of the GATT, we supplement these data by including the PTAs listed in Mansfield and Pevehouse (2000) and Goldstein et al. (2007), as well as arrangements identified by various newspaper databases (primarily Factiva and Lexis-Nexis).

As we noted in chapter 2, our focus is on the ratification of PTAs. Because countries can ratify the same PTA at different times, some arrangements have a set of different ratification dates. This issue will not affect our analysis in chapters 4 and 5, which is cast at the level of the directed dyad. But the fact that parties to a PTA often do not ratify the agreement simultaneously does affect some of the analyses in this chapter, particularly our analysis of *Form PTA$_t$*. Consequently, we consider PTAs as forming in the year when the agreement is signed and we code states as joining one when they become signatories to the agreement. In a few cases where we cannot identify the date when an agreement was signed, we used the date when it went into force instead.

We focus on explaining PTAs during the period from 1950 to 2005. We choose this temporal domain for three primary reasons: (1) because data on PTAs are much more difficult to identify prior to World War II, (2) because it is widely argued that PTAs have become increasingly important features of the international landscape over the past half century, and (3) because most empirical research on these groupings centers on the contemporary era. Only one dataset of which we are aware has the same coverage as ours. The World Trade Institute (WTI) has recently compiled a list of PTAs covering the period from 1948 to 2007 (Hufbauer and Schott 2009). It is important to recognize that our data is very similar to the WTI compilation, except that they include about thirty PTAs that we omit and we include about thirty that they exclude. However, the WTI data is not as well suited to our purposes as the data that we compiled. It does not identify the date when PTAs are ratified, which is central to our analysis. It also includes various partial scope agreements, which we do not consider PTAs. Nonetheless, in the following chapter, we analyze whether adding the PTAs listed by the WTI that are not included in our data influences our results and find no evidence of this sort.

In this chapter and throughout our study, we focus only on reciprocal PTAs, that is, agreements in which each party to the agreement grants all other member-states preferential market access. Consequently, we do not analyze "hub and spoke" arrangements or other agreements marked by one-way or nonreciprocal preferences, such as the Lomé Convention, in which the EC gave unilateral commercial preferences to various African countries. Nor do we analyze agreements that strengthen or supersede an existing PTA, since we do not consider these to be new ones. Finally, we do not include partial scope or economic complementary agreements, since they generally involve less extensive trade concessions and tend to cover far less overseas commerce than PTAs. As pointed out in chapter 1, we address five types of arrangements: (1) PAs, which grant each participant preferential access to select segments of the other members' markets; (2) FTAs, which eliminate trade barriers on many (if not all) products within the arrangement; (3) CUs, which eliminate trade barriers within the arrangement and impose a CET on third-party goods; (4) CMs, which are CUs augmented by similar product regulations and the free flow of factors of production among members; and (5) economic unions, which are CMs marked by the coordination of fiscal and monetary policies. In this chapter and most of chapter 4, we consider these arrangements as a group; in chapter 5, we analyze which type of arrangement governments choose to enter.

To distinguish countries from extra-sovereign entities entering a PTA, we require that actors are members of the United Nations (UN) in the year they joined a PTA in order to be coded as having acceded to it. The only exceptions to this coding rule are South Korea, Switzerland, and the members of the CMEA because of their sovereign status. South Korea was not a member of the UN until 1991, Switzerland only joined in 2002, and the parties to the CMEA did not join until after this arrangement was formed.

Independent Variables

Turning to the independent variables in models 3.1 and 3.2, $Hegemony_{t-1}$ is the percentage of total global trade (the sum of global imports and exports) conducted by the state engaging in the most commerce in year t-1. This is a widely used measure of hegemony in studies of the international political economy (Krasner 1976; Lake 1988; McKeown 1991; Mansfield and Busch 1995).[4] PTA_{t-1} is the number of existing PTAs in year t-1, and $Country\ PTA_{t-1}$ is the number of countries involved in at least one PTA in year t-1. The latter variables are included because the rates at which PTAs form and states join them may depend on the existing levels of PTAs and countries that are parties to a commercial bloc, respectively. Either rate, for example, may be characterized by "ceiling" or "saturation" effects. If the number of PTAs or countries involved in a PTA is relatively large, few countries may be left uncovered by such an arrangement.

---

[4] See Lake (1988) for a discussion of this measure's merits in studies of the international trading system. For each year analyzed here, the United States conducts more trade than any other state in the international system. Consequently, for each year, t-1, this measure is derived by summing U.S. imports and exports and dividing this total by the sum of global imports and exports. Data on these variables are expressed in U.S. dollars and are taken from the International Monetary Fund (IMF), *International Financial Statistics* (Washington, D.C.: International Monetary Fund, various years and cd-rom).

This, in turn, may reduce the number of states seeking PTA membership, thus depressing the rates at which PTAs form and states join them. If so, a quadratic relationship might exist between the number of existing PTAs and the frequency of PTA formation, as well as between the percentage of countries involved in a PTA and the frequency with which states join them. To address this possibility, PTA_{t-1}^2 and *Country PTA$_{t-1}^2$* are included in models 3.1 and 3.2, respectively, after we generate initial estimates of each one.

In addition, ΔGWP_{t-1} is the change in gross world product (or global income) from year t-2 to year t-1 and is a measure of the global business cycle.[5] *Democracy$_{t-1}$* is the percentage of states in the international system that are democratic in year t-1. To code this variable, we rely on the Polity IV dataset as updated by Marshall and Jaggers (2005), and coding procedures developed by Ted Robert Gurr and his colleagues (Gurr et al. 1989, 36–39; Jaggers and Gurr 1995; Marshall and Jaggers 2005). Gurr combines annual measures of the competitiveness of the process through which a country's chief executive is selected, the openness of this process, the extent to which institutional constraints exist on a chief executive's decision-making authority, the competitiveness of political participation within a country, and the degree to which binding rules govern political participation to create 11-point indices of each state's democratic (*Democ*) and autocratic (*Autoc*) characteristics. The difference between these indices (*Regime Type = Democ – Autoc*) is an overall measure of regime type that ranges from –10 to 10. In order to ease interpretation of the analyses conducted in chapters 4 and 5, we add 11 to each value, creating a variable that ranges from 1 (highly autocratic) to 21 (highly democratic). Following Keith Jaggers and Ted Robert Gurr (1995), we define democracies as states where *Regime Type* > 16.

Number of Countries$_{t-1}$ is the number of states in the system, based on the update of the Polity data by Marshall and Jaggers. This variable is included because, all things being equal, more countries are likely to form PTAs (and by extension more PTAs are likely to form) as the number of countries grows. *Post–Cold War$_t$* is a dummy variable that equals 0 until 1988 and 1 from 1989 onward. Finally, *Form PTA$_{t-1}$* and *Join PTA$_{t-1}$* are lagged endogenous variables that are included to indicate whether the rates of PTA creation and states' accession to PTAs are characterized by temporal dependence.

Figures 1.1 (in chapter 1) and 3.1 show the distribution of the dependent variables and most of our independent variables over time. Descriptive statistics for all of the variables used in this chapter are presented in table 3.1.

---

[5] GWP data are from the WTO (2005) available at http://www.wto.org/english/res_e/statis_e/its2005_e/appendix_e/a01.xls. (Last accessed July 26, 2011.)

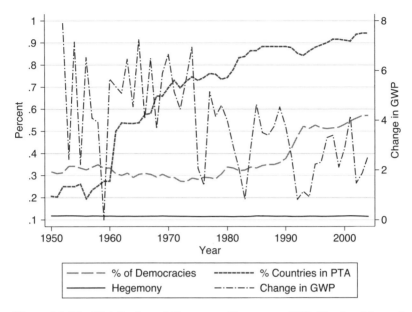

Figure 3.1: The Distribution of Hegemony, Democracy, PTA Membership, and the Change in GWP over Time, 1951–2004

Estimation Procedures

To estimate the parameters in models 3.1 and 3.2, we rely on two related discrete regression models (Maddala 1983; King 1989). We assume that the processes giving rise to the formation of PTAs and states' involvement in them are unobservable, but that a count of each outcome is observed at the end of each year, $t_1, \ldots, t_n$, where n is the number of years in the sample. Various analyses of international relations have used event count models in which the underlying process generating the events is assumed to have a Poisson distribution (e.g., Martin 1992; Pollins 1996). Based on a Poisson model:

$$Y_t \sim f(y_t|\lambda_t) = \frac{(\lambda_t)^{y_t} e^{-\lambda_t}}{y_t!}. \tag{3.3}$$

where, in the present case, Y_t refers to *Form PTA$_t$* in model 3.1 and *Join PTA$_t$* in model 3.2; λ_t is the annual rate of PTA formation for model 3.1 and the annual rate at which countries join PTAs for model 3.2; and y_t is the observed event count at year t. The expected value of Y at t is $E(Y_t) = \lambda_t = \exp(\mathbf{X}_t \boldsymbol{\beta})$, where $\mathbf{X}_t$ is a vector of independent variables and $\boldsymbol{\beta}$ is a vector of parameters.

TABLE 3.1
Descriptive Statistics

	Mean	Std Dev	Min	Max
Form PTA	5.170	7.416	0	30
Join PTA	18.962	20.326	0	79
Hegemony	0.143	0.009	0.126	0.163
Log of PTA	3.438	1.105	1.386	5.352
Log of PTA^2	13.019	7.620	1.922	28.642
PTA	53.849	58.324	4	211
Log of Country PTA	−0.455	0.462	−1.636	−0.058
Log of Country PTA^2	0.416	0.722	0.003	2.676
Country PTA	0.691	0.235	0.195	0.944
ΔGWP	3.825	1.903	0	7.895
Democracy	0.364	0.097	0.261	0.570
Post-Cold War	0.302	0.463	0	1
Number of Countries	128.5	23.3	79	157

Note: For each variable, N = 53. Std Dev = standard deviation, Min = minimum, and Max = maximum.

Central to the Poisson distribution is the assumption that the probability of an event occurring in a given period of time is independent of prior events in that period and that the rate at which events occur during this period, λ_t, is constant (or does not depend on prior events).[6] This assumption, however, may be violated in the present case if, as discussed above, decisions to form or join PTAs are characterized by strategic interdependence. Poisson regression will not be appropriate for estimating models 3.1 and 3.2 if the formation of a PTA or a country's decision to join a PTA in a given year influences the probability that another PTA will form or another state will join one in the same year.

One feature of the Poisson distribution is that the variance of Y_t, $\text{Var}(Y_t) = E(Y_t) = \lambda_t = \exp(\mathbf{X}_t \beta)$. The extent to which the independence of events occurring at a given time is violated can be assessed by expressing the variance of Y_t as $\text{Var}(Y_t) = \lambda_t \exp(\delta)$ and testing the hypothesis that $\delta = 0$ (King 1989, 126–27; Martin 1992, 78–79). If this hypothesis is not rejected, a Poisson distribution is the appropriate basis for the event count model. If it is rejected, the events are characterized by contagion (or λ_t is characterized by heterogeneity) and a negative binomial model should be used (King 1989, 56 and 126).

---

[6] See King (1989, 50–51). More precisely, the Poisson distribution occurs if: (1) the probability of an event occurring in a short period of time is proportional to the period's length; (2) the probability is zero that multiple events occur in a given period; (3) the events occurring in a given period are independent of each other; and (4) the probability that an event occurs in a very short period of time is invariant to when the period starts.

ESTIMATES OF THE PARAMETERS

Initially, we focus on estimating the parameters in model 3.1. The results of a likelihood ratio test based on this model lead us to reject the null hypothesis that $\delta = 0$. Since the formation of PTAs in a given year exhibits contagion, negative binomial regression is used to estimate these parameters, which are reported in table 3.2.

The results indicate that although the creation of PTAs is guided by positive contagion in a given year, it is not guided by positive feedback from one year to the next, since the coefficient estimate of *Form PTA$_{t-1}$* is negative and statistically insignificant. Equally, ΔGWP_{t-1} has little bearing on the incidence of PTA formation.

Our initial results suggest that there is an inverse relationship between the number of PTAs in the global system and the formation of additional trade agreements, since the coefficient estimate of *PTA$_{t-1}$* in the first column of table 3.2 is negative and statistically significant. Further analysis, however, reveals that this relationship is U-shaped. As shown in the third column of table 3.2, the estimated coefficient of PTA_{t-1}^2 is positive and statistically significant, indicating that new PTAs are most likely to form both when the global economy is dotted by few such arrangements and when it is marked by a plethora of them.

In addition, the estimated coefficient of *Number of Countries$_{t-1}$* is positive and statistically significant. As the number of countries increases, so does the likelihood of PTA formation. Hegemony and democracy strongly affect the rate of PTA formation as well. The negative and statistically significant coefficient estimate of *Hegemony$_{t-1}$* indicates that hegemony's erosion has spawned a rise in the development of PTAs. Equally, the positive and significant coefficient of *Democracy$_{t-1}$* reveals that PTAs have formed at a higher clip as the percentage of democracies in the world has increased. This is true even after controlling for the end of the Cold War, after which there was a marked rise in the number of democracies worldwide, as shown in figure 3.1. Yet whether we include *Post–Cold War$_t$* has little bearing on the remaining results. This variable does not have a statistically significant effect on PTA formation and when we remove it from the model (in the second column of table 3.2), the estimated coefficients of the remaining variables are quite similar to our initial results.

Figures 3.2 and 3.3 present the estimated effects of hegemony and democracy, respectively. The effect of hegemony is moderate while the effect of democracy is pronounced. An increase of one standard deviation in the mean value of *Hegemony$_{t-1}$* gives rise to about a 25 percent reduction in the predicted number of PTAs that are formed, holding constant the remaining continuous variables in model 3.1 at their mean values and assuming that the year in question was during the Cold War. Holding constant the other variables at their means (or modal value for *Post–Cold War$_t$*), increasing by one standard

TABLE 3.2
The Effects of Systemic Factors on PTA Formation, 1952–2004

Variable	Base Model	Omitting Post–Cold War	Including PTA Squared	Detrending Variables	Including Features of the GATT
Hegemony	−23.860*	−24.160*	−28.560***	−28.916**	−28.373**
	(13.182)	(13.303)	(9.923)	(11.657)	(11.586)
PTA	−1.875***	−1.942***	−6.363***	−1.158**	−6.931***
	(0.487)	(0.459)	(1.351)	(0.590)	(1.572)
ΔGWP	0.132	0.135*	0.053	0.090	0.062
	(0.084)	(0.081)	(0.080)	(0.083)	(0.075)
Lagged PTAs	−0.014	−0.015	−0.020***	−0.019	−0.016**
Formed	(0.010)	(0.010)	(0.006)	(0.013)	(0.007)
Democracy	17.482***	18.448***	13.972***	20.000***	13.069***
	(4.115)	(3.004)	(3.484)	(2.778)	(3.434)
Number of	0.085***	0.089***	0.151***	0.096***	0.158***
Countries	(0.024)	(0.023)	(0.025)	(0.024)	(0.028)
Post–Cold War	0.180		0.497		0.515
	(0.412)		(0.363)		(0.387)
PTA^2			0.474***	2.338*	0.505***
			(0.141)	(1.355)	(0.161)
Year				0.072***	
				(0.014)	
GATT Round					0.193
in Progress					(0.186)
Time since Last					−0.008
GATT Round					(0.015)
GATT Members					0.010
					(0.015)
Constant	−7.047**	−7.525**	−4.140	−140.986***	−4.147
	(3.401)	(3.385)	(3.004)	(27.898)	(2.973)
Log-Likelihood	−100.30	−100.37	−96.31	−98.21	−94.87
Chi square	211.46***	211.77***	272.29***	285.14***	413.17***
Overdispersion	0.02	0.03	0.00	0.00	0.00

Note: Entries are negative binomial regression estimates of model 3.1, with robust standard errors in parentheses. In each case, N = 53. Statistical significance is indicated as follows: *** $p <$ 0.01; ** $p < 0.05$; * $p < 0.10$. All tests of statistical significance are two-tailed.

deviation the mean value of *Democracy*$_{t-1}$ more than doubles the predicted number of PTAs that are established.

Having analyzed the factors contributing to the rate of PTA formation, we now turn to those influencing the rate at which states join PTAs. These factors differ in a variety of respects. Because the estimate of δ is again positive and

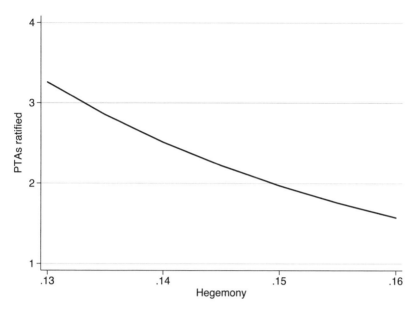

Figure 3.2: Substantive Effect of Hegemony on PTA Formation
Note: These results are generated from the base model in table 3.2. *Post–Cold War*$_t$ is
set to 0 and the other independent variables are set at their means.

statistically significant, we use negative binomial regression to estimate the parameters in model 3.2. One obvious reason why positive contagion marks the
rate at which states join PTAs is that any PTA's formation involves a joint decision by a group of countries to simultaneously become members. As we discuss below, however, these findings probably reflect strategic interaction among
countries competing in international markets as well.

The results of this analysis, presented in table 3.3, indicate that whereas a
state's decision to join a PTA increases the probability that others will do likewise in a particular year, the rate at which states join them is largely unrelated
from one year to the next. The estimate of the lagged dependent variable is
negative, but it is small and not significant.

Based on our initial estimates in the first column, only hegemony and (to
a lesser extent) the global business cycle have a marked influence on the rate
at which states enter PTAs. States enter such arrangements more frequently as
hegemony wanes, since the coefficient of *Hegemony*$_{t-1}$ is negative and statistically significant. That the coefficient estimate of ΔGWP_{t-1} is positive and mar-
ginally significant suggests that countries also enter these arrangements during
expansions in the business cycle, although the strength of this relationship is attenuated once we add *Country PTA*$_{t-1}^2$ in the third, fourth, and fifth columns. In
addition, there is scattered evidence that a rise in the percentage of democratic

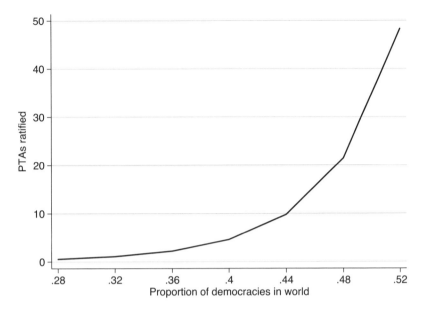

Figure 3.3: Substantive Effect of Democracy on PTA Formation
Note: These results are generated from the base model in table 3.2. *Post–Cold War₁* is
set to 0 and the other independent variables are set at their means.

countries is directly related to the incidence of states joining preferential arrangements: the estimated coefficient of *Democracy*$_{t-1}$ is positive, but it is only
statistically significant if we omit *Post–Cold War*$_t$ (the second column) or if we
detrend the variables in the model (a procedure that is discussed below).

Including *Country PTA*$_{t-1}^2$ in the model produces evidence of a nonmono-
tonic, inverse relationship between the number of countries that are currently
in PTAs and the rate at which states subsequently join (the third column), since
the coefficient estimates of both *Country PTA*$_{t-1}$ and *Country PTA*$_{t-1}^2$ are negative and statistically significant. These results suggest that the magnitude of this
inverse relationship becomes much more pronounced as the number of countries in PTAs grows larger. When we include this quadratic term, there is also
some indication that states entered PTAs at a more rapid clip in the aftermath
of the Cold War. Finally, there is no evidence that the number of countries
in the system affects the frequency of countries entering PTAs. The estimated
coefficient of *Number of Countries*$_{t-1}$ is always positive, but far from statistically
significant.

As shown in figure 3.1, *ΔGWP*$_{t-1}$ has declined over time, whereas *Democracy*$_{t-1}$ and *Country PTA*$_{t-1}$ have risen over time. Least squares regressions of
these variables on time confirm that each variable exhibits a statistically significant secular trend. These trends could pose a problem for our statistical analysis

TABLE 3.3
The Effects of Systemic Factors on Countries Joining PTAs, 1952–2004

Variable	Base Model	Omitting Post–Cold War	Including Country PTA Squared	Detrending Variables	Including Features of the GATT
Hegemony	−49.887***	−56.347***	−41.945***	−57.071***	−38.504***
	(15.128)	(16.346)	(15.104)	(16.758)	(14.679)
Country PTA	−0.504	0.140	−4.839**	1.385	−4.338*
	(1.285)	(1.243)	(2.445)	(2.339)	(2.582)
ΔGWP	0.150*	0.163*	0.077	0.131	0.059
	(0.081)	(0.084)	(0.091)	(0.097)	(0.089)
Lagged PTAs	−0.000	−0.000	−0.008	−0.005	−0.012
Joined	(0.008)	(0.008)	(0.007)	(0.008)	(0.008)
Democracy	3.679	8.847***	4.465	12.590***	5.428
	(3.758)	(2.479)	(3.218)	(4.415)	(4.116)
Number of	0.019	0.010	0.038	0.009	0.051
Countries	(0.029)	(0.028)	(0.028)	(0.033)	(0.041)
Post–Cold War	1.093		1.373**		1.428*
	(0.712)		(0.668)		(0.761)
Country PTA^2			−2.179**	2.404	−1.884*
			(0.954)	(4.107)	(0.984)
Year				0.067***	
				(0.017)	
GATT Round					0.318
in Progress					(0.230)
Time since Last					−0.030
GATT Round					(0.037)
GATT Members					−0.009
					(0.017)
Constant	4.674	5.564	0.065	−130.585***	−1.452
	(3.959)	(4.255)	(4.308)	(33.790)	(6.019)
Log-Likelihood	−186.25	−187.42	−184.22	−187.02	−183.46
Chi square	93.27***	80.12***	127.56***	86.18***	170.05***
Overdispersion	0.54	0.58	0.48	0.57	0.47

Note: Entries are negative binomial regression estimates of model 3.2, with robust standard errors in parentheses. In each case, N = 53. Statistical significance is indicated as follows: *** $p <$ 0.01; ** $p < 0.05$; * $p < 0.10$. All tests of statistical significance are two-tailed.

if they generate multicollinearity among our independent variables or if they contribute to a spurious correlation between these variables and our dependent variables. To address this issue, we regress $Hegemony_{t-1}$, ΔGWP_{t-1}, $Democracy_{t-1}$, PTA_{t-1}, and $Country\ PTA_{t-1}$, respectively, on time during the period from 1951 to 2005. For each variable, the residual of this regression in year t-1 is used as a measure of the variable in this year. Time is also included in both models: $Year_t$ is t and is introduced to directly assess whether there has been a secular increase in preferential arrangements. Because we include this measure of time, we omit *Post–Cold War_t* (which, of course, is highly correlated with $Year_t$) from the models. This detrending helps us deal with the fact that many of these variables are moving together over time.

The results in the fourth column of table 3.2 indicate that detrending the independent variables has little bearing on their effects on the rate of PTA formation. The only noticeable difference stemming from detrending is that the estimated coefficient of the lagged endogenous variable is no longer statistically significant. But as the results in the fourth column of table 3.3 make clear, various important differences arise when we focus on the rate at which states enter PTAs. Only $Year_t$, $Hegemony_{t-1}$, and $Democracy_{t-1}$ exert statistically significant effects on this outcome once we detrend the independent variables. Declining hegemony and a rising percentage of countries that are democratic both lead to a rise in the number of countries joining trade agreements. Equally, there is considerable evidence of a secular rise in both of our dependent variables, since the coefficient estimate of $Year_t$ is positive and statistically significant in both tables 3.2 and 3.3.

We mentioned earlier that the behavior of the United States with respect to PTAs could influence our results. The rapid spread of PTAs over the past two decades is often attributed to the U.S. government's decision to launch a set of these arrangements, beginning in the mid-1980s. It is widely argued that other states followed suit, creating a cascade of PTAs (e.g., Bhagwati 1993; Baldwin 1995 and 2008). To address this issue in a very preliminary manner, we supplement each model reported in tables 3.2 and 3.3 with a count of the number of PTAs to which the United States is a party in each year, t-1. For the purpose of this analysis, we consider the U.S.–Canada Free Trade Agreement and NAFTA to be a single PTA since some observers argue that the latter arrangement superseded the former (Fernández and Portes 1998, 199).

The results, although not presented here, indicate that the number of U.S. PTAs has a negative effect on both PTA formation and the rate of country accession. In almost every case, the estimated coefficient of this variable is statistically significant. The effect of this variable is puzzling: our results suggest that as the United States enters more PTAs, other countries form and enter fewer trade agreements. Nonetheless, including this variable has limited bearing on any of the remaining coefficients in our models. Although it is important to recognize the crudeness of this measure, these results imply that our results do not stem from U.S. behavior with respect to trade agreements.

THE GATT/WTO AND PTA FORMATION

One of the most distinctive features of the PTAs occurring since World War II is the multilateral framework in which they arose. Most contemporary PTAs have been established under the auspices of the GATT and the WTO. Article XXIV of the GATT stipulated that member-states were permitted to establish these arrangements provided that the PTAs eliminated internal trade barriers and did not increase the average level of members' external tariffs. Provisions for forming PTAs were made at the time of the GATT's establishment because it was apparent that this body would be hard-pressed to forbid states from doing so. In addition, some decision makers seemed to believe that Article XXIV's provision to completely eliminate trade barriers among PTA members would complement GATT initiatives to promote multilateral openness (Bhagwati 1993; Finger 1993).

Concerns about how the growth of PTAs is related to the multilateral economic system have spurred much recent attention. The GATT/WTO has been central to the international trading system, and it is therefore useful to examine whether features of the GATT/WTO influence the rates at which PTAs form and states join trade blocs. Before concluding this chapter, we address three such features.

First, we analyze whether the existence of a multilateral trade negotiation (MTN) influences when states elect to form or enter an existing PTA. Since its creation, GATT/WTO has sponsored eight rounds of MTNs: Geneva (1947), Annecy (1949), Torquay (1950–51), Geneva (1955–56), Dillon (1961–62), Kennedy (1963–67), Tokyo (1973–79), and Uruguay (1986–94), plus the Doha Development Agenda, launched in November 2001. One possibility is that PTAs will form less frequently during negotiating rounds than at other times. The central purpose of these rounds is to liberalize trade. If the round is successful, participants may view any trade liberalization fostered by entering a PTA as unnecessary, especially because the GATT/WTO covers trade relations among a much larger set of countries than any PTA.

Alternatively, MTN rounds may spur PTAs (Mansfield and Reinhardt 2003). Participants in MTNs that enter a PTA may be able to strengthen their bargaining position in these negotiations (Bhagwati and Panagariya 1996a; Whalley 1998). Heightened market power enhances the ability of members to use protectionist instruments to improve their terms of trade, thereby dampening their incentive to liberalize trade and bolstering their bargaining position in multilateral negotiations (Oye 1992, 527; Mansfield 1998). Further, by vesting each member with preferential access to the markets of other participants, PTAs can help states generate economies of scale. States entering a trade agreement thus face a reduced need for multilateral liberalization to achieve such economies, bolstering their leverage in multilateral negotiations (Bhagwati 1993; Fernández and Portes 1998, 201–2).

Second, the length of time since a round began may have an effect. Moreover, by forming a PTA with key trading partners during a multilateral negotiating round, parties to GATT/WTO can obtain insurance against the round stalling or failing to produce results in the specific areas they deem most important (Krugman 1993, 74; World Trade Organization 1995, 52; Fernández and Portes

1998, 212; Mansfield 1998, 535–36; Whalley 1998; Perroni and Whalley 2000). A deadlocked MTN round would place pressure on the multilateral regime and could threaten the stability of commercial relations between important trading partners. Such partners can minimize the severity of this threat by entering a PTA, since the grouping liberalizes commerce among members and limits their ability to raise trade barriers in the future. Hence, the longer a round continues, the more likely PTA formation will occur.

Third, the size of the GATT/WTO might influence whether participants elect to join PTAs. The GATT system has grown rapidly, from 23 states when it was created in 1948 to 153 states in 2008. It is widely recognized that as the multilateral system adds members, each member's leverage declines (Koremenos et al. 2001, 791–92; McCalman 2002, 154). This could give states (especially smaller countries, which have relatively little bargaining power) an incentive to band together by forming a PTA. Further, a rising number of parties to the multilateral regime has exacerbated collective action problems among members, making it harder to monitor the trade practices of others and increasing the incentives for members to cheat.

In addition, increased membership tends to introduce greater heterogeneity of preferences, as well as trade and business practices, within the GATT/WTO. Faced with heightened difficulty in arriving at any overarching agreement on economic matters as the number of members grows, parties to the GATT/WTO may find it advantageous to form smaller agreements composed of states with common interests on trade policy (Westhoff et al. 1994; Ethier 1998). Such arrangements provide insurance against future disruptions of trade that might occur if multilateral negotiations buckle under the weight of a large number of participants with disparate commercial preferences, thereby enhancing the members' bargaining power within the regime.

To address these hypotheses about the GATT/WTO, we add three variables to models 3.1 and 3.2: (1) a dummy variable indicating whether a MTN round is underway in year t *(GATT Round in Progress$_t$)*, (2) the number of years, as of t, since the last MTN round concluded *(Time since Last GATT Round$_t$)*, and (3) the number of GATT/WTO members in year t *(GATT Members$_t$)*. As shown in the final column of tables 3.2. and 3.3, none of these variables has a statistically significant bearing on either the incidence of PTA formation or the frequency with which states enter such arrangements. Furthermore, a comparison of the third and fifth columns of each table reveals that including these three variables has very little impact on the remaining coefficients in our models.

Conclusions

The purpose of this chapter has been to provide an initial analysis of the international political and economic factors that affect the rates at which PTAs form and states join these arrangements. Our results strongly indicate that eroding hegemony, the spread of democracy, and strategic interdependence promote trade agreements. There is also weaker evidence that the end of the Cold War led states to enter such arrangements.

Various observers have attributed the growth in these institutions to the decline in U.S. leadership and power. This echoes the argument advanced decades ago in a number of seminal studies about the effects of hegemony on international economic stability (Kindleberger 1973; Gilpin 1975 and 1987; Krasner 1976). Consistent with certain strands of hegemonic stability theory, we find evidence that PTAs form and states join them at increasingly rapid rates as hegemony erodes.

We also find that the global spread of democracy has spurred the formation of PTAs and has increased the rate at which states enter these arrangements. These results are consistent with the argument laid out in chapter 2, but it is clear that the analysis in this chapter is too highly aggregated to place much confidence in the conclusion that democracy promotes PTAs. The following two chapters will address this issue in much greater depth. Further, the rate at which states enter PTAs has been significantly higher since the Berlin Wall's collapse.

Evidence also exists of clustering in the rates at which PTAs form and states join PTAs. The results of this chapter suggest that PTAs often form in response to each other at a given point in time and that the decision by a country to enter one in a given year strongly affects the probability of other countries doing likewise in the same year. The fact that any PTA's creation requires a joint decision by multiple states to become members at the same time certainly contributes to this tendency. But more is probably at work here, including strategic interaction among countries competing in international markets. The decision by a state to join may prompt an economic rival to follow suit quickly rather than being left at a competitive disadvantage. In fact, the spate of states joining PTAs has led others—especially those in East Asia and many developing countries—to consider doing likewise rather than being left without adequate access to important foreign markets (Yarbrough and Yarbrough 1992, 105–6; de Melo and Panagariya 1993b, 5–6; Bhagwati and Panagariya 1996a; Perroni and Whalley 1996, 57). Illustrating the concerns of these countries, President Salinas of Mexico remarked early in the negotiations leading to NAFTA's establishment that "[w]hat we want is closer commercial ties with Canada and the United States, especially in a world in which big regional markets are being created. We don't want to be left out of any of those regional markets" (quoted in Fernández and Portes 1998, 211; see also Bhagwati 1991, 72). Positive contagion in the rate at which states join PTAs may also stem from the tendency for existing PTAs to conclude agreements with outside states contemporaneously rather than sequentially. EFTA followed this pattern, signing a series of preferential agreements with former Soviet republics and Eastern European countries in the early 1990s.

In sum, the results of this chapter indicate that certain systemic factors have contributed heavily to global patterns of commercial agreements; and that hegemony, the spread of democracy, and strategic interaction among both states and PTAs have been influential in this regard. In the following chapter, we turn to an analysis of the domestic politics of PTA formation, which is the central focus of this book. But we also account for many of the international factors that this chapter has shown to affect commercial arrangements.

CHAPTER 4

Regime Type, Veto Players, and PTA Formation

IN THIS CHAPTER, we test the theoretical propositions about domestic politics that we developed in chapter 2. Using a new dataset, we aim to identify the domestic and international factors that affect a country's decision to join and ratify a PTA. We review why democratic regimes are especially likely to enter PTAs and why a large number of veto players reduce the odds that a country will join such arrangements. Then we test these arguments after accounting for the effects of various other economic and international variables, including those that were of greatest importance in the systemic analysis we conducted in chapter 3. Our results provide strong support for these claims. Both regime type and veto players significantly influence whether and when states conclude trade agreements.

TWO THEORETICAL PROPOSITIONS

In chapter 2, we presented a model of international trade cooperation, arguing that two factors strongly influence whether political leaders decide to conclude trade agreements. Governments have to calculate the costs and benefits of entry into PTAs when considering whether to join one. We suggested that the economic costs and benefits of entry are not the sole factors, or even the most important ones, driving such decisions. Rather, politics shapes whether governments elect to seek membership in a PTA. In the previous chapter, we examined some systemic influences on PTA formation. Here, we focus on domestic political influences, while also controlling for international factors. More specifically, we examine whether the regime type and the number of veto players in a state influence whether it concludes a trade agreement. We explore the impact of these two factors on a government's decision to ratify the agreement, taking into account other domestic and international influences.

Political leaders face a tradeoff between pursuing the public interest—or the optimal national policy that a social planner would adopt—and responding to the pleas of special interests. This dilemma often generates higher trade barriers than many in the general public would otherwise prefer, since leaders have an incentive to respond to demands made by well-organized and highly concentrated interest groups, many of which have an interest in protectionism

(Schattschneider 1935; Magee et al. 1989; Grossman and Helpman 2002). Voters have different preferences for trade policy. Here, we assume that the average voter prefers some protectionism, but not too much since excessive protection can adversely affect a country's economy. Interest groups have diverse preferences on trade; some seek a liberal trade regime, while others seek protection from international competition. However, groups seeking protection tend to be highly concentrated and politically organized. Political leaders will be tempted by interest group pressures to adopt a level of protection that is too high from the standpoint of society as a whole. The public generally understands this and hence assumes its government will provide too much protection.

The more leaders' fortunes depend on public support, the more incentives they will have to find mechanisms to make a credible commitment to an open trade policy and reassure the public that they have not given in to special interest demands. In political systems where the public cannot vote leaders out of office, this problem is less severe. In systems with competitive elections, by contrast, this problem is acute. Voters do not actually cast ballots on the basis of a government's trade policy, but they do consider the state of the economy when going to the polls. Thus, governments are likely to be penalized when the economy degrades. Voters assume that such downturns are at least partly attributable to policies enacted in response to interest group pressures. As such, governments face a credibility problem: voters are more likely to remove them from office in bad economic times, even if they did not give in to special interest demands and overprotect the economy.[1]

Consequently, our first argument is that democracies are more likely to sign trade agreements than other countries because of their more competitive political systems. As we argued in chapter 2, a PTA not only lowers trade barriers among member-states, but it also does so publicly and provides for both monitoring and punishment if a participant reneges. The costs associated with the violation of a trade agreement bolster the credibility of a leader's claim not to raise trade barriers, which makes them less likely to be unfairly blamed for adverse economic conditions. Leaders who are not engaged in rent-seeking are therefore more likely to retain office. The public also gains from such an agreement since it limits the government's ability to grant demands for protectionism lodged by special interests. Both leaders and society at large benefit from PTAs, and these benefits rise in countries with more competitive political systems.

---

[1] A number of scholars have claimed that trade agreements can provide a "lock in" mechanism for countries to commit to economic reform (Gunning 2001; World Bank 2004; Crawford and Fiorentino 2005, 16; Büthe and Milner 2008). These arguments are similar to ours, except that we focus on trade policy and not general economic policy. Our model in chapter 2 also explicitly shows how such lock in occurs and why it is credible, unlike many of these claims.

Our second argument is that the odds of a country ratifying a PTA decline as the number of veto players rises. These groups occupy institutional positions that allow them to "veto" a trade agreement. As such, the head of government needs their approval to change policy. Furthermore, implementing policies often requires the tacit approval of veto players—especially legislatures. Veto players can thus check the executive and balance against his or her preferences at various stages of the process.

As we noted in chapter 2, an increased number of veto players raises the costs of making an international agreement. The number of such players affects what leaders must pay domestically to implement international agreements (Schelling 1960; Milner 1997a). Veto players often represent important interest groups and some may demand more protection than the government desires. When their preferences differ from those of the executive, the government has two ways to obtain their acquiescence. Both are expensive.

First, the head of government can try to craft an agreement to purchase the acquiescence of veto players. A chief executive, for example, could build enough flexibility into an agreement that its terms would be weakened in areas where domestic groups oppose it; or the government could simply exclude all sectors in which veto players would be adversely affected by trade liberalization. In this way, a leader could negotiate any agreement to minimize opposition by veto players. Research has suggested that governments do indeed respond to domestic conditions when designing international agreements (Downs and Rocke 1995; Koremenos et al. 2001; Rosendorff and Milner 2001). Nonetheless, there are several constraints on such behavior. For one thing, a government is likely to have trouble unilaterally insisting on terms that its domestic veto players favor because the other countries involved in the negotiations must agree to these terms. These countries are likely to press for precisely those concessions that the domestic veto players most fiercely oppose. Furthermore, these countries also have veto players who will reject the imposition of terms that are antithetical to their interests. For another thing, as the number of veto players grows, the demands of these groups for exclusions or flexibility also rise, which makes it more difficult for the set of chief executives involved in the negotiations to arrive at a mutually acceptable agreement.

Second, a government may respond to its veto players by attempting to buy their acquiescence to an agreement that they oppose rather than crafting an agreement that they find acceptable. Such bribery, however, contributes to the transaction costs an executive faces in concluding a PTA. Acting rationally, the government will only transfer as much utility as it gets from the agreement relative to the reversion point or status quo, thereby limiting its ability to bribe. As the number of veto players rises, the government is likely to have to make ever larger bribes, unless they are free traders. At some point, this will become prohibitively expensive. Hence, as the number of veto players grows larger, the odds of a government forming a PTA grow smaller.

EMPIRICAL TESTS OF THE HYPOTHESES

In this section, we explain and present a set of statistical tests of our two hypotheses. We begin by estimating the following baseline model:

$$
\begin{aligned}
(4.1)\quad PTA\ Ratification_{ij} = {} & \beta_0 + \beta_1\ Regime\ Type_i + \beta_2\ Veto\ Players_i + \beta_3\ Existing\ PTA_{ij} \\
& + \beta_4\ Trade_{ij} + \beta_5\ GDP_i + \beta_6\ \Delta GDP_i + \beta_7\ Dispute_{ij} + \beta_8\ Alliance_{ij} \\
& + \beta_9\ Former\ Colony_{ij} + \beta_{10}\ Contiguity_{ij} + \beta_{11}\ Distance_{ij} + \beta_{12}\ Hegemony \\
& + \beta_{13}\ Post{-}Cold\ War + \beta_{14}\ GDP\ Ratio_{ij} + \beta_{15}\ \%\ Dyads\ Ratifying\ PTA \\
& + \beta_{16}\ GATT/WTO_{ij} + \beta_{17}{-}\beta_{23}\ Regional\ Fixed\ Effects_i + \varepsilon_{ij}
\end{aligned}
$$

The Dependent Variable: PTA Ratification

Our dependent variable, *PTA Ratification$_{ij}$*, is the log of the odds that state i ratifies a PTA in year t with state j, where we observe 1 if this occurs and 0 otherwise. (For simplicity and because there is no danger of misunderstanding, t subscripts are not included in this and the following chapter.) Our analysis covers the period from 1951 (for variables measured in year t-1 and 1952 for variables measured in year t) to 2004. As in chapter 3, we focus on reciprocal agreements, which involve policy adjustments on the part of all members. Non-reciprocal arrangements, where one state unilaterally grants another country preferential access to its market, are excluded from the analysis, because our model assumes that all parties to an agreement must make commitments about trade barrier reductions. Note that the observed value of *PTA Ratification$_{ij}$* is 1 only in years when states initially ratify a PTA, not in subsequent years when the agreement is in force. It takes on this value if the country is joining an existing PTA or if it is forming a new one with other partners.

If the exact year of ratification could not be determined, we rely on the date that state i signed the PTA with state j. Since most agreements are ratified relatively soon after they are formed and since ratification dates are missing less than 30 percent of the time, this is a reasonable approach. Since states i and j need not—and, indeed, often do not—ratify a preferential arrangement in the same year, our unit of analysis is the annual "directed dyad." Thus, for each dyad in each year, there is one observation corresponding to state i and a second observation corresponding to state j. For example, in the case of the United States-Canadian dyad in 1985, we include one observation where the United States is i and Canada is j, and a second observation where Canada is i and the United States is j. Each monadic variable, as we explain below, is included in this model only once, for the country listed as i in each particular observation. Of course, analyzing directed dyads doubles the number of observations in the sample, thereby producing standard errors that are too small. To correct this problem, we cluster the standard errors over the undirected dyad.

We use directed dyads as our unit of analysis because we want to examine a government's decision to ratify a trade agreement. While it takes at least two countries to negotiate and sign an agreement, each then has to ratify it domestically to bring it into force. This ratification decision, which culminates the process of creating a PTA, is made by each country independently. We take into account the pressures of other countries and the international system on each government in our dyadic setup. But by using directed dyads, we are also able to focus on each government's separate ratification decision, which is what our theory highlights.

The Key Independent Variables: Regime Type and Veto Players

Our primary independent variables are the regime type and the number of veto players in each nation-state. First, *Regime Type$_i$* is country *i*'s regime type in year *t*. To measure each state's regime type, we rely on a widely used index constructed by Ted Robert Gurr, Keith Jaggers, and Will H. Moore (1989), and data drawn from the Polity Project (Jaggers and Gurr 1995; Marshall and Jaggers 2005).[2] This index combines data on five factors that help to capture the institutional differences between democracies and autocracies that we emphasized earlier: the competitiveness of the process for selecting a country's chief executive, the openness of this process, the extent to which institutional constraints limit a chief executive's decision-making authority, the competitiveness of political participation within a country, and the degree to which binding rules govern political participation within it. Following Gurr et al. (1989) and Jaggers and Gurr (1995), these data are used to create an 11-point index of each state's democratic characteristics (*Democ$_i$*) and an 11-point index of its autocratic characteristics (*Autoc$_i$*). The difference between these indices, *Regime Type$_i$* = *Democ$_i$* – *Autoc$_i$*, yields a summary measure of regime type that takes on values ranging from –10 for a highly autocratic state to 10 for a highly democratic country. In order to ease interpretation, we add 11 to each value, resulting in a range from 1 (highly autocratic) to 21 (highly democratic).

There are three principal reasons to rely on this measure in our empirical analysis. First, our theory treats regime type as a continuous variable, with the competitiveness of elections ranging from perfectly competitive to completely uncompetitive. As noted above, the index developed by Jaggers and Gurr has a range of 21 points, unlike some other measures of regime type (e.g., Przeworski et al. 2000) that treat regime type as dichotomous. Second, the Jaggers and Gurr index highlights a number of institutional dimensions of regime type that we stress. The ability of voters to choose the chief executive, which is central to our theory, is expected to rise as the process for selecting the executive becomes more competitive, that process becomes more open, and political participation becomes increasingly competitive. Jaggers and Gurr's index captures each of these three institutional elements, whereas various alternative measures do not

---

[2] We use the Polity IV data, generated in 2004.

(e.g., Gastil 1980 and 1990). Third, their index covers more countries during the period since World War II than most other measures of regime type (e.g., Bollen 1980; Gastil 1980 and 1990; Gasiorowski 1996). Nonetheless, after generating our initial results, we will assess their robustness using three alternative measures of regime type, each of which is a dichotomous indicator of whether a country is democratic or not.

From the standpoint of testing our theory, the second major independent variable in model (4.1) is *Veto Players$_i$*. This variable measures the degree of constraints on policy change in country i in year t, based on the number of independent, constitutionally mandated institutions that have different political preferences and can exercise veto powers over policy decisions. We rely on Witold Henisz's (2000 and 2002) index of veto players, which considers the presence of effective branches of government outside of the executive's control, the extent to which these branches are controlled by the same political party as the executive, and the homogeneity of preferences within these branches.[3] The strength of this measure is that it is not only internationally comparable but, as important, the theory underlying his measure is very similar to ours. His index, based on recent developments in positive political theory, is derived from a single dimensional, spatial model of policy choice that allows the status quo and the preferences of the actors to vary across the entire space. Since we focus on trade policy, a single policy dimension is useful. Because preferences range from protectionist to free trade in our analysis, Henisz's single policy dimension model capturing both domestic institutional arrangements and the preferences within those arrangements provides a simple yet powerful means to test our hypothesis. Indeed, Henisz's (2002, 363) research echoes our argument, revealing that

> (1) each additional veto point (a branch of government that is both constitutionally effective and controlled by a party different from other branches) provides a positive but diminishing effect on the total level of constraints on policy change and (2) homogeneity (heterogeneity) of party preferences within an opposition (aligned) branch of government is positively correlated with constraints on policy change.

The resulting measure is a continuous variable ranging from 0 to 1. When *Veto Players$_i$* equals 0, there is a complete absence of veto players in state i. Higher values indicate the presence of effective political institutions that can balance the power of the executive. In cases where effective institutions exist, the variables take on larger values as party control across some or all of these institutions

---

[3] We use the most recent version of these data, which were updated in 2006. Henisz has developed two measures of veto points, one that includes the judiciary and one that does not. We use the latter measure since there is little reason to believe that the judiciary would influence the decision to enter a PTA. However, our results are similar when we use the alternative measure.

diverges from the executive's party. For example, in the United States, the value of this measure is larger during periods of divided government.[4]

After conducting some initial tests using *Veto Players$_i$*, we analyze a second measure of veto players. *Checks$_i$* was developed by Thorsten Beck, George Clarke, Alberto Groff, Philip Keefer, and Patrick Walsh (2001 and 2005). This variable emphasizes the degree of electoral competition in a country, the number of different institutions that can check the executive, as well as the degree of partisan differences across these institutions. Countries with high levels of electoral competition for the legislature or chief executive, with numerous bodies that can check the executive, and with partisan differences in the control of those various bodies score very high on the checks measure. This rating is consistent with our idea that having many groups—with different preferences from those of the executive controlling institutions that affect policy outcomes—raises the transaction costs for leaders trying to sign and ratify PTAs. This measure has certain advantages over Henisz's measure: it is simpler, less highly correlated with *Regime Type$_i$*, and treats parliamentary and presidential systems slightly differently. However, it also has some key drawbacks, most notably a far shorter period of time over which data are available (1975 to 2005) and a smaller number of countries that are coded. To ensure that our temporal and country coverage is as broad as possible, we focus primary attention on Henisz's measure. Still, we use both scores to ensure that our results are robust to different calculations of veto players.[5]

For at least two reasons, we rely on these more general measures of veto players rather than constructing a measure that is specific to trade policy. First, constructing such a measure would require a great deal of detailed information that is unavailable for many countries. Equally, the countries that would be missing data would not represent a random collection. Instead, it is likely that states with low numbers of veto players or unstable institutions would be selected out of the sample, creating a potential source of bias. Second, it seems reasonable to assume that a measure of veto players for trade policy would look very similar to the ones that we are using because most changes in trade policy must endure the same institutional hurdles and ratification processes that all other policies face. In the United States, for example, trade policy initiatives have been contested by Congress and the president; both have the ability to block policy change. Fast track, the procedure often used to move trade legislation forward, simply reduces Congress's ability to amend a trade agreement. It

---

[4] For more details concerning this measure of veto players, see Henisz (2000 and 2002). The dataset is available at http://www.management.wharton.upenn.edu/henisz/POLCON/ContactInfo.html. (Last accessed August 17, 2011.)

[5] There is considerable agreement between Henisz's measure and Beck et al.'s measure; the correlation between a country's annual score on Henisz's measure of veto players and its score on the Beck et al.'s measure is about 0.72.

does not alter the legislative requirements for ratifying any such policy change. Veto players affect the ratification of changes in policy; trade agreements tend to require changes in policy in most countries and thus to invoke the usual institutional veto players.

Control Variables

We also include a battery of variables that previous studies have linked to the formation of PTAs to ensure that any observed effects of regime type or veto players are not due to other international or domestic factors, including the systemic factors that we analyzed in chapter 3. A number of the variables that we include also help to control in a very general way for similarities and differences in preferences between countries. All of these variables are measured in year t-1 to reduce the possibility of a simultaneity bias, since existing research indicates that PTA formation may influence some of these factors.

To begin, we include *Existing PTA$_{ij}$*, which indicates whether countries i and j are already members of the same PTA(s). There is reason to expect that participating in one arrangement is likely to affect a state's proclivity to create or join another with the same partner. Next, *Trade$_{ij}$* is the logarithm of the total value of trade (in constant 2000 U.S. dollars) between countries i and j.[6] Various observers argue that increasing economic exchange creates incentives for domestic groups that benefit as a result to press governments to enter PTAs, since these arrangements help to avert the possibility that trade relations will break down in the future (e.g., Nye 1988). Moreover, heightened overseas commerce can increase the susceptibility of firms to predatory behavior by foreign governments, prompting them to press for the establishment of PTAs that limit the ability of governments to behave opportunistically (Yarbrough and Yarbrough 1992).[7]

In addition to economic relations between countries, economic conditions within countries are likely to influence PTA formation. Particularly important in this regard is a state's economic size. Large states (in economic terms) may have less incentive to seek the expanded market access afforded by PTA membership than their smaller counterparts. We therefore analyze *GDP$_i$*, the logarithm of country i's GDP (in constant 2000 U.S. dollars). Moreover, fluctuations in economic growth may also affect whether states enter preferential arrangements. On the one hand, some research indicates that downturns in the business cycle lead states to seek membership in such arrangements (Mattli 1999). On the other hand, increased growth is likely to increase a country's demand

---

[6] We add .001 to all values of trade since some dyads conduct no trade in particular years and the logarithm of zero is undefined.

[7] Note that we use the International Monetary Fund's *Direction of Trade Statistics* as the main source for the trade data. Missing data are filled in with Gleditsch's (2002) data on trade flows. Like the IMF data, however, Gleditsch's data are in current dollars. We deflate these data using the U.S. GDP deflator.

for imports and supply of exports, creating an incentive to gain preferential access to overseas markets. To address this issue, we introduce ΔGDP_i, the change in GDP_i from t-1 to t.[8]

In addition, political relations between states may influence whether they join the same PTA, independent of their respective domestic political structures. Cooperation also depends on the extent of differences in preferences between countries' leaders. The further apart these preferences are, the less likely is cooperation. To account for these preferences, we include a number of variables that measure the foreign policy differences between states. Military hostilities between states signal large differences in preferences between countries and may discourage economic cooperation and thus their propensity to sign PTAs. Similarly, political-military cooperation may promote economic cooperation (Mansfield 1993; Gowa and Mansfield 1993; Gowa 1994). $Dispute_{ij}$ is coded 1 if countries i and j are involved in a dispute, 0 otherwise. Though many studies of political disputes rely on the militarized interstate disputes (MIDs) dataset (Jones et al. 1996; Ghosn and Bennett 2003), these data do not extend beyond 2001. To analyze the longest possible time frame, we therefore use the Peace Research Institute Oslo (PRIO) data on interstate armed conflict, which covers the period from 1951 to 2004.[9] $Alliance_{ij}$ equals 1 if countries i and j are members of a political-military alliance, 0 otherwise. We code this variable using the Alliance Treaty Obligations and Provisions (ATOP) data (Leeds et al. 2002).[10] To ensure that our results are robust to the measures of disputes and alliances that are used, however, we also measure disputes using the MIDs data and alliances using the Correlates of War (COW) data. Further, since previous research has found that a former colonial relationship between i and j increases the likelihood that they will enter the same PTA, we include $Former\ Colony_{ij}$, which equals 1 if countries i and j had a colonial relationship

---

[8] GDP data are also taken from Gleditsch (2002) but updated to 2004 and are already in constant dollars. They are available at http://privatewww.essex.ac.uk/~ksg/exptradegdp.html. (Last accessed August 18, 2011.)

[9] We use v4-2008 of the data from http://www.prio.no/CSCW/Datasets/Armed-Conflict/UCDP-PRIO/Old-Versions/4-2007/. (Last accessed July 15, 2011.) Their data includes four types of conflict: (1) extra-systemic armed conflict occurs between a state and a nonstate group outside its own territory; (2) interstate armed conflict occurs between two or more states; (3) internal armed conflict occurs between the government of a state and one or more internal opposition group(s) without intervention from other states; and (4) internationalized internal armed conflict occurs between the government of a state and one or more internal opposition group(s) with intervention from other states (secondary parties) on one or both sides. Type 3 conflicts are dropped. We keep the other three types and expand the data so that all possible dyads between the countries on side A and those on side B are created. Data that do not have an independent country as one of the sides are then dropped. These, then, should be all dyadic conflicts in the PRIO data. See Gleditsch et al. (2002) and UCDP/PRIO Armed Conflict Dataset Codebook, version 4-2008.

[10] For the ATOP data, we use version 3.0, specifically the atop3_0ddyr.dta file, which is the directed dyad dataset available at http://atop.rice.edu/. (Last accessed August 18, 2011.) Because the data only extend to 2003, data for 2004 are filled in with 2003 data. See Leeds et al. (2002).

that ended after World War II, 0 otherwise (Mansfield et al. 2002; Mansfield and Reinhardt 2003).[11]

Geographic proximity is another important influence on PTA formation. States often enter PTAs to obtain preferential access to the markets of their key trade partners. These partners tend to be located nearby, since closer proximity reduces transportation costs and other impediments to trade. We introduce two variables to capture distance. *Contiguity*$_{ij}$ is a dummy variable that is coded 1 if countries i and j share a common border or are separated by 150 miles of water or less. *Distance*$_{ij}$ is the logarithm of the capital-to-capital distance between i and j. It is useful to include both variables since some states have distant capitals (e.g., Russia and China) yet share borders, while other states do not share borders but are in relatively close proximity (e.g., Benin and Ghana).[12]

In addition, systemic conditions are likely to affect the prospects of PTA formation, as shown in chapter 3. Because we found that declining hegemony contributes to the proliferation of preferential arrangements, we include *Hegemony*, the proportion of global GDP produced by the state with the largest GDP (in our sample, the United States for each year). This variable therefore takes on the same value for each country in year $t-1$. We further include *Post–Cold War*, which equals 0 from 1950 to 1988 and 1 thereafter. Even though this variable had only a modest effect on the rate at which PTAs are formed and states enter them, we want to account for the spike in PTAs after the Berlin Wall's collapse. We also examine whether power disparities influence the establishment of preferential arrangements. To address this issue, we include *GDP Ratio*$_{ij}$, which is the natural logarithm of the ratio of the country GDPs for each dyad. In computing this variable, the larger GDP is always in the numerator; hence, a negative sign on the coefficient of this variable would indicate that a greater disparity between the countries decreases the likelihood of ratification.

Recall that the negative binomial regression results in chapter 3 revealed that both the rate at which PTAs form and the rate at which states join these arrangements are characterized by contagion. In this chapter, we continue to address whether countries sign agreements because others are doing so, thereby fueling the diffusion process (Simmons and Elkins 2004; Simmons et al. 2006). To this end, we include several variables. First, we add the percent of all dyads in the system that ratified a PTA in the previous year, *% Dyads Ratifying*. This variable is intended to tap global pressures for the diffusion of PTAs.

After conducting some initial estimates of our model, we include some additional variables to analyze whether the establishment of PTAs is marked by diffusion. We construct a measure of regional diffusion pressures (*Region PTA*$_i$). It is calculated as the number of PTAs in country i's geographical region—excluding

---

[11] Data on former colonial relations are taken from Kurian (1992).

[12] Data on distance and contiguity are taken from EUGene (Bennett and Stam 2000), available at http://eugenesoftware.org/. (Last accessed August 18, 2011.)

those arrangements in which country i participates—divided by the total number of countries in that region. We also analyze whether a diffusion process occurs through trade relationships. The variable *Trade Partner PTA*$_i$ measures the total number of PTAs that the top ten trading partners of country i belong to, excluding those in which country i is a member. If diffusion is occurring, we expect these variables to have positive signs, implying that the formation of PTAs around the world, in the region, or among trading partners is spurring country i to form its own trade agreements. Since these diffusion variables are highly correlated, however, we do not include them in the same models.[13]

Our final measure of diffusion is drawn from a recent study of PTA formation by Richard Baldwin and Dany Jaimovich (2010). They argue that country i is more likely to sign a PTA with country j if country j makes up a larger proportion of country i's exports, if country j is signing PTAs with other countries, and if it trades extensively with these PTA partners. As the percentage of country j's imports covered by PTA trade increases, exporters in country i will push for a PTA to maintain market in country j. Their measure of contagion is operationally defined as $Contagion_{ij} = (X_{ij}/X_i) \times (X_{kj}/M_j) \times PTA_{kj}$, where X_{ij} is the volume of exports from country i to country j; X_i is country i's total exports; X_{kj} is the flow of exports from countries k to country j; M_j is country j's total imports; and PTA_{kj} is a dummy variable indicating whether country j participates in at least one PTA with k, which collectively denotes country j's PTA partners. If j does not participate in any PTAs, the measure of contagion equals 0. To generate annual values of this variable, we generate the predicted value of exports (X_{ij}) and the predicted value of imports for each country-pair using a gravity model composed of dyad-specific fixed effects and the natural logarithm of the product of the country GDPs making up the dyad. We then sum: (1) the predicted export volumes across all of country i's trade partners to arrive at X_i, (2) the predicted import volumes across all of country j's trade partners to generate M_j, and (3) the predicted exports from each of country j's PTA partners to j itself to construct X_{kj}.[14]

Because the GATT and the WTO recognize and attempt to govern the establishment of PTAs, members of these global institutions may also be disproportionately likely to enter preferential arrangements (Mansfield and Reinhardt

---

[13] Interestingly, the diffusion process is highly correlated with the post–Cold War variable. The end of the Cold War seems to have increased diffusion pressures globally.

[14] Baldwin and Jaimovich (2010) generate a single value of this measure of contagion for each country-pair in the first year of their sample. They take this tack because PTA formation will affect the trade shares after the agreement is signed. The resulting endogeneity is a concern. However, their tack assumes that trade shares are extremely sticky, whereas such shares have varied substantially over time for many countries. Furthermore, our primary concern is to ensure that PTA contagion is not driving the effects of regime type or veto players on PTA formation. From that standpoint, we prefer to generate annual measures of this variable and accept any resulting endogeneity between PTA formation and this measure of contagion.

2003). To account for this possibility, we introduce $GATT/WTO_{ij}$ to the model. It equals 1 if countries i and j are both members of the GATT in each year prior to 1995 or if they are both members of the WTO in years from 1995 on, and 0 otherwise.[15] We also include regional fixed effects, using the eight regional categories identified by the World Bank since it is widely argued that the prevalence of PTAs varies across regions, as noted in chapter 1. Finally, ε_{ij} is a stochastic error term.

Descriptive statistics for all of these variables are presented in table 4.1. The sample in the following analyses is comprised of all pairs of states during the period from 1951 to 2004. Because the observed value of the dependent variable is dichotomous, we use logistic regression to estimate the model. Tests of statistical significance are based on robust standard errors clustered on the dyad to address any potential problems with heteroskedasticity or the directed dyad research design. To account for temporal dependence in the formation of PTAs, we include a spline function of the number of years that have elapsed (as of t) since each dyad last formed a PTA, with knots at years 1, 4, and 7, as suggested by Nathaniel Beck, Jonathan Katz, and Richard Tucker (1998). In the following tables, however, the estimates of this function are omitted to conserve space.

RESULTS OF THE EMPIRICAL ANALYSIS

In table 4.2, we report a series of results for different models. The first column (Base Model) shows our baseline results. In the second column (Dyadic Fixed Effects), we include dyad-specific fixed effects to account for any unobserved heterogeneity across the many country-pairs included in our data. The results in the third column (Dyad & Year Fixed Effects) are generated after including both dyad-specific and year-specific fixed effects. Adding year-specific effects helps to address the systemic factors that affect all dyads at a given point in time and that are not included in the model. In the fourth column (All Variables Lagged t-1), we measure *Regime Type*$_i$ and *Veto Players*$_i$ in year t-1, rather than year t. Our argument is that these factors should exert a contemporaneous rather than a lagged effect on PTA ratification. Furthermore, there is little chance that the observed effects of these variables are compromised by any simultaneity bias. After all, it seems highly unlikely that the decision to form a PTA, much less its ratification, would influence either a state's regime type or the number of domestic veto players. Nonetheless, measuring these variables in t-1, along with the other control variables in our model, should enhance the confidence in our results. In the final column of table 4.2 (COW Alliance/MID), we replace the ATOP alliance data and the PRIO disputes data with the COW Project's alliance and MIDs data. As we described earlier, the COW data covers less of the

[15] Data are taken from the WTO (2006a).

TABLE 4.1
Descriptive Statistics, 1952–2004

	N	Mean	Std Dev	Min	Max
PTA Ratification	1246407	0.008	0.088	0	1
Regime Type	1077348	11.126	7.507	1	21
Veto Players	1178204	0.199	0.216	0	0.71
Existing Dyadic PTA	1246407	0.061	0.240	0	1
Trade (logged)	1212889	−2.404	4.978	−6.908	12.923
GDP (logged)	1185246	16.888	2.099	9.397	23.046
ΔGDP (in $100 billion)	1171772	0.058	0.368	−18.627	4.815
Dispute (PRIO)	1212889	0.001	0.031	0	1
Dispute (MID)[b]	1136005	0.004	0.065	0	1
Alliance (ATOP)	1212889	0.097	0.296	0	1
Alliance (COW)[b]	1048468	0.070	0.255	0	1
Former Colony	1246407	0.006	0.076	0	1
Contiguity	1170650	0.033	0.178	0	1
Distance (logged)	1203572	8.254	0.781	1.609	9.421
Hegemony	1212889	0.222	0.019	0.204	0.287
Post–Cold War	1246407	0.457	0.498	0	1
GDP Ratio	1158018	2.374	1.792	0.000	13.635
% Dyads Ratifying PTA	1246407	0.008	0.008	0	0.031
GATT/WTO	1212889	0.340	0.474	0	1
Checks[a]	822886	2.445	1.688	1	18
Competitive Election	1041036	0.383	0.486	0	1
Regime Type (excluding executive constraints)	1041036	−0.289	5.000	−7	6
Dem (Regime Type ≥ 17)	1077348	0.374	0.484	0	1
ACLP Democracy	1126239	0.426	0.494	0	1
Regional PTA	1212889	0.624	0.785	−0.053	4.759
Trade Partner PTA	1212889	52.933	38.124	0	210
GATT Round in Progress	1212889	0.553	0.497	0	1
Time Since Last GATT Round	1212889	5.506	3.871	0	14
S Score	1021264	0.703	0.274	−0.714	1
Communist	1246407	0.098	0.297	0	1
Contagion	1031518	0.002	0.015	0	2.152

Note: Std Dev = standard deviation, Min = minimum, and Max = maximum. Regional dummy variables are not included in this table.

[a] Data for this variable are available from 1975–2004.

[b] Data for these variables are available from 1951–2001.

TABLE 4.2
The Estimated Effects of Regime Type, Veto Players, and Other Factors on PTA Ratification, 1952–2004.

Variable	Base Model	Dyadic Fixed Effects	Dyad & Year Fixed Effects	All Variables Lagged t-1	COW Alliance/ MID
Regime Type	0.028***	0.038***	0.020***	0.008***	0.029***
	(0.003)	(0.004)	(0.004)	(0.003)	(0.003)
Veto Players	−0.575***	−1.003***	−0.798***	−0.240***	−0.578***
	(0.095)	(0.109)	(0.113)	(0.088)	(0.101)
Existing PTA	0.156***	−2.008***	−1.925***	0.229***	0.114**
	(0.048)	(0.039)	(0.042)	(0.047)	(0.054)
Trade (logged)	0.016***	0.017***	0.023***	0.018***	0.011***
	(0.003)	(0.006)	(0.006)	(0.003)	(0.004)
GDP (logged)	0.027**	0.267***	0.441***	0.024*	0.053***
	(0.013)	(0.050)	(0.056)	(0.013)	(0.015)
ΔGDP (in $100 billion)	−0.065**	0.016	0.052*	−0.074**	−0.100***
	(0.030)	(0.031)	(0.031)	(0.030)	(0.020)
Dispute (PRIO)	0.154	−0.259	−0.265	0.158	
	(0.253)	(0.290)	(0.297)	(0.252)	
Dispute (MID)					−0.878***
					(0.242)
Alliance (ATOP)	0.491***	−0.537***	−0.384***	0.465***	
	(0.062)	(0.054)	(0.055)	(0.060)	
Alliance (COW)					0.468***
					(0.069)
Former Colony	−1.262***			−1.278***	−1.122***
	(0.339)			(0.339)	(0.340)
Contiguity	−0.648***			−0.673***	−0.554***
	(0.065)			(0.063)	(0.071)
Distance (logged)	−1.124***			−1.105***	−1.179***
	(0.057)			(0.056)	(0.058)
Hegemony	−6.416***	−15.614***		−6.052***	−6.548***
	(1.085)	(1.378)		(1.070)	(1.104)
Post–Cold War	0.807***	1.396***		0.804***	0.821***
	(0.032)	(0.042)		(0.032)	(0.033)
GDP Ratio	−0.156***	−0.043	−0.052	−0.155***	−0.174***
	(0.010)	(0.043)	(0.043)	(0.010)	(0.011)
% Dyads Ratifying PTA	35.789***	23.979***		37.233***	45.169***
	(1.349)	(1.244)		(1.311)	(1.383)
GATT/WTO	0.139***	0.214***	0.246***	0.161***	0.063**
	(0.030)	(0.042)	(0.044)	(0.029)	(0.032)

(continued)

Variable	Base Model	Dyadic Fixed Effects	Dyad & Year Fixed Effects	All Variables Lagged t-1	COW Alliance/ MID
South Asia	0.040			−0.093	−0.218
	(0.134)			(0.130)	(0.138)
Middle East &	0.601***			0.381***	0.629***
N. Africa	(0.091)			(0.085)	(0.101)
Sub-Saharan Africa	1.465***			1.265***	1.634***
	(0.076)			(0.070)	(0.089)
Europe & Central Asia	0.220**			0.130	0.043
	(0.086)			(0.080)	(0.106)
South America	0.817***			0.759***	0.871***
& Carib.	(0.094)			(0.089)	(0.108)
North & Central	0.399***			0.337***	0.391***
America	(0.085)			(0.079)	(0.100)
Western Europe	0.062			0.022	0.080
	(0.088)			(0.083)	(0.105)
Clusters	32307			32322	32154
Log-likelihood	−39108.93	−23086.01	−20516.02	−40541.17	−34020.41
N	1003363	182148	182148	1032040	915589

Note: Entries are logistic regression estimates with robust standard errors (clustered on dyad) in parentheses. Statistical significance is indicated as follows: *** $p < 0.01$; ** $p < 0.05$; * $p < 0.10$. All tests of statistical significance are two-tailed.

twenty-first century than the ATOP and the PRIO data; but analyzing the COW data provides a useful way of assessing the stability of our findings.

As expected, the odds of ratifying a PTA rise as countries become more democratic and as the number of veto players falls. In each model, the estimated coefficient of *Regime Type$_i$* is positive, the estimated coefficient of *Veto Players$_i$* is negative, and both of them are statistically significant. The magnitude of these effects is greatest when we examine the model including dyad-specific fixed effects, which indicates that within dyad variation in regime type and veto players has an especially potent impact on PTA ratification. The size of these effects is smallest when these variables are measured in year t-1, rather than year t. This confirms our argument mentioned earlier that both factors should have an immediate effect on PTA ratification. Furthermore, whether we measure alliances and disputes using the ATOP and PRIO data or the COW data has little bearing on the estimated effects of regime type and veto players. Figures 4.1 and 4.2 show the effects of regime type and veto players, respectively, on the probability of PTA ratification based on the results in the first column of table 4.2 (holding constant the remaining variables in the model).

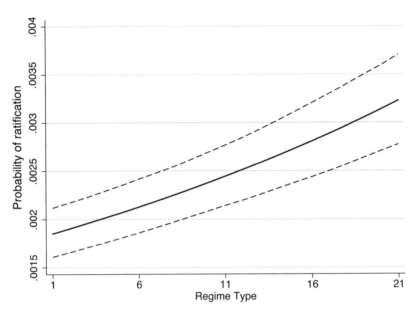

Figure 4.1: The Effect of Regime Type on the Probability of PTA Ratification
Note: Dashed lines represent 95 percent confidence intervals. To compute these predicted probabilities, we use the estimates in the first column of table 4.2. The continuous variables are set to their medians. *Post–Cold War* is set to 1 and the remaining dichotomous variables are set to 0.

To further illustrate the magnitude of these effects, we initially calculate the "relative risk" of state *i* ratifying a PTA with state *j* if the former state is democratic compared to if it is autocratic. More specifically, this risk is the predicted probability of state *i* entering a PTA with state *j* if state *i* is democratic (which we define here as *Regime Type*$_i$ = 19) divided by the predicted probability of state *i* entering a PTA if it is autocratic (which we define here as *Regime Type*$_i$ = 3), holding constant the remaining variables in the model.[16] If we focus on the first column of estimates in table 4.2, a democracy is about 55 percent more likely to enter a PTA than an autocracy. Figure 4.1 shows the effects of regime type on the predicted probability of ratification. As democracy rises, the probability of a PTA grows and the number of PTAs ratified rises rather quickly. Put differently, holding other continuous variables at their medians and the dichotomous variables at their modal values, a global system composed of autocracies

---

[16] The continuous variables are held constant at their median values and the dichotomous variables are held constant at their modal values.

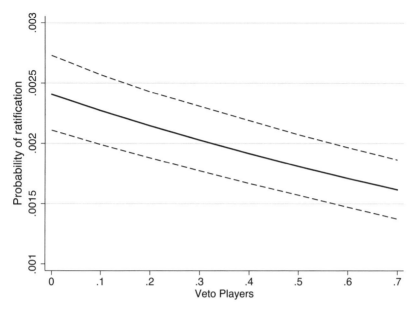

Figure 4.2: The Effect of Veto Players on the Probability of PTA Ratification
Note: Dashed lines represent 95 percent confidence intervals. To compute these predicted probabilities, we use the estimates in the first column of table 4.2. The continuous variables are set to their medians. *Post–Cold War* is set to 1 and the remaining dichotomous variables are set to 0.

would yield about 63 dyads ratifying PTAs per year. In a system composed of democracies, this predicted value is nearly 100.

Next, we compare the predicted probability of state *i* forming a PTA when it has few veto players—which we define as the 10th percentile in the data—to the predicted probability when it has many such players—which we define as the 90th percentile in the data—holding constant the remaining variables in the model. Based on the results in the first column of table 4.2, a state with few *Veto Players$_i$* is about 35 percent more likely to ratify a PTA than one with many *Veto Players$_i$*. These results clearly indicate that domestic politics plays an important role in shaping the decision to enter trade agreements.

Not surprisingly, however, various economic and international factors are also important in this regard. States that trade extensively and those that are economically large tend to form PTAs. In each case, the estimated coefficients of *Trade$_{ij}$* and *GDP$_i$* are positive and statistically significant. There is also evidence that recessions prompt states to ratify PTAs since the coefficient estimate of *ΔGDP_i* is negative in each case and is statistically significant in all but one.

In a variety of cases, it is not possible to estimate a coefficient when dyad-specific (*Former Colony*$_{ij}$, *Distance*$_{ij}$, and the regional fixed effects) or year-specific (*Hegemony*, *% Dyads Ratifying PTAs*, and *Post–Cold War*) fixed effects are included because they are time invariant or perfectly correlated with the year effects. For the most part, the influences of these variables are consistent across the remaining model specifications. States are unlikely to join PTAs with their former colonies and with geographically distant countries. In comparing different regions of the world, our results indicate that African countries have been most likely to ratify PTAs, followed by South American and Caribbean, Middle Eastern, and North and Central American countries. Countries in Asia (including both East Asia and South Asia) tend to be least likely to enter PTAs, although a few of these differences are not statistically significant. This finding is not unexpected since most Asian countries did not participate in PTAs until after 1998. Since then, however, PTAs have blossomed across Asia (Ravenhill 2003; Katada and Solis 2008). As such, we expect that this regional difference has probably attenuated of late.

Perhaps the most surprising cross-regional finding is that European states—both Eastern and Western—have formed PTAs less frequently than countries in various other regions. It is important to recognize, however, that Eastern European countries were part of the Warsaw Pact for most of the time period examined in this study. They only began seeking out other PTA partners after the Berlin Wall fell in 1989. Likewise, various Western European countries have granted unilateral preferences to their former colonies through hub and spoke agreements such as the Lomé Convention that are not included in our data, since our theory pertains to agreements in which all of the participants make trade concessions. This also helps to explain why our results indicate that states are less likely to form PTAs with their former colonies than other states (since the estimated coefficient of *Former Colony*$_{ij}$ is always negative and statistically significant).

Turning to the systemic variables, which cannot be estimated when we include year-specific effects in the model because they are perfectly predicted by these effects, there continues to be evidence of the diffusion of PTAs and that the odds of ratifying such arrangements rose in the Cold War's aftermath. The estimated coefficient of *Post–Cold War* is positive and statistically significant in each instance. So too is the coefficient of *% Dyads Ratifying PTAs*, which indicates that PTA formation tends to cluster over time. Consistent with the results in chapter 3, this implies a global diffusion process. States may be either strategically conditioning their behavior on their counterparts' actions or simply following the herd, an issue that we return to later.

Also consistent with the results in chapter 3, PTAs are especially likely to form when hegemony erodes. The estimated coefficients of *Hegemony* in table 4.2 are negative and statistically significant, indicating that the odds of ratifying a preferential arrangement rise as the portion of the world's output accounted for by the leading economy declines. This result tends to support theories of hegemonic stability (Krasner 1976; Gilpin 1981). These findings are interesting because many observers argue that the bipolar structure of the international system that marked the Cold War gave way to a unipolar system once the Soviet Union imploded (Wohlforth 1999), yet hegemony seems to inhibit PTA formation. One possibility is that our measure of hegemony reflects economic rather than military power and that economic hegemony inhibits PTAs whereas political-military hegemony promotes them. Another possibility, though, is that the effects of *Post–Cold War* reflect the efforts by countries formerly in the Soviet orbit to become more tightly integrated into the global (especially the Western European) economy once the Berlin Wall fell and the Soviet Union collapsed. One way that these countries tried to accomplish this goal was by forming PTAs with one another and with the advanced industrial countries of Western Europe.

In addition, the results in the first, fourth, and fifth columns of table 4.2 indicate that alliances, GATT/WTO membership, and existing PTA membership promote the ratification of other trade agreements. As expected, allies are more likely to form preferential arrangements than other states, and neither the size nor the strength of this relationship depends on whether we rely on the ATOP or the COW data. That members of the multilateral trade regime are more likely to form PTAs than other states might seem surprising at first blush since this institution was intended to combat regionalism and bilateralism. However, the GATT's Article XXIV made specific provisions for such agreements and PTAs have flourished among members of this regime. It also might seem surprising that countries that already participate in the same PTA are more likely to form another one than states that are not PTA partners. But in 2005, for example, 1,126 country pairs were parties to two preferential agreements; 415 pairs to three PTAs; 82 pairs to four PTAs; 27 dyads to five PTAs; and three pairs to six PTAs. In 1976, for instance, Papua New Guinea and Australia inked a bilateral agreement. Afterward both countries joined the South Pacific Regional Trade and Economic Cooperation Agreement (SPARTECA) in 1980. Singapore and New Zealand signed a bilateral agreement in 2000, after which both countries entered the Trans-Pacific Strategic Economic Partnership Agreement in 2005. In 1997, the Greater Arab Free Trade Area (GAFTA) was signed. Among the members were three countries (Morocco, Tunisia, and Libya) that were also parties to the Arab Maghreb Union, as well as six members (Iraq, Egypt, Syria, Yemen, Kuwait, and the United Arab Emirates) that were already joined under the Council of Arab Economic Unity (CAEU).

The results in the first, fourth, and fifth columns also show that contiguous states are unlikely to form PTAs. In combination with the observed effects of *Distance$_{ij}$*, this suggests that PTAs are most likely to form between states that are nearby but do not share a border. Finally, while many observers assume that PTAs are formed between a large, rich country and small, poor ones, our results indicate otherwise. The coefficient estimate of *GDP Ratio$_{ij}$* is negative and statistically significant, implying that greater imbalances in national income discourage the ratification of PTAs. Since countries that are equally powerful may be better able to conclude agreements that involve reciprocal concessions, this result may not be that surprising. But the idea that most small countries are forced into PTAs with larger ones against their will does not seem to be borne out (Gruber 2000).

The effects of alliances, the change in GDP, existing PTA membership, and the GDP ratio change in key ways when we introduce fixed effects in the model. This undoubtedly reflects the fact that the vast bulk of dyads (fully 84 percent of the country-pairs in our sample) never form a PTA. These dyads are not used to generate the parameter estimates because introducing fixed effects leads us to assume that none of the independent variables in our model other than the fixed effects influence the probability of these dyads ratifying a PTA. It is for this reason that Beck and Katz (2001, 487–99; see also King 1989) warn that using fixed-effects models to analyze time-series cross-section data with a binary dependent variable is "pernicious" and yields "estimates that are so far off as to be completely useless." This problem is exacerbated in our case because some independent variables—such as $Alliance_{ij}$—display little or no change over time, even among dyads that do form PTAs. These dyads are also excluded when estimating the coefficients of such variables. The upshot is that, given the sparseness of our data, very few dyads are used to estimate the model's parameters when including fixed effects, and fewer still are used to estimate certain coefficients. There is no reason to expect that these few pairs are a representative sample of the population of all dyads. Consequently, while we have included some results based on a fixed-effects specification because certain studies advocate this modeling strategy (Green et al. 2001), we think it is prudent to view the results in columns two and three only with the greatest caution and to place primary emphasis on the remaining results in table 4.2.

Our analysis shows that a wide variety of factors influence PTA formation. We find strong evidence that regime type and veto players shape the political calculus of governments contemplating PTAs even after accounting for domestic economic conditions, regional factors, and international influences. However, our argument is not that the effect of domestic politics is larger than that of all these other influences. In fact, some international factors have a more sizable impact than either regime type or veto players. Countries, for example, were almost two and a half times more likely to enter a PTA after the Cold War than during this era. Similarly, if the geographical distance between a pair of states is at the 90th percentile found in our dataset, then they are about eight times less likely to form a trade agreement than a pair whose distance is at the 10th percentile in the data. On the whole, however, the effects of many other factors—such as GATT/WTO membership, alliances, trade, GDP, the change in GDP, conflict, existing PTA membership, and hegemony—are roughly the same or smaller than those of regime type and veto players. Moreover, in light of the short shrift that the existing literature on PTAs has given domestic politics, the strong and fairly sizable impact of regime type and veto players is important.

It is also interesting to note that our data do not suggest that interactions between our domestic and international factors are of importance. When we interact *Regime Type*$_i$ or *Veto Players*$_i$ with the international variables in the base model (i.e., *Existing PTA*$_{ij}$, *Trade*$_{ij}$, *Dispute*$_{ij}$, *Alliance*$_{ij}$, *Hegemony*, *GDP Ratio*$_{ij}$, % *Dyads Ratifying PTA*, and *GATT/WTO*$_{ij}$), there is no case when the coefficient estimate of an interaction term is statistically significant. Hence, regime type and veto players have an important and autonomous role in influencing governments' decisions to launch trade agreements.

Robustness Checks

At this point, we turn to a battery of supplemental tests that are intended to assess the robustness of our initial findings. First, it is important to determine whether our results are sensitive to the particular measure of veto players that is used. Thus far, we have analyzed Henisz's (2000 and 2002) data and his measure of these players. As we discussed earlier, Beck et al. (2001 and 2005) have developed an alternative measure, *Checks*$_i$, which emphasizes the extent of electoral competition, the number of domestic institutions that can check the chief executive, and the partisan differences across these institutions. To assess the robustness of our findings with respect to the measure of veto players, we replace *Veto Players*$_i$ with *Checks*$_i$. As a result, this analysis spans the period 1975 to 2004 since Beck et al. do not provide data prior to 1975. In the first row of table 4.3, we present the estimates of *Checks*$_i$ and *Regime Type*$_i$ based on this analysis. The remaining variables in model (4.1) are included in this analysis, but are not presented in the table to conserve space and because there are few differences between their coefficient estimates in table 4.2 and those based on this analysis.

The results continue to indicate that states are increasingly unlikely to ratify PTAs as the number of veto players rises, since the estimated coefficient of *Checks*$_i$ is negative and statistically significant. However, the quantitative influence of this variable is even larger than that of *Veto Players*$_i$. We again compare the predicted probability of state i forming a PTA when it has few veto players (which we define as the 10th percentile in the data) to the predicted probability when it has many such players (which we define as the 90th percentile in the data), holding constant the remaining variables in the model. Based on this analysis, a state with few *Checks*$_i$ is about 55 percent more likely to ratify a PTA than one with many *Checks*$_i$.

Second, it is useful to address whether our results are sensitive to the particular measure of regime type that we are using. While *Regime Type*$_i$ is particularly

TABLE 4.3

Supplemental Tests of the Effects of Regime Type and Veto Players on PTA Ratification, 1952–2004

	Regime Type		Veto Players	
	β	se	β	se
Checks (1975-2005)	0.029***	(0.003)	−0.109***	(0.012)
Competitive Election	0.239***	(0.038)	−0.221***	(0.082)
Competitive Election + Regime Type[a]	0.252***	(0.071)	−0.712***	(0.118)
Regime Type excluding XCONST	0.027***	(0.005)	−0.335***	(0.095)
Dem (Regime Type ≥ 17)	0.384***	(0.040)	−0.487***	(0.088)
ACLP Democracy	0.131***	(0.043)	−0.265***	(0.089)
No EC/EU Dyad	0.027***	(0.003)	−0.578***	(0.095)
No EC/EU Country	0.022***	(0.003)	−0.648***	(0.102)
Rare Events	0.028***	(0.003)	−0.575***	(0.095)
Only 1st PTA in Dyad	0.034***	(0.004)	−0.695***	(0.117)
Exclude Zero Trade	0.021***	(0.004)	−0.273**	(0.116)
WTI PTAs	0.026***	(0.003)	−0.479***	(0.093)

Note: Entries are logistic regression estimates with robust standard errors (clustered on dyad) in parentheses. Statistical significance is indicated as follows: *** $p < 0.01$; ** $p < 0.05$. All tests of statistical significance are two-tailed. The remaining variables in model (4.1) are included when generating these estimates, but are omitted from the table to conserve space.

[a] This model includes both Competitive Election and Regime Type, as well as both dyad-specific and year-specific fixed effects. The estimated coefficient listed in the column labeled Regime Type is that of Competitive Election. The estimated coefficient of Regime Type is 0.006, and the corresponding standard error is 0.006.

well-suited to testing our argument, the Polity Project has also developed an indicator of whether a given state holds competitive elections (Marshall and Jaggers 2005, 22). In our view, political leaders that have to stand for competitive elections should exhibit a particular interest in entering a PTA because elections increase the possibility that leaders will be removed from office due to economic conditions that may actually be beyond their control. We therefore replace Regime Type$_i$ with Competitive Elections$_i$, which equals 1 if state i is coded by the Polity Project as holding competitive elections as of year t, 0 otherwise.[17] As shown in the second row of table 4.3 (Competitive Election), the estimated coefficient of this variable is positive and statistically significant. It is also large. Holding constant the remaining variables in the model, states with competitive elections are approximately 27 percent more likely to join a

[17] Formally, this variable equals 1 if the regulation of executive recruitment is coded as "regulated," if the competitiveness of executive recruitment is coded as "elections," and if the openness of executive recruitment is coded as "open."

PTA than other countries. Furthermore, as shown in the third row of this table (Competitive Election + Regime Type), the estimated coefficient of *Competitive Elections$_i$* remains positive and significant even if we also include *Regime Type$_i$* and both dyad-specific and year-specific fixed effects. These results provide very strong support for our argument that competitive elections underlie the decision by democracies to enter trade agreements.

To further address the effects of regime type, we undertake a number of analyses. We begin by recoding *Regime Type$_i$* after excluding the constraints on the chief executive (XCONST)—which is one of the institutional features used to measure it—because these constraints may be closely related to the veto players that exist in a country. We would like to avoid including factors related to veto players in our measure of regime type. Next, we recode *Regime Type$_i$* as a dichotomous variable. Consistent with various studies, we consider state *i* to be democratic in year *t* and assign it a score of 1 if *Regime Type$_i$* ≥ 17. Otherwise, we consider the state to be nondemocratic and assign it a value of 0. We also analyze a different dichotomous measure of regime type (ACLP) developed by Adam Przeworski and his colleagues (2000).[18] The results of these analyses are presented in the fourth, fifth, and sixth rows of table 4.3. They continue to provide strong evidence that democracy promotes the ratification of PTAs since the coefficient estimates of *Regime Type$_i$* remain positive and statistically significant.

Third, although *Regime Type$_i$* and *Veto Players$_i$* are analytically distinct concepts, they are related empirically. In fact, the correlation between the Polity Project's 21-point index of regime type and Henisz's measure of veto players is roughly 0.83. This raises the possibility that our results may exhibit multicollinearity, a situation in which independent variables are so highly correlated that there is not enough information to accurately estimate their coefficients. Multicollinearity can inflate the standard errors of coefficient estimates; it can also produce estimated coefficients with the wrong sign (Greene 2003, 56–57). In our case, the estimated coefficients of *Regime Type$_i$* and *Veto Players$_i$* are highly significant and the sample size is very large, dampening concern about inflated standard errors.

In an effort to ensure that the coefficient estimates of *Regime Type$_i$* and *Veto Players$_i$* do not have the wrong sign, we drop each variable, one at a time, and then re-estimate the model. When *Veto Players$_i$* is dropped, the estimated coefficient of *Regime Type$_i$* is 0.016, smaller than in our earlier analysis but still positive and statistically significant (its standard error is 0.003). When *Regime Type$_i$* is dropped, the estimated coefficient of *Veto Players$_i$* remains negative (–0.050), but it is relatively small and statistically insignificant. It is important to recognize, however, that deleting *Regime Type$_i$* from the model creates an omitted

---

[18] The ACLP dataset is available at https://netfiles.uiuc.edu/cheibub/www/datasets.html. (Last accessed August 18, 2011.)

variable bias, since we know that regime type has a large and strong influence on PTA formation. There is no way to determine whether the relatively weak effect of *Veto Players*$_i$ stems from this bias or from its collinearity with *Regime Type*$_i$. But further analysis reveals that even if multicollinearity is the apparent culprit, the statistically insignificant effect of *Veto Players*$_i$ when *Regime Type*$_i$ is removed from the model is actually due to two countries. To assess whether our results are unduly sensitive to the inclusion of any given country in our sample, we eliminate each country, one at a time, from the model that includes veto players and excludes regime type.[19] When either the Congo or Mauritius (or both) is omitted, the coefficient estimate of *Veto Players*$_i$ is negative and statistically significant; in every other case, it is not significant. Since it makes little sense to base the estimated effect of *Veto Players*$_i$ for all countries on these two nation-states, these results strongly suggest that neither the influence of regime type nor that of veto players is an outgrowth of multicollinearity.

Fourth, we analyze whether our results are driven by the EC and EU, which are composed of democratic members. We find, however, that excluding members of the EC/EU in the seventh row of table 4.3 (No EC/EU Dyad) has little bearing on the estimated coefficients of *Regime Type*$_i$ or *Veto Players*$_i$ (or the remaining variables in the model). In the eighth row of the table (No EC/EU Country), we show the results when we exclude all EC/EU countries (in any dyad) from the analysis. Again there is no change to the effects of regime type or veto players.

Fifth, we examine whether the rarity of PTAs affects our findings. As shown in the ninth row of this table (Rare Events), our results are virtually unchanged when we estimate the base model using a rare events logit specification (King and Zeng 2001). Sixth, we analyze whether the results are sensitive to our inclusion of all instances in which a given pair of states form a PTA. As we explained earlier, the observed value of our dependent variable is 1 only in those years t when states i and j enter a PTA. We do not remove observations after the pair ratified an agreement because various dyads established more than one arrangement during the period we analyze. In many cases, they formed a second PTA without terminating the first. Nonetheless, it is important to assess the implications of this modeling strategy. For any pair of states that form a PTA, we therefore eliminate every observation after the arrangement is established and then re-estimate the model. As shown in the tenth row of table 4.3 (Only 1st PTA in Dyad), the influence of regime type and veto players does not depend on whether we include or exclude these observations.

Seventh, although we have analyzed all dyads for which data on the variables in equation (4.1) are available, we also assess whether our results hold

---

[19] Similarly, we eliminate each country, one at a time, from the model that includes regime type and omits veto players. In every case, the estimated coefficient of *Regime Type*$_i$ is positive and statistically significant.

up after excluding cases where the flow of bilateral trade is reported as zero in a given year. The IMF's *Direction of Trade Statistics*, which is the source of the trade data we have relied on, does not distinguish between situations in which no trade was conducted by a pair of countries and cases where no trade was reported by the pair to the IMF. As such, it is not clear how to interpret situations in which the flow of trade is zero in the dataset. Moreover, those dyads that actually did not conduct any trade in a given year could be considered unimportant to the international trading system and particularly unlikely to form any type of PTA. In the eleventh row of table 4.3 (Exclude Zero Trade), we report the estimated coefficients of *Regime Type$_i$* and *Veto Players$_i$* after excluding dyad-years in which the value of bilateral trade is zero. Clearly, omitting these observations has little bearing on our earlier findings.

Eighth, we analyze whether our results are influenced by adding the PTAs listed by the WTI (Hufbauer and Schott 2009; World Trade Institute 2009) that are not included in our data. As we mentioned in chapter 3, the WTI has compiled a dataset on PTAs covering the period 1948 to 2007. Although there is a very high degree of agreement between this dataset and ours, it includes a number of arrangements that we do not consider to be PTAs and hence exclude from our list of trade agreements, particularly partial scope agreements. As shown in the final row of the table (WTI PTAs), there is no evidence that including these arrangements influences our results.

Ninth, we address whether the diffusion of PTAs affects our findings. We have found that the coefficient of *% Dyads Ratifying PTAs* is positive and statistically significant, indicating that PTAs may be marked by a global diffusion process. To further address this issue, we analyze the three other measures of diffusion described earlier. In the first two columns of table 4.4, we report the results of tests in which *Regional PTA$_i$* (which is the number of PTAs in country *i*'s geographical region—excluding those arrangements country *i* participates in—divided by the total number of countries in that region) and *Trade Partner PTA$_i$* (which is the total number of PTAs that the top ten trading partners of country *i* belong to, excluding those in which country *i* is a member) are added to the base model. We present the estimated coefficients of these variables, as well as the coefficients of *Regime Type$_i$* and *Veto Players$_i$*; but we do not report the coefficients of the remaining variables in the model to conserve space. The results provide further evidence that PTA formation is guided by diffusion. As a country's regional neighbors form PTAs (*Regional PTA$_i$*), the likelihood rises that it will enter one too, suggesting that diffusion pressures exist at the regional level. Furthermore, when a country's major trading partners sign more PTAs (*Trade Partner PTA$_i$*), that country is more likely to ratify such an arrangement.

To further investigate this issue, we follow Baldwin and Jaimovich (2010) by including *Contagion$_{ij}$* and *Contagion$_{ij}^2$* in our model. They find evidence of an inverted U-shaped relationship between their measure of contagion and PTA formation. As shown in the seventh column of table 4.4, we find that this

TABLE 4.4
Effects of Regime Type and Veto Players on PTA Ratification, Controlling for Regional Diffusion, Features of the GATT/WTO, and UN Voting, 1952–2004

	1	2	3	4	5	6	7
Regime Type	0.028***	0.029***	0.027***	0.026***	0.032***	0.027***	0.037***
	(0.003)	(0.003)	(0.003)	(0.003)	(0.003)	(0.003)	(0.004)
Veto Players	-0.594***	-0.638***	-0.540***	-0.431***	-0.449***	-0.579***	-0.724***
	(0.096)	(0.095)	(0.095)	(0.094)	(0.095)	(0.095)	(0.121)
Region PTA	0.055***						
	(0.021)						
Trade Partner PTA		0.002***					
		(0.000)					
GATT Round in Progress			0.155***				
			(0.024)				
Time Since Last GATT Round				0.052***			
				(0.003)			
S Score					2.186***		
					(0.086)		
Communist						-0.051	
						(0.084)	
Contagion							-3.755**
							(1.674)
Contagion^2							3.094***
							(0.848)
Constant	3.294***	3.045***	3.262***	2.116***	-0.382	3.458***	4.472***
	(0.537)	(0.546)	(0.535)	(0.535)	(0.586)	(0.530)	(0.573)
Clusters	32307	32307	32307	32307	31689	32307	29426
Log-likelihood	-39106.06	-39090.63	-39089.85	-38966.71	-35982.32	-39108.47	-24557.53
N	1003363	1003363	1003363	1003363	888357	1003363	876139

Note: Entries are logistic regression estimates with robust standard errors (clustered on dyad) in parentheses. Statistical significance is indicated as follows: *** p < 0.01; ** p < 0.05. All tests of statistical significance are two-tailed. The remaining variables in model (4.1) are included when generating these estimates, but are omitted from the table to conserve space.

relationship is U-shaped since the estimated coefficient of $Contagion_{ij}$ is negative and the estimated coefficient of $Contagion_{ij}^2$ is positive. The differences between Baldwin and Jaimovich's results and ours may stem from the fact that their study covers fewer countries (113) and a shorter time frame (1977–2005). It may also stem from collinearity between $Contagion_{ij}$, on the one hand, and $Trade_{ij}$, $Alliance_{ij}$, and $Distance_{ij}$, on the other. When these three variables are dropped from the model, we find that the relationship between $Contagion_{ij}$ and PTA ratification has an inverted U-shape.

Although there seems to be some indication of diffusion pressures through trade competition, it is important to interpret these results cautiously. The trade shares that help to make up both $Trade\ Partner\ PTA_i$ and $Contagion_{ij}$ are likely to be affected by PTA formation. Even though the effects of these variables on $PTA\ Ratification_{ij}$ are lagged by a year, trade flows tend to be relatively sticky and change only gradually from one year to the next. This, in turn, raises the specter of a simultaneity bias that complicates any effort to draw firm conclusions about the effects of diffusion and contagion pressures on the formation of preferential groupings (Baldwin and Jaimovich 2010, 12). Of central importance for present purposes, however, is that adding these three measures of diffusion has no bearing on the observed effect of regime type or veto players. Regardless of which measure is used, the estimated coefficient of $Regime\ Type_i$ is positive, that of $Veto\ Players_i$ is negative, and both of them are statistically significant.

Tenth, we include a variable indicating whether state i was a post-Communist regime, as of year t, in order to ensure that our results are not driven by those countries in Eastern Europe and the former Soviet Union that rushed to enter PTAs during the 1990s and 2000s (Kornai 1992; U.S. Central Intelligence Agency 2010; U.S. Department of State 2010). As shown in table 4.4, however, this is not the case. The estimated coefficient of $Communist_i$ is not statistically significant and including this variable has very little bearing on our other results.

Eleventh, our earlier findings show that members of the GATT/WTO are more likely to form PTAs than other states. In chapter 3 we analyzed whether the formation of PTAs was influenced by the existence of a GATT/WTO negotiating round or the length of time since such a round ended. To return to this issue, we include a variable indicating whether a GATT/WTO negotiating round is ongoing in year t. Some have claimed that countries are more likely to sign PTAs before a round begins rather than in the middle of one to increase their bargaining leverage (OECD 2001, 7; Crawford and Fiorentino 2005, 16). Others suggest that it is during the round itself that signing a PTA is most useful in this regard (Mansfield and Reinhardt 2003). We also explore whether the length of time since the last GATT/WTO round concluded might affect PTA formation. Some have argued that a long period of time between rounds might induce countries to seek PTAs (e.g., Fiorentino et al. 2007; Katada and Solis 2008).

The estimated coefficients of *GATT Round* and *Time Since Last GATT Round* are positive and statistically significant, as shown in table 4.4. Consequently, states tend to form preferential arrangements during GATT/WTO rounds and long after they end. Taken together, these results suggest that PTAs are used strategically by GATT/WTO members. They form PTAs during rounds and on the eve of rounds (after some time has elapsed since the last one ended) to improve their bargaining position in GATT/WTO negotiations. It is often argued, for instance, that the United States negotiated what became NAFTA due to frustration about the slow pace of the Uruguay Round; the United States hoped that NAFTA would pressure other countries to conclude a global trade agreement (Whalley 1993, 352). Features of the multilateral regime, in sum, have clear and important effects on the proliferation of PTAs. However, including these features has no influence on the observed effects of regime type or veto players.

Twelfth, we examine whether accounting for the similarity of foreign policy preferences between states i and j affects our results. Curt Signorino and Jeffrey Ritter (1999) argue that the $S\ Score_{ij}$, which is a measure of the similarity of UN voting patterns between states i and j, provides a reliable estimate of the extent of such similarity. As such, it is not surprising that the coefficient of this variable in table 4.4 is positive and statistically significant, indicating that states with more similar foreign policy preferences are especially likely to enter into PTAs. But adding this variable has no impact on the observed effects of regime type and veto players.

Finally, although we have treated the effects of regime type and veto players as linear, we also analyze whether these factors have an interactive effect on PTA ratification. We find no evidence of this sort. When we add $Regime\ Type_i \times Veto\ Players_i$ to the base model, its estimated coefficient is neither large nor statistically significant. The results indicate that regardless of the number of veto players, more democratic countries have a greater probability of ratification than less democratic ones. Regardless of the country's regime type, a rising number of veto players reduces the probability of ratification. As such, treating the effects of regime type and veto players as linear seems quite reasonable.[20]

[20] In addition, we test our argument using a research design that Poast (2010) has recently proposed. He warns against potential drawbacks of a dyadic research design when analyzing outcomes that involve more than two states and instead recommends a "k-adic" design, where k is the number of countries involved in a given outcome. The method he proposes is interesting but not well-suited to our study. First, his approach would only allow us to analyze the initial creation of a PTA; it would not permit us to address the many cases where countries join an existing agreement. Second, as the size of k increases, Poast's approach becomes increasingly cumbersome computationally and gives substantial influence to a very few observations. Many of the PTAs in our dataset are quite large, shedding doubt on the usefulness of his technique for our purposes. Nonetheless, we use Poast's method to create a k-adic dataset that only includes the initial signatories of PTAs. Because of the undue influence of PTAs with six or more members, any PTAs with more than five members were dropped. To implement this procedure, we measure regime type using the minimum value

CONCLUSIONS

In this chapter, we have examined the two core propositions developed in chapter 2. We have done so after accounting for a wide variety of domestic economic conditions, regional factors, and international variables, including some that we identified in chapter 3. Based on a battery of tests covering all country pairs from 1951 to 2004, we found strong support for our hypotheses. States become more likely to ratify PTAs as they become more democratic and as the number of veto players shrinks. This provides evidence in favor of our argument that leaders calculate whether to join based in part on domestic politics. They have to weigh the political costs of joining against the benefits. When the political benefits are likely to outweigh the costs, they are more likely to join. Empirically, then, we expect the decision to join PTAs depends on both veto players and regime type.

Holding constant transaction costs, greater democracy in a country induces a higher likelihood of cooperation. On the other hand, holding constant the degree of democracy, a greater number of veto players is associated with a lower probability of ratifying an agreement. Both factors have a statistically significant and substantively important impact. Moreover, these results are quite robust.

In addition to domestic politics, economic conditions and international factors guide PTA formation. Eroding hegemony and the end of the Cold War have prompted states to form PTAs. Very distant states are unlikely to form PTAs, but so are states that are contiguous. States with a former colonial relationship seldom form (reciprocal) PTAs, but allies tend to form such arrangements. GATT/WTO members tend to enter PTAs, and countries tend to be more likely to ratify agreements with equals than with those of much greater or smaller capability. Global and regional diffusion pressures are evident as well. But in addition to these influences, we find strong evidence that domestic politics has a strong and sizable impact on the proliferation of PTAs since World War II.

---

for each k-adic observation. We measure veto players using the maximum value for each observation. As expected the coefficient estimate of regime type is positive and statistically significant; the coefficient of veto players is negative and significant. These findings provide further support for our argument, but they are clearly preliminary.

CHAPTER 5

Auxiliary Hypotheses about Domestic Politics and Trade Agreements

WE EXAMINE a variety of additional hypotheses that flow from our core argument in this chapter. These tests will allow us to probe aspects of our argument's logic and distinguish it from alternative models linking domestic politics to PTA formation.

Recall that we posit that leaders are caught between demands for protection from various interest groups and the need for economic growth, which helps them retain office. Governments have a hard time committing to not granting too much protection to interest groups. Voters, including interest groups that prefer free trade, focus attention on a country's economic situation, holding governments accountable for economic downturns at the ballot box unless they can be convinced that lagging growth was beyond the control of an otherwise competent leader. As a result, competent chief executives value possessing a means of convincing voters that bad economic times were not an outgrowth of government rent-seeking or incompetence. But voters understand that granting protection to interest groups benefits the head of government, at least in the short term. As such, voters may turn a chief executive out of office, suspecting that he or she furnished too much protection to interest groups, even if this is not the case. This possibility prompts these leaders to search for ways to commit publicly to limit protection. Signing PTAs is one way to do so because these agreements reduce trade barriers and provide mechanisms to monitor leaders' compliance with their terms.

A number of implications flow from this argument. First, if PTAs help governments in situations where voters play an important role in determining a head of government's tenure, then democratic leaders that sign PTAs should enjoy a longer tenure than those that do not. If PTAs are a commitment device that reassures the public, democratic governments that sign them should benefit from greater longevity.

Second, the degree to which governments—democratic and nondemocratic alike—need to demonstrate credibility to voters may depend on their partisan composition. Left-wing governments, which tend to engage in more economic intervention and are more likely to enact protectionist policies than other governments, might have a particular need to establish a credible commitment by entering into a trade agreement. If so, they should be more likely than centrist or right-wing governments to sign PTAs.

Third, in countries with greater exposure to foreign trade, the government is more likely to face domestic constituencies that have greater knowledge of and interest in its trade policy. Such domestic political dynamics will lead the government to be particularly interested in trade agreements that reassure the informed public and interest groups that prefer open commerce. We thus expect democracies, in which leaders must be highly attuned to the public, will be particularly likely to sign trade agreements when they are more exposed to trade than when they are less exposed. This exposure should have little impact on whether autocratic governments enter trade agreements.

Fourth, whereas our argument is that domestic political competition spurs democratic governments to form PTAs, nondemocracies have signed such arrangements as well. However, not all nondemocracies are created equal; one source of variation among them is the extent of domestic political competition. Our argument implies that nondemocratic states characterized by more domestic political competition are more likely to sign PTAs than less competitive ones. Consequently, we address whether the degree of competition influences the likelihood of nondemocracies entering preferential arrangements.

Fifth, democratic governments are more likely than nondemocratic governments to sign agreements that provide extensive credibility. As we argued in chapter 2, leaders that encounter serious electoral competition face the prospect of losing office unless they can commit to refrain from catering to special interests. Hence, we expect that PTAs involving more extensive commitments should be preferred by democratic governments, since they experience greater electoral competition than their nondemocratic counterparts. We analyze two hypotheses stemming from this argument. Initially, we examine whether democracies are especially likely to enter PTAs that aim to achieve deeper levels of economic integration. We then address whether democracies are more prone to entering preferential arrangements that include a DSM.

In addition to a country's regime type, we have emphasized that the number of veto players influences the likelihood of its establishing a PTA. Such integration arrangements generate benefits for leaders but also have distributional consequences that threaten certain domestic sectors and groups. Further, trade agreements limit the government's ability to shield these segments of society from foreign competition. Adversely affected segments are likely to respond by withholding campaign contributions and other forms of political support. Leaders must either craft an agreement that avoids harming veto groups or compensate these groups. Consequently, as we argued in chapter 2 and showed empirically in chapter 4, the more veto players in a country, the lower the likelihood of its forming a trade agreement.

In this chapter, we add to this argument by further testing three hypotheses. First, in countries with more veto players it is less likely that political leaders will be able to form deeper integration agreements. As trade agreements become more constraining, they will prompt greater resistance from more groups.

Hence, countries marked by a large number of veto players are unlikely to accede to agreements that aim to achieve more extensive integration. Second, in the same vein, political leaders are also unlikely to enter PTAs that include more constraints, such as a DSM. Finally, in countries with more veto players, we expect greater delays between signing and ratifying agreements. As the number of veto players rises, so does the time needed for the government to convince these groups of the agreement's value and to design ways of compensating those that will be harmed by it.

PTAs and the Longevity of Political Leaders

One implication of our argument is that, among democratic governments, those that sign PTAs are likely to enjoy a longer tenure than those that do not. PTA membership reassures the public that their government is not engaged in rent-seeking and economic mismanagement. As a result, the public is less likely to vote the government out of office, especially if poor economic conditions arise that are seen as beyond its control. But if governments do not worry about the possibility of losing office because there is no competition, then they have less reason to enter PTAs for domestic political reasons. Hence, we focus our analysis on democratic regimes and examine whether those governments that sign trade agreements last longer in office than other governments.

To address this issue, we replicate and then extend a well-known model of leadership tenure developed by Bruce Bueno de Mesquita and his colleagues (Bueno de Mesquita et al. 2003, ch. 7; hereafter BDM2S2). BDM2S2 examine the effects of two political conditions on such tenure: (1) the size of a country's selectorate (S), which is the set of individuals in a country who choose the state's leadership, and (2) the size of the winning coalition (W), which is the portion of the selectorate needed for a leader to win office (BDM2S2 2003, 41–55 and 134–35). The authors argue that the likelihood of a chief executive being removed from office increases as W increases and as S decreases (BDM2S2 2003, 276–89), while assuming that the risk of being removed also depends on the length of time a leader has been in office. To test these arguments, BDM2S2 use a Weibull regression model to analyze the tenure in office for 2,960 state leaders during the nineteenth and twentieth centuries. This technique involves modeling event times as a function of a baseline hazard and the effects of covariates (the scale parameter). Technically, the baseline hazard of the Weibull regression follows the form $h_0(t) = pt^{p-1}\exp(\beta_0)$, where p is an ancillary shape parameter that indicates how the hazard rate shifts over time and β_0 is the scale parameter for the regression constant term. When $p > 1$, the hazard rate is monotonically increasing, so that over time the risk of a leader leaving office increases. When $p < 1$, the hazard rate is decreasing, indicating that a leader benefits from an incumbency effect that increases the likelihood of his or her survival over time. With the effects of covariates added, the hazard for the Weibull model is expressed as $h(t \mid x_j) = pt^{p-1}\exp(\beta_0 + x_j \beta_x)$. BDM2S2 (2003, 298—300) start by estimating both the scale parameter and the shape parameter as a function of W.

We extend the BDM2S2 base model by including a variable, *Sign PTA*, which equals 1 if a given leader has signed a PTA in the current year or previously in his or her term in office, and 0 otherwise.[1] Because the model is specified in the logarithmic relative hazard form, a positive (negative) coefficient indicates that a given variable increases (decreases) the hazard rate and thereby increases (decreases) the likelihood that a leader will be turned out of office. Thus, we expect the estimated coefficient of *Sign PTA* to be negative for the democratic leaders in our sample. Here we rely on the Archigos Data on Political Leaders (Goemans et al. 2009), which improves and expands upon the original BDM2S2 data of political leaders' longevity.[2]

Figure 5.1 displays the Kaplan-Meier estimator of the survivor function of democratic leaders (i.e., the probability of leaders remaining in office past time t) for heads of government who signed PTAs and for those who did not. To define democracies, we rely on the same procedure used in chapters 3 and 4. Recall that *Regime Type$_i$* is the 21-point measure of regime type developed by Gurr and his colleagues (Gurr et al. 1989; Jaggers and Gurr 1995; Marshall and Jaggers 2005). States are coded as democratic in year t if *Regime Type$_i$* ≥ 17. A higher proportion of democratic leaders signing a PTA survived over a period slightly longer than the first six years in office. After about seven years in office, the probability of leaders surviving appears to be the same, whether they have signed a PTA or not.[3] But note that 90 percent of democratic leaders do not last more than eight years in office.

The Weibull regression results, shown in table 5.1, confirm this initial observation. The results in the first column replicate the BDM2S2 model about the effects of W. The second column reports the effect of our key variable, *Sign PTA*. Its estimated coefficient is negative and statistically significant, indicating that signing a PTA decreases the likelihood that a leader will leave office.

---

[1] Because our data on PTAs do not include specific information on the executive who signed the agreement, we rely on the Archigos Data on Political Leaders, which is described in footnote 2, below. If a PTA was signed within a leader's term in office, that leader is given credit as signing the PTA. For instances where the exact sign date was unknown, it is treated as January 1 of the sign year.

[2] The Archigos project's "A Data Base on Leaders 1875-2004" is available at http://www.rochester.edu/college/faculty/hgoemans/data.htm. (Last accessed November 26, 2009.) This database has some advantage over the BDM2S2 data. It has corrected some errors in BDM2S2. It also has expanded the time coverage from 2001 to 2004. Nonetheless, our results are not substantially affected by those differences between the two datasets.

[3] Between 1948 and 2004, the average time in office for democratic leaders is roughly 3.55 years. BDM2S2 (2003, 295) provide a similar analysis.

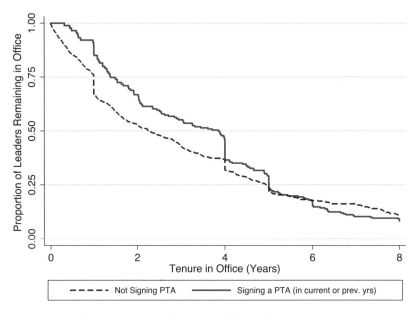

Figure 5.1: Kaplan-Meier Survival Estimates for Leaders in Democracies

In columns 3 and 4, we add W and S to the model. Inclusion of these variables does not change the sign or significance of *Sign PTA*; signing a PTA continues to reduce the likelihood of a leader being removed from office.

We use the Weibull regression estimates to calculate the expected values of survival times for leaders signing a PTA versus those not signing a PTA. From day one in office, the mean (4.00 years compared to 3.49 years) and the median (3.05 years compared to 2.27 years) survival times are both over a half-year longer for democratic leaders who join trade agreements. Given that the median time in office for all democratic leaders is only 2.4 years, this is a substantial improvement.

We recognize the potential limitations of our analysis, which stem from a number of practical constraints. For one thing, many factors that might also affect longevity are not accounted for in our model, in part because many are not readily measureable. In particular, leaders' competence might be a third factor that contributes to both their political achievements (i.e., signing trade agreements) and their longevity in office. For another, leaders that remain in office longer may be more likely to sign PTAs, perhaps simply because they have more time to negotiate and conclude an agreement, suggesting that *Sign PTA* may be endogenous. Unfortunately, in nonlinear models such as the ones we have estimated in this section, the use of instrumental variables is inappropriate and

TABLE 5.1
Weibull Analysis of Leadership Survival in Democracies

		(1) *BDM2S2* *1840–2003*[a]	*(2)* *Democ.* *1948–2004*	*(3)* *Democ.* *1948–2003*	*(4)* *Democ.* *1948–2003*
Xβ	W	−0.073		−0.616	−0.412
		(0.220)		(0.855)	(0.856)
	Sign PTA		−0.528***	−0.596***	−0.573***
			(0.204)	(0.210)	(0.212)
	S				−1.321***
					(0.345)
	Constant	−0.877***	−1.124***	−0.576	0.545
		(0.110)	(0.114)	(0.722)	(0.610)
Ancillary parameter, ln(p)	W	0.535***		0.192	0.115
		(0.109)		(0.312)	(0.317)
	Sign PTA		0.218**	0.226**	0.216**
			(0.088)	(0.089)	(0.089)
	S				0.363
					(0.279)
	Constant	−0.651***	−0.077	−0.238	−0.524*
		(0.059)	(0.049)	(0.284)	(0.318)
Summary Statistics	Countries	165	109	106	106
	Log-likelihood	−4445.54	−1215.01	−1164.31	−1160.78
	N	12041	3237	3105	3105

[a] Replicated results from BDM2S2 (2003, 299).

Note: All models assume that the event times follow a Weibull distribution with ancillary parameters parameterized as a function of *W*, *Sign PTA*, and/or *S*, following the modeling scheme of BDM2S2. Standard errors are in parentheses and clustered by country. Our analysis relies on the Archigos Data on Political Leaders (Goemans et al. 2009). Columns 2–4 are restricted to democracies (*Regime Type* ≥ 17) for the years 1948–2003/4. Statistical significance is indicated as follows: *** $p < 0.01$; ** $p < 0.05$; * $p < 0.10$. All tests of statistical significance are two-tailed.

other solutions to this problem are very difficult to identify (Box-Steffensmeier and Jones 2004, 112; Angrist and Pischke 2009, 190–92). Further, we do not have data on term limits, another factor that might well affect our results. These issues are clearly important and our results should therefore be considered preliminary and interpreted with great caution. Despite these caveats, however, our findings accord with the hypothesis that trade agreements are associated with greater leadership longevity in democracies and show promise for future studies about this relationship.

Partisanship and PTAs

Entering a PTA helps governments credibly commit to not engage in excessive protectionism. Some governments, however, may need such credibility more than others. Democracies have a greater need because of the high degree of political competition their leaders face. But the partisan nature of a government may also affect its need for credible commitments, regardless of a country's regime type.

In general, left-wing governments are considered more likely than others to intervene in the economy and to enact protectionist trade policies.[4] Citizens may be especially worried about the willingness of such governments to accede to special interest demands for protection. Consequently, leftist governments may face a more skeptical public if the economy is performing poorly and may need to demonstrate greater credibility to generate public support. One way to do this is to propose policies that risk hurting their own constituents, at least in the short run. As José Tavares (2004, 2451) argues, "by pursuing policies that are costly and against the immediate interests of their constituents, policymakers provide information [and this] signaling [of] policy commitment improves the chances of the [policy] adjustment being successful." Hence, by signing a trade agreement that constrains the government to lower trade barriers and comply with the agreement even in difficult times, left-wing governments can show that they are strongly committed to limiting state involvement in the economy. This helps reassure voters that the government will refrain from giving in to interest group demands for protectionism.

---

[4] There is mixed evidence on this score. Milner and Judkins (2004) show that in advanced industrial countries, left-wing parties seem to be more protectionist and interventionist in their policy statements. On the other hand, Dutt and Mitra (2005), following a Heckscher-Ohlin model, show that leftist governments in poor countries are less protectionist than other governments. They note that a left-wing government that is generally more interventionist and is committed to state control of the economy may, under certain conditions, have a preference for free trade. Hence, their explanation for our finding would simply revolve around the preferences of leftist governments, not their need for credibility.

We therefore expect leftist governments to be more likely to sign PTAs than more centrist or right-wing governments.[5]

To test this hypothesis, we add a series of partisanship variables to our baseline model in chapter 4 (see the first column of table 4.2). These variables, taken from the World Bank's Database on Political Institutions (Beck et al. 2005), indicate whether a country's head of government is from a right-wing party, a centrist party, a left-wing party, or is unclassified, respectively. We set the reference category to a head of government whose party is classified as rightist, so that the two opposite ends of the political spectrum can be easily compared.[6] This measure of government partisanship is crude, but it is the only available measure that covers a wide variety of countries over a fairly long period of time (1975 to 2005).

Table 5.2 shows the results of this analysis. Note that only those pertaining to the effects of regime type, veto players, and partisanship are reported in table 5.2 to conserve space. Clearly, partisanship has an important influence on PTA formation. Left-wing governments are more likely than right-wing governments to enter such arrangements, as indicated by the positive and statistically significant estimated coefficient of *Left Gov$_i$*. *Center Gov$_i$* and *Unclassifiable Gov$_i$* also differ from *Right Gov$_i$* in their likelihood of PTA formation. Based on this analysis, left-wing governments are approximately 30 percent more likely to sign trade agreements than right-wing governments, and this difference is statistically significant.

REGIME TYPE AND EXPOSURE TO THE INTERNATIONAL ECONOMY

Our argument assumes that the public and interest groups have some knowledge about PTAs and about whether the government complies with the terms of these institutions. The extent to which this is the case, however, is likely dependent on how important overseas commerce is to a country's economic performance. If trade plays a substantial role in the economy, it will have more impact on citizens who in turn will seek more information about foreign commerce and the government's trade policy. This implies that in democracies—where

[5] An additional implication seems to be that left-wing governments might benefit from PTAs more and thus have greater longevity in office. However, our preliminary analysis yields little support for this hypothesis. We thank Johannes Urpelainen for his thoughts on this issue.

[6] The coding scheme is based largely on parties' economic policy positions. Right includes parties that are defined as conservative, Christian democratic, or right-wing. Left includes parties that are defined as communist, socialist, social democratic, or left-wing. Center includes parties that are defined as centrist or when party position can best be described as centrist (e.g., the party advocates strengthening private enterprise in a social-liberal context). Unclassifiable includes those cases that do not fit into the above-mentioned categories (i.e., the party's platform does not focus on economic issues, or there are competing wings), or where no information exists.

TABLE 5.2
The Effects of Partisanship on PTA Formation, 1952–2004

	Model 4.1 + Partisanship
Regime Type	0.030***
	(0.003)
Veto Players	−0.502***
	(0.097)
Left Gov	0.264***
	(0.041)
Center Gov	0.153**
	(0.073)
Unclassifiable Gov	0.263***
	(0.043)
Constant	16.662***
	(0.970)
Clusters	31724
Log-likelihood	−32716.21
N	728320

Note: Entries are logistic regression estimates with robust standard errors (clustered on dyad) in parentheses. Right-wing government is set as the reference category. Statistical significance is indicated as follows: *** $p < 0.01$; ** $p < 0.05$. All tests of statistical significance are two-tailed. The remaining variables in model (4.1) are included when generating these estimates, but are omitted from the table to conserve space.

governments generate political gains from entering PTAs—there is a particular impetus to signing these agreements if the exposure to international trade is pronounced. Conversely, autocracies may be less affected by exposure to trade since they are less affected by societal political pressure. In short, there may be an interaction effect between regime type and the degree of exposure to international trade.

To test this claim, we start with the base model in chapter 4. To increase the ease of interpreting our results, we initially replace *Regime Type$_i$* with *Dem$_i$*, a dummy variable that equals 1 if *Regime Type$_i$* ≥ 17, and 0 otherwise. To this baseline model, we add two variables. First, *Open$_i$* is a widely used measure of trade exposure that is computed as the sum of country i's imports and exports in year t divided by its GDP in t.[7] Second, we add *Dem$_i$* × *Open$_i$* and we expect the coefficient of this variable to be positive.[8] Then we estimate a second model

[7] Data on *Open$_i$* are taken from the World Bank's World Development Indicators and the variable is defined as (exports + imports)/GDP.

[8] We do not expect the interaction between veto players and openness to be important. And indeed we find that the effect of this interaction is small. Countries with fewer veto players always

TABLE 5.3
The Effects of the Interaction between Openness and Democracy, 1952–2004

	Dem	Regime Type
Veto Players	−0.717***	−0.832***
	(0.089)	(0.095)
Dem (Regime Type ≥ 17)	−0.001	
	(0.070)	
Regime Type		0.005
		(0.005)
Open	−0.001**	−0.002***
	(0.001)	(0.001)
Dem × Open	0.005***	
	(0.001)	
Regime Type × Open		0.000***
		(0.000)
Clusters	30235	30235
Log-likelihood	−35879.91	−35887.78
N	806382	806382

Note: Entries are logistic regression estimates with robust standard errors (clustered on dyad) in parentheses. Statistical significance is indicated as follows: *** $p < 0.01$; ** $p < 0.05$. All tests of statistical significance are two-tailed. The remaining variables in model (4.1) are included when generating these estimates, but are omitted from the table to conserve space.

that includes *Regime Type$_i$* and *Regime Type$_i$* × *Open$_i$* instead of *Dem$_i$* and *Dem$_i$* × *Open$_i$*.

The results in table 5.3 confirm our expectation. The estimated coefficients of both *Dem$_i$* × *Open$_i$* and *Regime Type$_i$* × *Open$_i$* are positive and statistically significant. Figure 5.2 shows the substantive effects of the interaction between *Dem$_i$* and *Open$_i$*. As trade dependence rises, democratic countries are more likely to sign PTAs. And as countries become more democratic, trade openness has an increasingly positive effect on their probability of entering a PTA. For autocratic governments, on the other hand, trade dependence has a much less pronounced effect, as expected, and heightened trade exposure seems to dampen enthusiasm for trade agreements. Finally, more democratic countries are always more likely to sign PTAs than less democratic ones. These findings accord with our claims about leaders' calculations and the reassurance that PTAs provide.

have a higher probability of ratifying a PTA, but as openness grows very high, the probability of ratification across different values of veto players begins to converge.

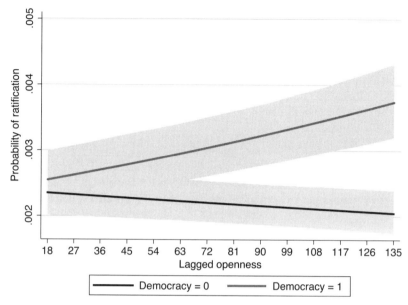

Figure 5.2: The Probability of Ratification at Different Levels of Openness
Note: To compute these predicted probabilities, we use the estimates in the first column of table 5.3. The continuous variables are set to their medians. *Post–Cold War* is set to 1 and the remaining dichotomous variables are set to 0. The shaded panels represent 95 percent confidence intervals.

AUTOCRACIES, POLITICAL COMPETITION, AND PTAS

Our results in chapter 4 established that democracies are more likely to form PTAs than other states. It is obvious, however, that nondemocracies have formed PTAs as well. Indeed, various trade agreements that were established during the initial wave of PTAs after World War II included autocratic countries in the developing world or the Soviet orbit (Mansfield and Milner 1999).

Nondemocracies vary along a number of institutional dimensions, including the extent of political competition. One implication of our argument is that more politically competitive autocracies are more likely to sign PTAs than less competitive ones because of the credibility that these agreements provide. Nondemocratic governments may need to make credible commitments to their supporters to remain in office (Gandhi and Przeworski 2006; Weeks 2008). So while electoral competition may not be central for them, maintaining the allegiance of their key supporters is important. Moreover, autocrats who break commitments may suffer domestic audience costs, in a way similar to but perhaps less apparent than democracies (Weeks 2008). From these claims, it follows that less secure autocratic leaders might face a similar dynamic to democracies. They may be pressed by important interest groups to furnish protection, but fear losing office if they alienate other supporters by taking actions that inhibit economic growth. Many have suggested, for example, that this is the situation that the current Chinese government faces (Shirk 2007; Shih 2008). China's recent efforts to enter trade agreements (for example, with ASEAN, New Zealand, and South Korea) may stem in part from the government's (or factions' within it) attempts to restrain domestic interest group pressures for protection and subsidization at the expense of overall economic growth. China, a one-party autocracy, is nevertheless marked by a certain amount of domestic political competition, as factions within the party vie vigorously for power (Shirk 1993; Lieberthal 2004; Shih 2008). Leaders in nondemocratic systems may thus find trade agreements appealing as they can lengthen their tenure in office by reassuring domestic groups that leaders are not rent-seeking too extensively and are also concerned with the overall economic situation. To the extent that autocratic leaders can be replaced, such a dynamic is more likely and hence trade agreements are more appealing.

To address this issue, we rely on three datasets. First, we use Barbara Geddes's (2003) coding of autocracies and Joseph Wright's (2008) update of these data, combined with Wright's (2008) data on the same classification scheme. The most comprehensive and widely used scheme for coding autocracies, Geddes's typology involves identifying regimes by their governance structure. As she notes,

> [d]ifferent kinds of authoritarianism differ from each other as much as they differ from democracy. Their leaders emerge from different groups and via different selection processes. They rely on different segments of society for support. They have different procedures for making decisions, and different interest groups influence policies. [And] they deal with ordinary citizens and opposition in different ways (Geddes 2004, 5).

She classifies them into three main types, with intermediate categories as well: single party, personalist, and military. Geddes points out that "[i]n military regimes, a group of officers decides who will rule and influences policy. In single-party regimes, one party dominates access to political office and controls policy, though other parties may legally exist. In personalist regimes, access to office and the fruits of office depends on the discretion of an individual leader. . . . The whims of the ruler prevail" (Geddes 2004, 5–6). Personalist regimes, then, are marked by the least political competition since they are dominated by one individual or family. As Geddes (2004, 13–14) mentions, "[i]n personalist regimes, one individual dominates the military, state apparatus, and ruling party (if one exists). Because so much power is concentrated in the hands of one individual, he generally controls the coalition-building agenda. . . . In contrast to single-party regimes, the leader's faction in a personalist regime may actually increase benefits to itself by excluding the rival faction from participation."

In single-party systems, by contrast, factions compete against one another and provide competition. In personalist systems, one faction dominates (Geddes 2004).[9]

Jessica Weeks (2008) has updated Geddes's (2003) coding of regime type and used that scheme to test the presence of audience costs in nondemocratic regimes.[10] She codes such states as personalist, single-party, military, hybrid (military/single-party), monarchy, or mixed over the period from 1816 to 2001 for 147 countries. Weeks argues that personalist regimes can most easily suppress any competition domestically, and that single-party systems have the most domestic political competition. Given her claims and those of Geddes, we expect single-party regimes to be the most politically competitive, personalistic ones to be the least competitive, and military regimes to lie somewhere in between.

Like Weeks, Wright (2008) has coded regime type according to Geddes's categorizations. In addition, though, he includes categories for personalistic-military, single-party-personalistic, and single-party-military-personalistic governments. Since Wright's data (1946 to 2003 for 122 countries) cover more recent years than Weeks's and coincide well with our PTA dataset, we organize his data to fit Weeks's simpler categorizations. Since the Weeks data do not include categories for personalistic-military, single-party-personalistic, and single-party-military-personalistic, these are grouped with single-party-military (which she calls hybrid) into a general hybrid category.

Second, we measure competition among nondemocratic regimes using the National Elections across Democracy and Autocracy (NELDA) data developed by Susan Hyde and Nicolay Marinov (2010). They code 139 developing countries that held elections during the period from 1960 to 2006.[11] The unit of analysis in the dataset is an individual election. For a given country at time t, electoral competitiveness is coded based on the most recent election in that state. A country retains the same value for competitiveness until January 1 after

---

[9] Because power is less concentrated in single-party regimes, they are less vulnerable to the death or illness of leaders. Thus, we should expect single-party regimes to last longer than either military or personalist regimes. Because the dominant strategy of the ruling coalition in single-party regimes is to coopt potential opposition, these regimes tend to respond to crises by granting modest increases in political participation, increasing opposition representation in the legislature, and granting some opposition demands. They attempt to give the opposition enough to deter them from risky plots and uprisings while continuing to hang onto power (Geddes 2004, 17).

[10] The crucial question in generating international credibility is whether the relevant domestic audience can and will coordinate to sanction the leader, and whether the possibility of coordination is observable to foreign decision makers. While the small groups of supporters in autocratic regimes differ from the more inclusive audiences that can punish democratic leaders, autocratic elites can nevertheless visibly remove incumbents when elites have incentives to coordinate to punish the leader, and domestic politics are stable enough that outsiders can infer this possibility (Weeks 2008, 36).

[11] Data used are from a version dated April 20, 2009, available at http://hyde.research.yale.edu/nelda/. (Last accessed, August 18, 2011.)

the next election. To construct an electoral competitiveness measure, three component questions from the NELDA dataset are used. The measure is coded as 1 if an observation had "yes" answers to all questions: "Was opposition allowed?" (NELDA3); "Was more than one party legal?" (NELDA4); and "Was there a choice of candidates on the ballot?" (NELDA5). All observations with a "no" answer to any of these questions are coded as noncompetitive.

Third, Jennifer Gandhi (2008) provides similar data on electoral competitiveness, though her data are drawn from legislatures. Gandhi's data cover 199 countries from 1946 to 2002. A country-year is coded as competitive if a legislature met the following criteria: the legislature is open and over half of members are elected (CLOSED = 2); two or more political parties exist (by legal statute) (DEJURE = 2); two or more political parties exist (de facto, allowing for government fronts) (DEFACTO2 = 2); and two or more political parties hold seats within the legislature (LPARTY = 2). Though this is as restrictive a measure as the data allow, the coding of the observations remains the same even if the LPARTY condition is dropped.

To analyze the effects of different types of nondemocratic regimes on PTA formation, we again define all countries for which $Regime\ Type_i \geq 17$ in year t as democratic (Dem_i). All remaining countries are then coded as single-party, military, personalistic, or hybrid/mixed (which is referred to as $Other_i$ below) based on Wright's data. To analyze the NELDA and the Ghandi data, we code nondemocratic states as anocratic if $4 < Regime\ Type_i < 17$ or autocratic if $Regime\ Type_i \leq 4$. Among the autocracies, we then distinguish among competitive regimes, noncompetitive regimes, and those that lack election data. Then we reestimate the baseline model in chapter 4. In the analysis based on Wright's data, $Personalistic_i$, the least competitive form of autocratic regimes, is designated as the reference category. In the analysis based on the NELDA and Gandhi data, the reference category is a noncompetitive autocracy. Note that we estimate all of the parameters in this model, but only present those pertaining to regime type because they are of central interest and in order to conserve space.

The results shown in table 5.4 support our argument that democracies are more likely than every type of nondemocratic regime to form a PTA. Further, the difference between the estimated coefficient of Dem_i and that of each type of autocracy is statistically significant. Especially important for present purposes, however, is the tendency for more competitive nondemocracies to have a greater likelihood of forming PTAs than less competitive ones. The estimated coefficients of both $Single\ Party_i$ and $Military_i$ are positive and statistically significant, indicating that single-party and military governments are more likely to form PTAs than personalistic ones. Both of these coefficients are also significantly larger than that of $Other_i$. Furthermore, the estimated coefficient of $Single\ Party_i$ is the largest among the nondemocratic categories, although it is not significantly different from that of $Military_i$. Turning to the NELDA and the Gandhi data, there is considerable evidence that competitive autocracies are

TABLE 5.4
The Effects of Different Types of Autocracies on PTA Formation, 1952–2004

	(1) Wright/Weeks 1951–2003	(2) NELDA 1960–2004	(3) Gandhi 1951–2002
Veto Players	−0.516***	−0.683***	−0.677***
	(0.088)	(0.089)	(0.089)
Dem (Regime Type ≥ 17)	0.477***	0.714***	0.653***
	(0.052)	(0.053)	(0.050)
Single Party	0.352***		
	(0.056)		
Military	0.306***		
	(0.075)		
Other	−0.042		
	(0.049)		
Competitive Autocracy		0.271***	0.198**
		(0.052)	(0.087)
Anocracy (4 < Reg Type < 17)		0.389***	0.325***
		(0.041)	(0.038)
Clusters	32307	32307	32307
Log-likelihood	−39042.65	−38776.88	−39057.37
N	1003363	957168	1003363

Note: Entries are logistic regression estimates with robust standard errors (clustered on dyad) in parentheses. Statistical significance is indicated as follows: *** $p < 0.01$; ** $p < 0.05$. All tests of statistical significance are two-tailed. The remaining variables in model (4.1) are included when generating these estimates, but are omitted from the table to conserve space. In column 1, the reference category is "personalistic autocracies." In columns 2 and 3, the reference category is "noncompetitive autocracies" and "autocracies with no election data," as coded by NELDA and Gandhi.

more likely to establish PTAs than noncompetitive ones, since both estimated coefficients of *Competitive Autocracy$_i$* are positive and statistically significant.

In sum, the results of this analysis provide some support for the hypothesis that the extent of political competition in nondemocracies influences their propensity to sign PTAs. Although these findings should be interpreted cautiously, competitive autocracies are more likely to establish PTAs than their noncompetitive counterparts. Equally, single-party regimes are more likely than other nondemocratic governments to sign trade agreements and personalistic ones are especially unlikely to do so. This suggests that political competition—even in a country where there is only one organized party—can affect leaders' incentives to make credible commitments. Single-party systems often have internal factions and fierce competition among them that makes retaining power a paramount concern. Leaders in such systems may be driven to try to resist pressures exerted by special interests so that they can generate broader support by promoting economic growth. Trade agreements thus may appeal to leaders in such competitive autocratic systems.

The Extent of Proposed Integration and Enforcement

As we noted in chapter 1, PTAs come in different forms. One of the most important distinctions among them is the extent of integration they aim to achieve. All PTAs attempt to promote economic integration by improving and stabilizing the access that each member offers to the other participants' markets. Nonetheless, important differences exist among these arrangements in terms of the constraints on domestic actors in member countries. In a preferential agreement (PA), member-states grant the other participants preferential access to selected segments of their market; in a free trade area (FTA), members mutually reduce or eliminate trade barriers on many (if not all) products; in a customs union (CU), members eliminate barriers to trade with other participants and erect a common external tariff (CET) vis-à-vis third parties; in a common market (CM), countries augment a customs union by implementing similar product regulations and permitting the free flow of factors of production between members; and in an economic union, members participate in a CM and coordinate their fiscal and monetary policies.

Different types of trade agreements thus aim to achieve different degrees of economic integration among members, with PAs being the least integrative and economic unions being the most. The magnitude of domestic change needed to comply with a trade agreement and the associated political costs borne by leaders for entering it depend on the extent of integration that the agreement aims to achieve. As the proposed degree of economic integration rises, so does both the degree of commitment made by a government and the expected adjustment costs for adversely affected domestic actors. Rational leaders then will prefer different levels of integration given their domestic political situations.[12]

---

[12] There have been disagreements regarding the way in which trade agreements may impact the degree of democracy. Some have argued that democracy may be adversely affected by trade agreements, especially as their level of integration rises. As more policy areas and more domestic institutions are touched by the presence of this international agreement, domestic legislatures lose the authority to set trade policy and are stripped of policy mechanisms, yet international institutions may not step in to fill the resulting gap in the public's needs. Once a state decides to enter a CU, for example, its trade barriers on the products of third parties are replaced with a common external tariff negotiated at the supranational level. In CMs and economic unions, rising numbers of issues such as monetary policy as well as labor and immigration policy are also handled by international institutions that may or may not be responsive to the domestic politics of member-states. In contrast, others have argued that trade agreements may enhance democracy by reigning in the role of special interests (Keohane et al. 2009). Our argument is closer to this perspective.

Another key difference among trade agreements is whether they include mechanisms for enforcing trade integration. DSMs provide PTA members with legal recourse to settle disagreements concerning the arrangement, and hence to impose constraints on member countries. Whether to include such mechanisms in an agreement is another decision with which political leaders are faced. Governments that seek to enforce the terms of a PTA and want their publics to be aware of this are more likely to desire such a mechanism. As such, leaders rationally designing a trade accord are likely to include or exclude DSMs on the basis of domestic political conditions.

Why countries choose to sign different types of agreements rarely has been studied. In one of the most important studies on this topic, Beth Yarbrough and Robert Yarbrough (1992) argue that the structure of the trading relationship helps determine whether trading partners form a unilateral, bilateral, or multilateral agreement. Our explanatory and dependent variables are quite different from theirs, however, because central to our argument are the domestic political factors that influence the proposed level of integration in the PTAs that leaders choose to enter.

From a political perspective, (neo)functionalists have argued that integration occurs when economic transactions become dense enough among a group of countries that organized economic interests benefiting from these transactions pressure governments to manage economic interdependence by centralizing policies and creating common institutions (e.g., Mitrany 1943; Haas 1958 and 1964; Sandholtz and Stone-Sweet 1998). Neofunctionalists stress that any initial decision to integrate because of such dense transaction networks produces, and unintentionally creates, both economic and political spillovers that push regional integration forward and deeper. The theory of spillover predicts that cooperation between countries on certain sectors of the economy is likely to trigger sequential cooperation (both intended and unintended) in other related areas (Lindberg 1963). This claim is ultimately about international externalities leading to greater levels of integration, and it has been examined most thoroughly in the case of the European Union. We do not disagree with this argument, but we expect that domestic politics will play an important role as well.

Regime Type

Our argument suggests that democracies should be particularly likely to sign agreements that aim to promote more extensive integration. In effect, deeper integration provides them with greater credibility since it increases the costs they have to pay for violating the agreement. As Jon Pevehouse (2007) shows, democratic leaders tend to sign more binding and legalistic agreements than nondemocracies. He attributes this to the desire of democratic leaders to be locked into agreements in order to deter future policy changes.

Our claim is similar. Electoral competition creates the possibility that leaders will be removed from office by voters who punish them for their lack of a credible commitment to withhold protection of special interests. PTAs can ameliorate these credible commitment problems, and deeper integration agreements can provide increasing amounts of credibility for leaders. Democratic leaders thus have greater incentives to sign agreements that aim to achieve fairly extensive integration, while autocrats do not. Autocratic governments bear the ever greater costs and constraints of deeper integration, but they do not benefit from greater credibility as democratic governments do. Thus, we hypothesize that democracies are more likely to sign deeper integration agreements than other regimes. Likewise, where leaders need a vehicle to generate a more credible commitment, they are more likely to include a DSM. Hence, we also hypothesize that democratic countries are more likely to include DSMs in the PTAs that they join than autocratic states.

Veto Players

In addition to the effect of a country's regime type, we also expect that a greater number of veto players, by increasing the government's transaction costs, will inhibit a state from entering arrangements that aim to achieve deeper integration. The magnitude of domestic change needed to comply with a trade agreement, and the associated political costs borne by leaders for entering it, depend on the extent of integration that the agreement aims to achieve. Arrangements that envision more extensive integration are likely to cover more goods and services and therefore to affect more sectors and a larger segment of society. Specifically, deeper arrangements tend to reduce the decision-making power of certain veto players (such as domestic legislatures), increase the adjustment costs and the portion of society affected, and attenuate the ability of domestic groups to lobby the government. The result is likely to be mounting opposition to trade agreements among the segments of society that anticipate being adversely affected. The number of veto players that represent those affected groups will grow as the proposed depth of integration rises, thereby adding to the transaction costs that governments must pay for ratification.

Under FTAs, for instance, increased competition from partner countries will lead to contraction of noncompetitive industries (Hillman 1982; Van Long and Vousden 1991; Richardson 1994). As a result, workers in these industries will be displaced and the industries' "lobbying activities [will] decrease and the level of protection from non-members granted [them] by policy-makers also [will] decrease" (Richardson 1993, 320; see also Cassing and Hillman 1986). If individuals affiliated with such industries anticipate that the FTA will threaten their employment and hamper their ability to lobby, then they have reason to exert considerable effort to block the formation of the FTA in the first place.

It is even harder to successfully lobby for changes in trade policy within a CU than within an FTA. Since the former involves the adoption of a CET, an industry can no longer influence trade policy by lobbying its home government alone. The industries that expect to be adversely affected by the CET or the heightened integration of members' markets will fight particularly hard to block the CU. Of course, these industries may find allies in other member-states, raising the possibility that they could join forces to lobby for a higher CET. These efforts are likely to be frustrated by free-riding, however. The likely consequence, as Arvind Panagariya and Ronald Findlay (1996) and Martin Richardson (1994) have shown, is that the level of external protection will actually be lower in a CU than in an FTA. A domestic industry will assume that its foreign counterparts will lobby hard for a higher CET and will therefore reduce its own lobbying efforts. Since all industries are likely to behave in this way, the result is less lobbying within the CU and a lower level of protection. Foreseeing this possibility, industries will attempt to scale back integration goals. As Richardson (1994, 88) points out, "just as firms lobby for tariff levels, presumably they also lobby for their preferred arrangement."

Finally, trade agreements that aim to achieve greater economic integration also tend to entail heightened political integration among members and often the loss of power for domestic institutions. Domestic legislatures lose the authority to set trade policy and are stripped of policy mechanisms that can be used to pressure foreign or domestic executives. Once a state decides to enter a CU, its trade barriers on the products of third parties are replaced with a common external tariff negotiated at the supranational level. In common markets and economic unions, issues such as monetary policy as well as labor and immigration policy are also handled by international institutions that may or may not be responsive to the domestic politics of member-states. Thus, the effectiveness of institutional veto players in blocking policy change can be mitigated by trade agreements if policymaking shifts from the domestic to the supranational level. Moreover, the ability of veto players to influence policy becomes increasingly attenuated as the agreement aims to achieve progressively deeper integration. This effect is quite separate from the effects of societal interests, but stems from the institutions that give voice to those interests, which may themselves oppose a loss of independent power. Veto players may pose increasingly onerous transaction costs for governments as proposed agreements affect the powers of the domestic institutions that empower them.

Testing the Hypotheses

In order to test these hypotheses, we conduct a variety of analyses. We begin with the baseline model in chapter 4 (see the first column of table 4.2), but redefine the dependent variable as the proposed level of integration in a PTA signed by a pair of states, i and j, in year t. We code this variable on a 6-point ordinal scale: 0 if states i and j did not form a PTA in year t; 1 if they formed a PA; 2 if they created an FTA; 3 if they established a CU; 4 if they entered a CM; and 5 if they joined an economic union. The coding of these agreements is based on an analysis of each PTA. Some arrangements set integration goals that are not realized, but we are interested in the aims of the treaty itself. If, for example, states decide to enter a common market, they likely have every hope and expectation that this type of institution will come to fruition even if that does not actually happen. Moreover, domestic interests are more likely to respond to the proposed level of integration than to an ad hoc calculation about the level of integration that will eventually be achieved.

Because the observed value of the dependent variable is ordered, we use an ordered probit regression to estimate the model. The first column of table 5.5 presents the initial parameter estimates of regime type and veto players. The remaining variables are included in this analysis, but are not in the table to conserve space. The estimated coefficient of *Regime Type$_i$* is positive and statistically significant, which indicates that the proposed level of integration increases as states become more democratic. In addition, the coefficient estimate of *Veto Players$_i$* is negative and statistically significant, indicating that as the number of veto players rises, this level declines.

Because the use of an ordered probit specification places certain restrictions on the parameter estimates—namely, imposing the assumption that each independent variable has the same effect on the odds of all levels of the dependent variable—we also estimate the model using a multinomial logit treatment, which allows us to eliminate this restriction on the parameter estimates and to relax the assumption that the different types of PTAs are ordered. To conduct this analysis, we use the no agreement group as the reference level and separate PTAs into three categories: PAs, FTAs, and CUs/CMs/economic unions. The latter three types of arrangements are grouped together because there are relatively few customs unions and economic unions in our data.

The results, presented in the second column of table 5.5, suggest that the effects of regime type and veto players on entry into trade agreements may differ across different proposed levels of integration in a way that does not accord with our expectations. The estimated coefficients of *Regime Type$_i$* are positive and statistically significant at all levels, but the size of this coefficient falls substantially when we examine the ratio of the probability of entering FTAs to that of not entering any agreement. The coefficient estimates of *Veto Players$_i$* exhibit even more varying impacts across different degrees of proposed integration. *Veto Players$_i$* is statistically insignificant when a model for PAs relative to no agreement is considered, and somewhat surprisingly it is positive and statistically significant when we examine the probability of entering FTAs relative to the probability of not entering any agreement. It is negative and statistically significant, however, when focusing on the most extensive integration (customs unions/common markets/economic unions) and the size of the coefficient is

TABLE 5.5
The Effects of Regime Type and Veto Players on the Depth of Proposed Integration, 1952–2004

		Ordered Probit	Multinomial Logit
	Regime Type	0.010*** (0.001)	
	Veto Players	−0.230*** (0.037)	
1: PA	Regime Type		0.034*** (0.012)
	Veto Players		−0.258 (0.397)
2: FTA	Regime Type		0.009* (0.006)
	Veto Players		0.437*** (0.158)
3: CU/CM/EU	Regime Type		0.022*** (0.004)
	Veto Players		−1.019*** (0.120)
	Clusters	32307	32307
	Log-likelihood	−49218.97	−43853.47
	N	1003363	1003363

Note: Entries are ordered probit and multinomial logit estimates with robust standard errors (clustered by dyad) in parentheses. Statistical significance is indicated as follows: *** $p < 0.01$; ** $p < 0.05$; * $p < 0.10$. All tests of statistical significance are two-tailed. The remaining variables in model (4.1) are included when generating these estimates, but are omitted from the table to conserve space. We use all five categories of PTAs in the ordered probit models. But since there are few customs unions and economic unions (which are referred to as EUs in this table), we collapse them and common markets into a single category for the purpose of estimating the multinomial logit model.

much larger than those of the other two groups. This suggests that the presence of more veto players reduces the prospect of states concluding agreements that aim to achieve the deepest levels of integration.

We further analyze this relationship with a different modeling strategy. In order for states to choose a given type of PTA, they must first decide to sign a trade agreement. In other words, the decision about whether to join a PTA that aims to achieve extensive or modest integration can only be made by states that have selected themselves into the set of PTA members. With this consideration in mind, we estimate a probit model with sample selection. This model has two stages. The first stage estimates the probability of entering a PTA, and the second stage estimates the odds of being in a particular type of PTA, given that a state has selected itself into the sample of PTA members. In order to identify this type of model, there must be some factors influencing whether states join a PTA that do not affect the type of arrangement they join. While there are few theories to guide us on this decision, there is little reason to expect the systemic determinants of PTA formation—namely hegemony and the percentage of dyads worldwide that are members of a PTA—to affect the degree of integration that an arrangement aims to achieve.[13]

We again group CUs, CMs, and economic unions together because there are relatively few customs unions and economic unions in our data, and all of these groupings are marked by a CET. In the same vein, we combine PAs and FTAs since these arrangements lack a CET. In table 5.6, we present the second stage estimates based on this analysis; that is, the estimates of whether countries entering a PTA select one with a CET (a CU, CM, or economic union) or not (a PA or FTA). As expected, the estimated coefficient of $Regime\ Type_i$ is positive, that of $Veto\ Players_i$ is negative, and both of them are statistically significant. These results provide some evidence that democratic governments opt for PTAs that aim to achieve greater integration and that countries marked by a large number of veto players eschew highly integrative arrangements.

As mentioned earlier, in addition to the degree of proposed integration, states must choose whether or not to enter PTAs with a DSM. We expect leaders to select arrangements with a DSM when they need to create a more credible commitment; as such, we expect that democratic countries are more likely to include DSMs in the PTAs that they join than autocratic ones.[14] To test this hypothesis, we estimate another probit model with sample selection. In this case, the first stage estimates the probability of entering a PTA and the second stage estimates the odds that the arrangement has a DSM. Again, we identify this model by excluding hegemony and the percentage of dyads worldwide that are members of a PTA from the second stage.

The results in the second column of table 5.7 indicate that the estimated coefficient of $Regime\ Type_i$ is positive, that of $Veto\ Players_i$ is negative, and both

---

[13] We do, however, include the indicator variable for the post–Cold War in both stages, since a very large portion of arrangements formed after the collapse of the Berlin Wall were FTAs (Mansfield and Pevehouse forthcoming).

[14] Smith (2000) and Kono (2007) code DSMs for a sample of PTAs in much greater detail than we do here. In future research, it would be useful to undertake such detailed coding for all PTAs. We expect, in their terms, that more legalized DSMs should be more likely in PTAs involving democracies.

TABLE 5.6
Second Stage of Probit Model with Sample Selection, Depth of Proposed Integration, 1952–2004

Regime Type	0.011**
	(0.005)
Veto Players	−0.929***
	(0.123)
Existing Dyadic PTA	1.070***
	(0.045)
Trade (logged)	−0.021***
	(0.006)
GDP (logged)	−0.075***
	(0.015)
ΔGDP	−0.009
	(0.029)
Armed Conflict (PRIO)	−0.033
	(0.368)
Alliance (ATOP)	0.106*
	(0.057)
Post–Cold War	0.719***
	(0.048)
GDP Ratio	0.027*
	(0.016)
GATT/WTO	0.270***
	(0.041)
South Asia	——[a]
Middle East & North Africa	1.304***
	(0.151)
Sub-Saharan Africa	2.257***
	(0.154)
Europe & Central Asia	0.489***
	(0.148)
Latin America & Carib.	1.681***
	(0.172)
North & Central America	0.452***
	(0.169)
Western Europe	1.207***
	(0.150)
Constant	−1.505***
	(0.343)
Athrho	0.246***
	(0.067)
Clusters	32307
Log-likelihood	−42125.97
N	1003350

Note: Two-stage probit analysis with a first-stage Heckman selection model. Robust standard errors clustered on dyads are in parentheses. All tests of statistical significance are two-tailed. Statistical significance is indicated as follows: *** $p < 0.01$; ** $p < 0.05$; * $p < 0.10$. Note that athrho is the inverse hyperbolic tangent of rho.

[a] The coefficient of South Asia cannot be estimated because no CUs, CMs, or economic unions have formed in that region.

of them are statistically significant.[15] Thus, democratic governments are more likely to enter PTAs with a DSM than other countries. Further, states become less likely to accede to PTAs with such a mechanism as the number of veto players rises.

Ratification Delay and Veto Players

A final implication of our argument is that the number of veto players influences the length of time that it takes to ratify a PTA. The process of agreeing to enter a PTA involves two steps. One is the decision to sign the agreement and second is the decision to ratify it domestically. Usually there is some lag between the first and second phase. Why this lag occurs is interesting. We expect that much of this delay stems from domestic political negotiations. Leaders do not want to lose ratification votes, since these can be no-confidence votes in the government itself. Political leaders need to make sure that they can convince legislators and voters to agree to the proposed PTA. If they oppose it, then leaders need to devise domestic compensation strategies to buy off this opposition.

Reaching agreement at home can take time, however, and larger numbers of veto players may make quick ratification even more difficult. As some observers have noted, delay often indicates political division and sometimes it is necessary for governments to delay proposed actions until they are sure they can gain the needed support (e.g., Lesbirel 1987; Alesina and Drazen 1991; Cramton 1992; Drazen 1996; Martin and Vanberg 2003; Manow and Burkhart 2008). We follow this line of argument, which implies that a large and rising number of veto players are associated with greater delay between signing and ratifying a trade agreement. Governments, however, are expected to anticipate that more veto players are likely to cause them problems. From the start of negotiations, they know the number of veto players they will face at each stage, and they rationally anticipate the resistance of those players. If governments are fully rational and informed, they should never experience ratification failure (Milner 1997a). The problem for a government arises when the number and composition of veto players changes over the course of the negotiations or after signing but before ratification. When such a change brings an increase in the number of veto players, delay is likely to occur prior to ratification as the government seeks to work with the new veto players to satisfy their concerns. Hence, we expect, that adding more veto players after signing an agreement will cause ratification delays.

---

[15] An additional hypothesis that we do not explore in detail concerns whether more competitive autocracies are more likely than less competitive ones to ratify PTAs that include DSMs. Our preliminary results provide some support for this hypothesis when Gandhi's (2008) data are analyzed.

TABLE 5.7
Second Stage of Probit Model with Sample Selection, Ratification of PTAs That
Include Dispute Settlement Mechanisms, 1952–2004

	Model 1	Model 2
Regime Type	0.036***	0.037***
	(0.005)	(0.006)
Veto Players	−0.382**	−0.376**
	(0.164)	(0.164)
Trade (logged)	−0.039***	−0.038***
	(0.005)	(0.006)
GDP (logged)		−0.020
		(0.018)
ΔGDP		0.104**
		(0.045)
Armed Conflict (PRIO)	0.027	0.023
	(0.372)	(0.380)
Alliance (ATOP)	−0.436***	−0.428***
	(0.046)	(0.047)
GATT/WTO	0.133***	0.138***
	(0.048)	(0.049)
GDP Ratio	0.044***	0.044***
	(0.016)	(0.017)
Existing Dyadic PTA	0.297***	0.303***
	(0.054)	(0.055)
Post–Cold War	0.717***	0.742***
	(0.067)	(0.073)
Constant	1.978***	2.258***
	(0.135)	(0.270)
Athrho	−0.814***	−0.788***
	(0.094)	(0.099)
Clusters	32307	32307
Log-likelihood	−38302.93	−38299.73
N	1002970	1002970

Note: Two-stage probit analysis with a first-stage Heckman selection model. Robust standard errors clustered on dyads are in parentheses. Statistical significance is indicated as follows: *** $p <$ 0.01; ** $p < 0.05$; * $p < 0.10$. All tests of statistical significance are two-tailed. Note that athrho is the inverse hyperbolic tangent of rho.

To test this hypothesis, we use an event-history technique referred to as log-logistic regression, following a growing literature on ratification delay (Fredriksson and Gaston 2000; Boockmann 2001; Neumayer 2002; von Stein 2008) and legislative delay (Golub 1999 and 2007; Schulz and König 2000; Chau and Kanbur 2001; König 2007 and 2008; Daubler 2008). As in our earlier analysis of political survival, event history models allow us to consider how the time path of an agreement affects its likelihood of ratification, thus setting it apart from ordinary binary-link models, such as logit or probit models.

We choose to estimate a log-logistic model for both substantive and statistical reasons. First, it does not force researchers to assume a monotonic hazard rate (Box-Steffensmeier and Jones 2004, 31). This fits well with a plausible scenario about the general ratification process. That is, it is reasonable to assume that the likelihood of the ratification of a PTA initially rises (as most agreements take at least an initial period to gain the approval of legislatures), peaks, then declines (as the probability that an agreement will be ratified declines after a certain amount of time has elapsed). It is therefore not surprising that past studies investigating delay often take similar approaches (e.g., Schulz and König 2000; König 2007 and 2008; Daubler 2008).[16] Second, the Akaike Information Criterion (AIC), a goodness-of-fit test frequently used for model selection, confirms that the log-logistic model is the best description of the hazard function of our data.[17]

The log-logistic regression is estimated in the accelerated failure time metric, with the dependent variable as the log of time. Hence, in our analysis, the event in question is ratification and a coefficient with a positive sign, for instance, would indicate a lengthening in delay in ratification. To achieve the greatest possible precision, we calculate the delay between the exact date each PTA in our sample was signed and the exact date it was ratified and then scale

---

[16] Despite the relatively similar topics tackled by the literature outlined above, a wide variety of event history approaches have been used with frequent debate over the use of parametric versus semiparametric models in terms of their distributional assumptions and their ability to deal with time-varying explanatory variables. Golub (2007), Collett (2003), and others criticize the use of parametric models due to the fact that these analyses often do not lay out clear, a priori arguments for the assumption of a particular distribution. A number of studies have utilized a Cox proportional hazards (PH) model (Chau and Kanbur 2001; von Stein 2008), which has the benefit of not assuming an underlying distribution of hazard rates. As implied by its name, however, the Cox PH model makes the assumption that the effect of included covariates does not change as a function of duration time—that is, if these effects are not constant relative to a baseline hazard function, they are not *proportional*. For this reason, others have used parametric models, most frequently the log-logistic model, to avoid the need for a PH assumption (Golub 1999; Schulz and König 2000; König 2008), though the log-logistic model does maintain the assumption that the log-odds ratio is constant over time (Collett 2003; Golub 2007 and 2008).

[17] The AIC provides a goodness of fit measure and is commonly used to identify the correct distribution among parametric models in event-history analysis (Box-Steffensmeier and Jones 2004, 44–45). The lowest AIC score indicates the best parametric model based on the underlying distribution. We find that among parametric models with different measures of veto players as covariates, the log-logistic distribution has the lowest AIC. This remains the case even when a number of other independent variables are included. Thus, a log-logistic distribution is best for analyzing ratification delay.

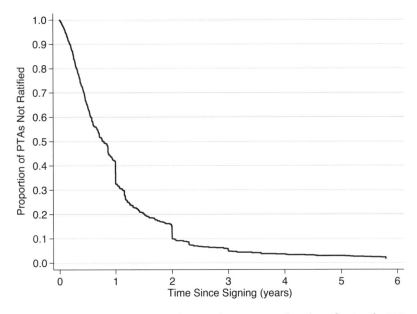

Figure 5.3: Kaplan-Meier Estimate of Survival Function, Delay of Ratification for PTAs

this value to years by dividing it by 365.25.[18] The model is specified as $\log(T) = \beta'_j X + \gamma\varepsilon$, where T is a random variable denoting the event time that follows a log-logistic distribution, X is a vector of covariates, β is a vector of coefficients associated with X, ε is the error term that assumes the standard logistic distribution, and γ is some ancillary parameter that scales the shape of the distribution. The log-logistic hazard function is expressed as $h(t) = \{\lambda(1/\gamma)(\lambda t)^{[1/\gamma]-1}\}/\{1+(\lambda t)^{1/\gamma}\}$. When $\gamma < 1$, the log-logistic hazard increases, peaks, and then decreases, and when $\gamma \geq 1$, the hazard function is monotonically decreasing (Box-Steffensmeier and Jones 2004, 31–32; Cleves et al. 2004).

We start by plotting the Kaplan-Meier survival function in figure 5.3, or the estimated probability of ratifying agreements after time t. The plot exhibits the pattern of ratification occurrences that we anticipate; the vast majority of the signed agreements are quickly ratified after signing. Approximately 70 percent of the signed agreements are ratified a year after signing, and about 90 percent

---

[18] This results in some agreements lacking date information. We fill in such missing information conservatively. Specifically, there are a few instances where only a month and year are available. For such cases, the first day of that month is used as the starting date. Additionally, the ratification data are supplemented with exact "in force" dates where the ratification dates are not known. Finally, we drop a small number of cases where an agreement is signed and then not ratified to avoid overestimating delay (i.e., to avoid assuming right-censoring when the reason was missing data).

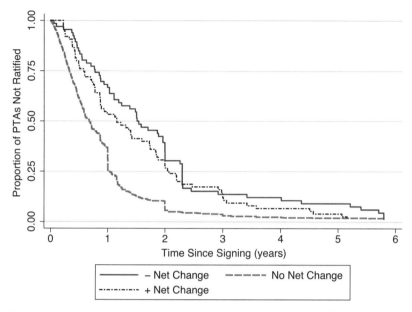

Figure 5.4: Kaplan-Meier Estimate of Survival Function, Delay of Ratification for PTAs by Percentage Change in Veto Players

are ratified by the end of the second year. Once past this early peak, however, the pace of ratification slows down.

In line with a veto player framework, figure 5.4 shows the survival function distinguished by the percentage change in *Veto Players$_i$*.[19] This graph describes a possible relationship between changes in veto players and ratification delay. It shows that ratification is more likely (the survival rate is lower, which conversely implies the hazard rate is higher) when there is no change in veto players from signing to ratification (indicated in the dashed line) than when there is some change between the two time periods. When there is a change in the number of veto players between the two periods (a decrease indicated by the solid line; an increase by the dash-dot line), the ratification process slows down. It is not yet clear, however, that there are differences in the effect of an increase and a decrease in veto players on ratification delay.

To examine if these initial, nonparametric results hold when other covariates are considered, we estimate a log-logistic regression model.[20] The models

---

[19] Due to the fact that *Veto Players$_i$* can assume a value of 0, the percentage change variables were calculated as the log difference in *Veto Players$_i$*, that is, *% Change Veto Players$_i$* ≈ ln(*Veto Players at Ratification$_i$* + .001) − ln(*Veto Players at Signing$_i$* + .001).

[20] All models are clustered by country to account for country-specific characteristics.

we use introduce a number of covariates that are similar to the ones employed in the existing literature. One widely used covariate is regime type (Boockmann 2001; von Stein 2008). Another commonly used covariate in the ratification or legislative delay literature is a measure of the specifics of agreements or pieces of legislation (e.g., Fredriksson and Gaston 2000; Chau and Kanbur 2001). These studies, however, focus on a narrow number of agreements. Due to the fact that our dataset employs a large number of PTAs, the specific details of individual agreements are abstracted to the level of proposed integration, and agreement type dummy variables are consequently included (for PA, FTA, CU, CM, and economic union).

The veto players measure used here is the annual percentage change in *Veto Players$_i$* relative to the previous year, calculated as the log difference. This measure has some key advantages. First, since it is a percentage change, it is expressed in relation to the initial level of veto players. Second, unlike the percentage change in veto players at the date of ratification relative to veto players at the date of PTA signing, this measure allows us to identify a change in veto players that occurs in the year prior to an agreement signed and ratified in the same (calendar) year. Using the percentage change in veto players relative to the previous year then allows the analysis of agreements where a change has occurred in the year before signing that may affect ratification delay nonetheless. Relying on the percentage change between signing and ratification in such a case would always produce a value of 0. Finally, as implied above, the use of the percentage change relative to the previous year allows for more variance in the variable both because there are fewer values of 0, but also because this variable allows for veto player changes in the opposite direction over the course of a (particularly) long delay (e.g., the cases of Ecuador [Latin American Integration Association (LAIA)], Armenia [Commonwealth of Independent States (CIS)], and Benin [AEC]).[21]

Table 5.8 presents the results of the log-logistic model. Most notably, the estimated coefficient of the change in veto players is positive and highly significant across all models, indicating that an increase in veto players relative to the previous year increases ratification delay. The values of gamma range from 0.55 to 0.58, suggesting an initial increase and then a peak of ratification for PTAs after a period of time, followed by a gradual decline as time elapses after the agreement is signed. This is in line with our expectation. But most importantly, these results uncover a tendency for increases in the number of veto players to lengthen the time needed for domestic ratification of the trade agreement. Political delay grows as the number of veto players rises. Once more, support for this hypothesis provides additional evidence for our argument in chapter 2.

---

[21] Nonetheless, the same models conducted using the percentage change between signing and ratification produce consistently similar results in terms of the coefficients' signs.

TABLE 5.8
The Effects of Veto Players and Other Factors on PTA Ratification Delay,
1952–2004

	(1)	(2)	(3)	(4)
% Change in Veto Players	0.071***	0.073***	0.084***	0.084***
	(0.026)	(0.028)	(0.028)	(0.027)
Regime Type		−0.033***	−0.021**	−0.015*
		(0.006)	(0.009)	(0.009)
Veto Players at Ratification			−0.475*	−0.519*
			(0.281)	(0.280)
Free Trade Area				−0.219**
				(0.112)
Customs Union				−0.467***
				(0.165)
Common Market				0.124
				(0.122)
Economic Union				−0.238
				(0.247)
Constant	−0.355***	0.063	−0.002	0.093
	(0.056)	(0.075)	(0.074)	(0.126)
Ln(γ)	−0.543***	−0.576***	−0.597***	−0.605***
	(0.030)	(0.033)	(0.034)	(0.033)
γ	0.581	0.562	0.551	0.546
	(0.018)	(0.019)	(0.019)	(0.018)
Countries	181	160	160	160
Country-Agreements	899	852	815	803
Log-likelihood	−1274.86	−1185.21	−1146.94	−1122.28
N	1636	1554	1479	1465

Note: All models assume that the event times follow a log-logistic distribution, based on the lowest AIC score relative to Weibull, Gompertz, and Log-normal distributions. Standard errors are clustered by country. Statistical significance is indicated as follows: *** $p < 0.01$; ** $p < 0.05$; * $p < 0.10$. All tests of statistical significance are two-tailed.

CONCLUSIONS

In this chapter, we have examined a set of auxiliary hypotheses that flow from the argument we presented in chapter 2. Finding support for these hypotheses suggests that the effects of regime type and veto players on PTA formation actually reflect the causal processes advanced in our argument.

The tests presented in this chapter are tentative and sometimes rather crude. A more exhaustive set of tests would take us far afield from the book's main themes and would require data that are often lacking. But we have tried to show through the accumulation of different pieces of evidence that there is some support for all of these propositions. None of our claims has been definitively proven. The accretion of evidence for each one, however, helps to build support for our particular causal model.

We have tested the following hypotheses:

1. Democratic governments that sign trade agreements last longer in office than those that do not sign them.
2. Left-wing governments are more likely to sign and ratify PTAs than are centrist or right-wing ones.
3. Democracies that are more exposed to international trade are more likely to sign PTAs than those that are less exposed.
4. Autocracies with more domestic political competition are more likely to sign PTAs than uncompetitive autocracies.
5. The more democratic a country, the deeper the proposed level of integration in a PTA it is likely to agree to and the more likely it is to enter an arrangement with a DSM.
6. The more veto players in a country, the shallower the proposed level of integration a country will choose in a PTA and the less likely it is to agree to a DSM.
7. A heightened number of veto players increases the delay between the signing and ratification of a PTA.

In chapter 2, we argued that democratic leaders seek PTAs as a means of demonstrating a credible commitment to voters that they will not overprotect the economy in response to interest group demands. Their incentive to do so lies in the domestic political gains they receive from joining: they are less likely to be rejected from office in bad economic times when they demonstrate this credible commitment. PTAs should therefore help democratic leaders last longer in office, a hypothesis for which we find some support.

In addition, we have argued that leaders in more politically competitive settings have greater need for credible commitments. But any leader who has more need for a credible commitment to resist interest group pressures should have more desire to sign a PTA. This suggests that partisanship may affect the demand for credibility. Left-wing governments—which are more likely to intervene in the economy and to raise trade barriers—should have a greater need for devices that credibly commit them not to do so. Hence, we anticipate that left-wing governments should be more likely to sign international trade pacts than right-wing or centrist governments. Our results accord with this hypothesis, adding support to our claim in chapter 2 about the domestic political incentives leaders realize from trade agreements through the credible commitment mechanism. We also addressed whether and how greater exposure to trade affects political leaders' decision-making process in terms of entering trade agreements. We argued that leaders in more trade-dependent economies can use PTAs as a stronger mechanism for reassuring the public, but that this motivation should be greatest in democratic countries because foreign trade is usually on the policy agenda and can have important electoral consequences. The public in such economies is more likely informed about trade agreements and their leaders' behavior toward them through their daily economic activities, the news media, and public discourse, thereby creating pressures for governments to seek out trade agreements to respond to the public's interests and demands. In chapter 4, we found that dyadic trade flows have a positive and significant effect on PTA formation, but this might simply imply that greater trade exposure increases the number of interest groups in favor of trade. Our further analysis in this chapter, however, calls that alternative interpretation into question by revealing that the degree of a country's trade openness has a positive and significant effect in democracies but a different one in autocracies. The political story that we spell out about leaders and their quest for political support is more in line with our findings.

It is puzzling that autocracies sign trade agreements since these agreements constrain them to some (varying) extent, but may not provide many domestic political benefits otherwise. Our argument suggests, however, that nondemocratic governments marked by greater political competition should be more likely to sign PTAs than less competitive regimes. The available data allow us to engage in only a rough test of this hypothesis, but the results are consistent with our conjecture. Among nondemocracies, personalistic regimes are less likely than either single-party regimes or militarist ones to sign trade accords, a finding that fits with our model; so does the fact that politically competitive autocracies are more likely to enter PTAs than noncompetitive autocracies.

Recent research has emphasized the design of international agreements and institutions. In this vein, we have analyzed the domestic political conditions under which leaders choose to enter PTAs that aim to achieve different degrees of integration. We conjecture that democratic leaders should seek deeper agreements and PTAs containing a DSM since credibility is more of a factor than in less politically competitive systems. We also hypothesize that a higher number of veto players should constrain not just the possibility of an agreement but also its proposed depth of integration. We find some support for these hypotheses. The design of trade agreements does seem to arise from a rational response to domestic political conditions.

Finally, domestic political conditions can affect the timing of agreements and their ratification. Leaders can and should rationally anticipate the impact of veto players. If they understand the extent and type of veto players at the start of negotiations, they can incorporate this into the international bargaining process. But should their number or type change after the international signing of the agreement and domestic ratification, leaders face a new challenge. If the number of veto players increases (or their type changes dramatically), leaders will have to negotiate anew with these newly empowered domestic groups. This is likely to slow the process down and cause delay. Hence, we expect that increases in veto players between signing and ratification will cause delay; greater increases will mean longer delay as leaders seek a way to get approval from the new groups. Our data provide strong evidence for this dynamic. The timing of the process also responds to domestic political pressures.

We have found at least some support for almost all of the hypotheses analyzed in this chapter. These results increase our confidence in the underlying logic of our theory. They also show that the theory is fruitful since it can generate new hypotheses that are testable. In the next chapter, we conclude and develop more implications for broader themes in international relations and international political economy.

CHAPTER 6

Conclusions

INTERNATIONAL TRADE AGREEMENTS are key features of the global political economy. For centuries, countries have coordinated their trade policies and more recently regulated many other forms of economic exchange through these agreements. Lately, however, PTAs have proliferated at an especially rapid rate. The EU, NAFTA, Mercosur, ASEAN plus three, SADC, and other PTAs have a significant bearing on the current world economy and are among the most important regional and international institutions. Trade agreements are also central instruments through which countries can promote international cooperation. The purpose of this study has been to explain why and when governments elect to enter PTAs.

It is widely recognized that PTAs have important consequences. Many economists believe they enhance economic growth (Baier and Bergstrand 2004 and 2007) and there is considerable evidence that they affect trade flows. Such agreements can also enhance the flow of foreign investment into poor countries, thus affecting development prospects (Büthe and Milner 2008). As Albert Hirschman (1980 [1945]), Jacob Viner (1950), and John McLaren (1997) have argued, they create webs of interdependence that can be exploited politically and thereby influence power relations. By affecting trade patterns, PTAs also have the potential to alter domestic politics in important ways (Hirschman 1980 [1945]; Rogowski 1989). Further, empirical research shows that PTAs affect the tenor of political relations among states, including dampening conflict among member-states (Mansfield et al. 1999; Mansfield and Pevehouse 2000). Trade agreements may also help countries enforce other agreements that they develop, including those that promote human rights and environmental standards (Hafner-Burton 2005 and 2009; Limão 2005). Taken together, there are a wide variety of reasons why PTAs demand our attention.

The establishment of PTAs has been marked by considerable variation over time and across countries. We exploit this variation to gain a better understanding of the microfoundations of international cooperation by addressing why and when decision makers enter these agreements. In the most general terms, we agree with Judith Goldstein (1996, 541) that "[i]nstead of envisioning domestic politics as a constraint upon those nations that enter into international agreements, signing an agreement is suggested to be a strategy whereby domestic actors further their own interests. Here, the answer to a commonly asked question of why nations would agree to specific rules of international conduct is that these rules present a solution to a domestic problem."

We focus on the domestic political conditions that motivate leaders to seek trade cooperation. Our tack is not intended to dismiss the importance of international factors, which are also crucial in this regard. Rather, we aim to highlight the domestic political incentives faced by leaders, which have received too little attention in studies of the international political economy. These domestic benefits are not just economic; they are political and bear heavily on the ability of leaders to retain office. Leaders enter PTAs to reassure their publics about their policies in the hope that this will increase their longevity in power. We thus provide a domestic political rationale for why leaders might consider these agreements. More specifically, this study shows that both regime type and veto players are key influences on why and when states choose to enter and ratify PTAs. We also show that the design of trade agreements responds to domestic political factors.

THE ARGUMENT AND EVIDENCE IN BRIEF

Our theory posits that leaders are pulled in at least two directions. Interest groups, which can provide rents and campaign contributions to politicians, often seek protection from imports. The public wants to retain competent leaders and replace those who are incompetent or predatory. Leaders want to retain office and hence bolster public support; at the same time, however, they also want rents and campaign contributions. Voters understand the preferences of leaders, but they do not know the details of the trade policies that heads of government choose. Voters tend to oust leaders if the economy performs badly and they often attribute adverse economic conditions to leaders having done too much for special interests. Chief executives usually lack domestic mechanisms to reassure the public that they are not rent seekers or captured by special interests. However, entering a PTA can help to redress this problem. The act of signing a trade agreement can serve as a public reassurance mechanism that helps competent leaders avoid being turned out of office by proving to the public that economic downturns are not due (entirely) to rent-seeking behavior of the executive. This, in turn, provides an important political motivation for leaders to sign such agreements. The public also gains in that it rejects fewer competent leaders and experiences less protectionism than would otherwise exist.

Leaders are more likely to enter trade agreements in competitive domestic political settings, where they can be turned out of office relatively easily. Hence, chief executives of more democratic countries are particularly likely to sign PTAs. This argument was spelled out in chapter 2 and then tested in chapters 3, 4, and 5. In chapter 3, we found strong support for this claim based on an analysis cast at the international or systemic level of analysis. We found further evidence that accords with our argument based on an analysis of country pairs from 1951 to 2004 in chapter 4. Finally, the auxiliary hypotheses that we derived from this argument received support in chapter 5.

Domestic political pressures can also incline leaders against entering PTAs. These arrangements yield domestic benefits for leaders, especially in competitive political systems. But they also generate political costs, including transaction costs stemming from ratification. Trade accords involve the exchange of market access among countries and sometimes aim to coordinate members' trade and other economic policies. These features have distributional consequences. Some groups gain from these trade barrier reductions; others lose. If the distributional losers have political clout, they can delay, block, or veto such policy change.

Veto players have the institutional capacity to prevent policy change. Assuaging these groups can be time-consuming and expensive. Leaders may have to alter their preferred trade policy proposals or bribe veto players to gain their acquiescence to ratification. For instance, in the recent EU–South Korea FTA negotiations, concessions were made to the EU automobile industry to convince enough national representatives to ratify the agreement. Conversely, blockage of the proposed US–South Korea FTA grew out of opposition from the American auto and beef industries, labor unions, and their representatives in Congress (Castle 2010). The more veto players that exist, the greater are the potential costs for leaders. In countries with a large number of veto players, policy change is inhibited (Tsebelis 2002; Mansfield et al. 2007). Consequently, leaders face a trade-off that they try to address rationally by weighing the benefits against the costs of ratification stemming from veto players. We view this trade-off as central to the domestic politics of PTAs. When the benefits of trade agreements are likely to outweigh their costs, leaders are more likely to join. Thus, we expect the decision to join to depend on both veto players and regime type. From an empirical standpoint, we expect that greater democracy in a country should increase its likelihood of cooperation. On the other hand, we expect that a larger number of veto players should reduce its probability of entering an agreement. Consistent with this argument, there is strong evidence in chapter 4 that democracy promotes the ratification of PTAs and that a heightened number of veto players discourages ratification.

Of course, PTAs are not shaped by domestic politics alone. In chapters 3 and 4, we found that international political factors—including the distribution of capabilities, alliances, diffusion pressures, and the GATT/WTO—bear heavily on the formation of PTAs. We also found that certain economic and geographic factors affect entry into such arrangements. But even after accounting for these factors, regime type and veto players exert a pronounced influence on the establishment of preferential groupings. Our claim is not that domestic political factors are the most important determinants of PTA ratification, but rather that they have been underemphasized in existing research on this topic and that they have a strong and systematic influence on trade cooperation, even when other factors are taken into consideration.

Clearly, we need to be cautious in interpreting these findings. There could be variables that we did not include in our statistical models that influence either regime type or the number of veto players, on the one hand, and PTA formation, on the other. However, we have tried to account for as many of these variables as possible. Alternatively, PTA ratification could in principle affect regime type or the number of veto players, which could raise questions about the causal direction of these relationships. But it is hard to identify more than a small handful of cases where a PTA could have had an influence on a country's domestic political institutions. Even in these cases, such change is more likely to happen over a very long period of time, not the short time periods that we analyze in this study. Furthermore, our results are robust with respect to whether we lag the effects of regime type and veto players. As such, we are confident that our results are not threatened by endogeneity.

In chapter 5, we tested a series of auxiliary hypotheses that flow from our argument and that help to assess its internal logic. Our argument implies that, especially in competitive political systems, leaders who sign PTAs should enjoy a longer tenure since the agreement will reassure the public that the head of state is neither incompetent nor predatory. Consistent with this hypothesis, we did find that democratic leaders who sign PTAs enjoy a longer tenure in office. Although we cannot rule out the possibility that leaders who sign PTAs also take other actions that promote their durability, this result offers some evidence that supports the internal logic of our theory.

Just as democracies may have more need for mechanisms to reassure their publics, so might left-wing governments. Leftist governments may have a harder time convincing domestic groups and voters that they are not intervening in the economy on behalf of special interests and therefore may have a greater need than other governments for establishing credible commitments about their economic policies. Trade agreements may thus be more appealing to them than to centrist or right-wing governments, which have an easier time reassuring voters because of the voters' ideological presumption against government involvement in the economy. We expect left-wing governments to be more likely to sign and ratify PTAs, and the tests we conducted in chapter 5 provide support for this hypothesis.

We also expect that the degree of trade dependence might affect leaders' political calculations. When an economy faces greater exposure to trade and is more dependent on overseas commerce, the public is more likely to pay attention to trade issues and therefore to know more about them. Recognizing this, heads of government are more likely to use PTAs as a reassurance mechanism. Hence, we expect that in politically competitive regimes, a greater level of trade dependence will increase the probability of ratifying a PTA, and the analysis we performed in chapter 5 supports this hypothesis.

The search for ways to reassure the public about leaders' intentions—in order to enhance a leader's longevity in power—may not be restricted to democracies. Some nondemocracies are more politically competitive than others. Our argument implies that those nondemocratic leaders who are especially vulnerable to turnover in office should be more likely to seek external reassurance mechanisms, such as PTAs, than leaders of less competitive nondemocracies. Other theories that point to democracy's role in promoting trade agreements do not suggest this result. Consistent with this hypothesis, we found that, among nondemocratic regimes, those that are more politically competitive are most likely to enter PTAs.

We also conducted a number of tests that bear on the recent literature about the optimal design of international agreements (Koremenos et al. 2001; Hawkins et al. 2006). Not all trade agreements are identical, as some aim to achieve much deeper integration than others. We have analyzed five types of PTAs in this study: PAs, FTAs, CUs, CMs, and economic unions. PAs aim to achieve the least integration and involve the least extensive trade barrier reductions and interstate cooperation in setting trade policies. Economic unions aim to achieve the greatest integration and entail the most cooperation. As the proposed level of integration rises, so do the domestic political benefits and costs for leaders stemming from PTA membership. We argued that since more democratic countries are in greater need of the political benefits provided by PTAs, they should also prefer deeper integration, since it provides even more reassurance to voters. We further argued that as the number of veto players rises, it will become harder to enter arrangements that aim to generate extensive integration.

In addition, we examined another important feature of PTAs: whether or not they include a dispute settlement mechanism. These mechanisms also serve to reassure publics that their leaders are going to be less likely to relent to special interest pressures. DSMs allow other PTA members and domestic groups an opportunity to publicly challenge a government for violating an agreement. We expect that more democratic countries will be more likely to include DSMs in trade agreements; countries with more veto players may find it harder to include them because they are a monitoring mechanism that might constrain leaders' ability to respond to interest group pressures. In chapter 5, we found evidence that is generally supportive of these hypotheses, although the strength of this support varies across the tests we conducted. Hence, this evidence provides further corroboration that trade agreements are rationally designed by governments to take into account the international environment and their domestic political situation.[1]

[1] We did not explore whether our argument also explains why countries sign other types of economic agreements, but one could extend it this way. Today countries have the opportunity to sign many types of economic agreements, such as bilateral investment treaties (BITs), double taxation

Finally, we analyzed the problem caused by changes in the number of veto players over the course of negotiating a PTA. Leaders, we presume, understand the number and composition of veto players at the start of an international negotiation. They can rationally adapt their strategies in these negotiations to avoid returning home with an agreement that will be vetoed. But when the number or character of the veto players changes over the course of negotiations or during the domestic ratification process, then leaders face a more difficult problem. They have to accommodate the new veto players with an agreement that was designed for a different situation. This type of change is likely to stimulate a delay between signing and ratifying an agreement. More specifically, based on the logic of our model, an increase in the number of veto players between the signing and ratification of a PTA should lengthen the period of time between these two events. Delay is consequently an outgrowth of domestic political problems, and our empirical results in chapter 5 supported this conjecture.

These supplemental tests help to establish the logic put forward in our theory by addressing the internal connections underlying the argument and by extending the claims driving it. This type of exercise lends further credence to our argument. We cannot establish that these auxiliary empirical claims are causal. But the fact that there is some support for most of them should enhance the confidence that can be placed in our argument. Moreover, the fact that many of the claims could not be derived from alternative theories about PTAs provides further support. This accumulation of different types of evidence provides us with the strongest corroboration of our claims about the domestic political incentives for trade agreements. The additional evidence also shows that our argument is progressive in the sense that it can generate new and interesting insights (Lakatos 1974; Elman and Elman 2003).

Other parts of our argument could be tested if the necessary data were collected. Future studies might fruitfully conduct such tests. For example, our argument relies on the idea that some voters are informed about the trade agreements their government has signed. As we explained in chapter 2, public opinion evidence drawn from various parts of the world supports this idea. Nonetheless, it would be interesting to more systematically document public opinion about PTAs and determine if signing them did change public attitudes toward governments. Equally, while we found in chapter 5 that entering PTAs and leadership duration are positively related, we were not able to establish that this relationship is causal. It would be useful to have more information on whether voters view leaders who sign agreements more positively than those who do not, or if they are more likely to reelect leaders who sign and abide by an international trade agreement.

---

treaties, services agreements, and overall economic integration agreements. Rationally, they may use these as complements and substitutes, making patterns more difficult to discern.

SOME IMPLICATIONS FOR THE STUDY OF INTERNATIONAL RELATIONS

This book has several novel implications for the study of PTAs, but it also sheds new light on a number of longstanding issues and debates in the field of international relations.

Economic versus Political Motivations

We have attempted to demonstrate that political considerations are an important impetus for PTAs. Leaders do not enter these arrangements for economic reasons alone.[2] The political roots of PTAs may extend to other international economic institutions as well. For instance, BITs may also generate domestic political benefits for leaders and not just economic gains. While trade accords may yield economic benefits, we have emphasized that they also have the potential for delivering important political benefits for leaders.

Our theory focuses on how PTA membership helps leaders retain office. Since staying in office is a critical goal of leaders, this constitutes a powerful motivation. We argue that trade agreements are costly to negotiate and leaders will only undertake them if they expect to realize benefits as a result. In many cases, the benefits are primarily political. Other scholars have advanced a related argument about how such membership can help "lock in" economic or political reforms, tying the hands of current leaders and rendering it difficult for future leaders to roll back reforms. Our argument is different, but the political benefits that leaders derive from locking themselves in are consistent with our theory. Politics remains very important to the understanding of economic phenomena. Domestic political motivations can help us understand international economic cooperation.

International versus Domestic Factors

Our argument focuses attention on domestic politics and its role in promoting and retarding international cooperation. As we have noted, however, international factors also influence PTA formation. Indeed, some of these factors may be more influential than the domestic ones that we have stressed.

Our empirical results reveal that systemic factors—such as the distribution of capabilities and pressures generated by international diffusion mechanisms—shape PTA formation. Bilateral influences—including alliance ties, political-military disputes, and geography—are also important. So too is

---

[2] As Eicher and Henn (2009, 17) have recently concluded, "PTAs are formed between countries that have all along been sharing characteristics favorable to mutual trade. In this case, tariff reduction may simply be an afterthought."

the GATT/WTO. The multilateral trade regime seems to have contributed to the creation of trade agreements. And some observers believe that it has made those agreements more open and less discriminatory than would otherwise be the case (Freund 2000a). Interestingly, conflicts, contiguity, greater distance, past colonial relations, global hegemony, and asymmetric power capabilities reduce the likelihood of PTA formation among pairs of countries. In contrast, greater trade flows, alliance relations, and other dyads forming PTAs throughout the international system increase the odds that countries will sign and ratify PTAs. Taken together, these findings provide ample evidence that international factors have a salient influence on the establishment of international trade agreements.

We have not fully explored the interaction of domestic and international politics in this study, although research on "two-level games" suggests that this interaction may be important (Putnam 1988; Milner 1997a). One related issue that we addressed briefly in chapter 5 involves the interaction between trade dependence and democracy. For those democracies that are more integrated into the international economy, the utility of PTAs may be greater than ever. In these countries, the public is likely to know and care more about trade; and leaders, recognizing this, can use PTAs as a reassurance device with more confidence. The effect of the interaction between a country's regime type and its international economic dependence on its foreign policy is an interesting avenue for further inquiry, but one that would also benefit from additional theoretical insights.

Societal Interests versus Institutions

A large literature focuses on the role of interest groups in affecting a country's trade policy (e.g., Baldwin 1985; Rogowski 1987; Milner 1988; Magee et al. 1989; Bailey et al. 1997; Hiscox 2002; Ladewig 2006). Much of this research has centered on whether these groups are best understood as factors of production or export-oriented and import-competing sectors, and thus whether class cleavages or sectoral interests have the most significant bearing on trade policy. Some studies also point to the role of interest groups in making or breaking trade agreements (Grossman and Helpman 1995; Milner 1997a; Chase 2005; Manger 2005; Katada and Solis 2008; Pahre 2008).

While we do not focus on the role of interest groups, we do view them as having an impact. First, our argument explicitly incorporates special interests. Governments are trying to maximize both rents (which can be used as campaign contributions) from interest groups and their probability of retaining office, which depends on the public more generally.[3] The difficulty that

---

[3] Gawande et al. (2009) show that countries vary greatly in the extent to which governments pay attention to special interests relative to the public interest (and social welfare maximization). And

governments experience revealing their true willingness to resist special interest demands creates an especially serious dilemma. The public (or some segments of it) realizes that governments find it very hard to resist interest group demands and satifying these demands can hurt the economy; it is this political problem that helps motivate governments to sign trade agreements. Interest groups thus play a role in our theoretical argument.

Second, veto players represent interest groups. Those groups that matter most have access to institutional capabilities that give their demands greater weight in the political process. Not all interest groups get what they want; in fact, some of them rarely get what they want. We need a better way to determine which ones are influential, when, and why. Political institutions are a crucial piece of this puzzle. Interest groups that have the ear of political actors who occupy critical institutional positions are of the greatest importance. The views of these interest groups will be heard and their representatives will have the greatest chance to advance their interests. To ratify agreements, governments need the acquiescence of these veto players and hence they will be able to exercise influence over the terms and timing of the agreement. Our focus on veto players allows us to combine the impact of interest groups and political institutions.

Finally, two hypotheses flow from interest group arguments. One hypothesis bears on who initiates a trade agreement. Interest group arguments suggest that the main initiators and demanders are domestic social groups, not the government. Interest group arguments about PTAs emphasize that the initiation of the trade agreement is due to the pressure of domestic lobbies. Since these arguments view interest groups as the main beneficiaries of PTAs, they see the initial impetus for the agreements as stemming from such groups. The government then should not be the primary instigator; rather, interest groups should prompt the government to undertake negotiations with other countries over trade access. But it is not clear that interest groups generally prompt governments to initiate PTAs or play much of a role in negotiating them, as our brief case studies in chapter 2 illustrate. In many cases, heads of government have made decisions to enter PTAs, regardless of interest group preferences. Similarly, governments that propose a program of liberal economic reforms and encounter (or expect to encounter) domestic opposition may enter a PTA to bind themselves to these changes (Summers 1991; de Melo et al. 1993; Haggard 1997; Whalley 1998). Mexico's decision to enter NAFTA, for example, is frequently discussed in such terms (Tornell and Esquivel 1997, 54; Whalley 1998, 71–72). Finding additional evidence about the respective roles of interest groups and governments in the initiation of trade agreements would be useful.

---

they show that political institutions are important factors in explaining this difference. But they view electoral competition as leading to more power for special interests.

A second hypothesis stems from claims that interest groups press for PTA membership because of the associated gains they can secure. The more trade diverting the agreement, the more of these gains they can capture (Grossman and Helpman 1995). Hence, if PTAs are driven by interest groups, they should be trade diverting and thus degrade the welfare of the participating countries. The debate over the economic impact of PTAs is extensive, as we pointed out in chapters 1 and 2. Nevertheless, the majority of evidence seems to suggest that most recent PTAs are not trade diverting and that many are trade creating on balance (Lawrence 1996; Krueger 1999; Panagariya 2000; Freund 2000b; Baier and Bergstrand 2004 and 2007; Freund and Ornelas 2010). This result implies that interest group arguments may be less potent than their advocates maintain. In sum, interest groups undoubtedly affect PTA membership. But leaders choose to negotiate these agreements only under certain conditions, and interest group arguments have limited ability to explain these conditions.

Rather than focusing on societal actors, we have placed primary emphasis on domestic institutions. Regime type is crucial in this regard. Democracies ensure greater political competition for leaders than do other regime types, and governments in democracies turn over more than in other regimes. The set of institutions that support vigorous electoral competition is the main focus of our theory. Where those institutions promote political competition, we expect the greatest interest in PTA membership. Other domestic institutions that allow or prevent governments from revealing their intentions and making credible commitments are also likely to be important, including divided government, electoral rules, and party systems (e.g., Milner 1997a; Martin 2000; Rogowski and Kayser 2002; Gawande et al. 2009). It would be useful to address the effects of these other institutions more fully in future research.

The Democratic Difference

Democratic government has been a focus of much recent literature in the field of international relations. A large literature exists on the impact of regime type on a variety of international outcomes, from war to trade to intergovernmental organizations. The democratic difference in matters of war and peace has generated a voluminous body of research (e.g., Doyle 1983a and 1983b; Russett 1993); and the democratic difference in economic policy has also been analyzed (Leeds 1999; Mansfield et al. 2000; Pahre 2008).

We contribute to this literature by showing that more democratic governments are particularly likely to enter PTAs. The recent spread of democracy throughout the global system has helped accelerate the trend toward trade agreements, as chapter 3 suggested. The first wave of democratization after World War II also produced a surge in the number of PTAs. During this early period, however, there were fewer democracies, which may help to explain why the number of PTAs formed was noticeably smaller than in more recent years.

As chapter 3 demonstrated, the global spread and retrenchment of democracy influences the spread of PTAs. If democracy retreats globally, we expect one upshot to be a slowdown in the formation of trade agreements. Political institutions affect international economic cooperation, and none more so than democracy.

International Cooperation and Externalities

A number of scholars have argued that international externalities are a major impetus for international cooperation (e.g., Milner 1997a; Maggi and Rodríguez-Clare 1998; Bagwell and Staiger 2002; Ossa 2011). When countries take actions that affect others and the cost of these actions is not included in the first country's utility function, a negative externality is produced. It is in the interest of the adversely affected countries to change the behavior of the state producing the externality. When countries mutually create externalities, these scholars claim, the possibility of cooperation rises.

Cooperation is particularly useful when externalities exist and markets cannot resolve the problem directly. Trade policy need not be made cooperatively; governments can set such policy unilaterally. This poses a puzzle for international trade theory. It is not clear why governments should ever need to conclude trade agreements. Only in the presence of externalities and other market failures is there a role for trade agreements in an economic context. Government action to "fix" the market failure results in cooperation that can leave the participants better off. In the most abstract sense, then, international trade cooperation depends on some sort of market failure, and externalities from the independent actions of interdependent actors within and across countries are prime sources of such failure.

But are externalities and market failures so pervasive that the world needs some four hundred trade agreements? Why is the WTO unable to rectify the major terms-of-trade externalities on which many economists focus (e.g., Bagwell and Staiger 2002 and 2010)? Indeed, since the use of MFN treatment is central to their argument about addressing such externalities, it appears that PTAs cannot be explained by this argument because they violate MFN explicitly. PTAs may be a response to some form of externality, but whether it is the commonly cited terms-of-trade variety remains unclear. Our findings about hegemony also indicate that PTAs may not be so much about international economic externalities. Declining hegemony is associated with a rise in PTAs, but this decline should alleviate concerns over terms-of-trade competition.

Incomplete Information, Credible Commitments, and International Relations

An important issue in international relations is the problem of incomplete information and credible commitments (Schelling 1960; Jervis 1978; Fearon

1995; Powell 1999). Many interstate conflicts arise from the fact that countries possess incomplete information about each other, cannot communicate truthfully, and are unable to credibly commit. Time inconsistency problems loom large; a government would like to commit to an action at the moment but has no incentive to carry it out in the future (e.g., Kydland and Prescott 1977; Barro and Gordon 1983). Knowing this, other governments do not believe it and hence do not change their actions. Various scholars of international relations view conflict as an outgrowth of incomplete information, incentives to misrepresent information, and governments' inability to make credible commitments (e.g., Fearon 1995; Powell 1999). Cooperation may also suffer because of these informational problems (Leeds 1999; Powell 1999; McGillivray and Smith 2004).

One implication of our analysis is that incomplete information problems also matter at the domestic level. Our argument emphasizes that governments have difficulty reassuring their own publics about their ability to resist special interest demands. Voters realize that governments are tempted by such demands because of the rents they can obtain. Further, they are uncertain of exactly how willing to resist protectionist pressures their government is and what trade policies their government adopts. Governments want to convey to voters that interest groups are not being excessively accommodated, but voters cannot simply believe them. Moreover, governments would like to rebuff interest groups, but they have a hard time doing so when pressed. Reassuring various domestic groups and the public about the government's behavior plays a similarly important role in domestic and international politics.

Leaders have found a variety of mechanisms in trade to deal with these problems. As U.S. legislators found out in the 1920s and 1930s when pressed for protection, it is sometimes better to relinquish the power to set trade policy (Schattschneider 1935; Goldstein 1993). As Raymond Bauer, Ithiel de Sola Pool, and Lewis Dexter (1972, 37) note, "[t]o protect their own freedom, congressmen needed to reduce their power [over trade policy] to be immediately helpful to their constituents." The same situation can face the executive branch when it is given responsibility for trade policy. Pressures on the executive to grant interest group demands can become overwhelming and harmful to the executive. Giving up the freedom to set trade policy by signing an international agreement can help governments maintain their power and retain office.

Relinquishing control over a policy realm can benefit leaders, as scholars have suggested in research on monetary policy and exchange rates (Kydland and Prescott 1977; Barro and Gordon 1983; Taylor 1983; Obstfeld and Rogoff 1995; Lane 1999). Central bank independence is a prime example of this phenomenon. Such delegation of policy to more independent entities can relieve political leaders from the incessant and noxious pressure of interest groups. The decision to tie one's hands has its costs, since governments lose some control over a policy lever that could yield future rents. But sometimes that loss of control can be advantageous. Because they are flexible, PTAs vest governments with the ability to protect certain segments of the economy but avoid unnecessary protection in other segments. Consequently, they may be especially prized by governments. Being able to reassure publics that they will not always accommodate interest groups may produce a sizable political advantage for governments. Doing so thus may be an important impetus to international trade cooperation.

Institutional Design and Rational Choice

Recent research has emphasized the importance of the particular features of international agreements (Goldstein et al. 2001; Koremenos et al. 2001; Hawkins et al. 2006). It has identified a number of dimensions along which international institutions vary. However, no consensus exists on which institutional dimensions are most important. Judith Goldstein, Miles Kahler, Robert Keohane, and Anne-Marie Slaughter (2001) address the increasing legalization of world politics. Part of this process is the increasing use of dispute settlement mechanisms, especially ones that invoke third party arbitration. Our argument about when DSMs are included in PTAs is consistent with their claims. We view DSMs as more likely when democracies design PTAs because of the domestic political significance of these mechanisms. This position seems to fit with their claim that legalization can increase credible commitments for governments.

Barbara Koremenos, Charles Lipson, and Duncan Snidal (2001), in contrast, identify five different dimensions of international agreements: membership, scope, centralization, control, and flexibility. They assert that these characteristics are rationally chosen by the founders to maximize the institution's ability to adapt to its environment and succeed. PTAs vary along these dimensions as well, and we have not discussed most of these characteristics. However, we do focus on membership. In this study, membership depends on rational decisions made by governments. We show that domestic politics can affect this decision substantially. Koremenos et al. (2001) tend to view membership from an international point of view (i.e., its relationship to international enforcement, uncertainty, and distributional concerns), and they do not consider domestic politics. Further research on PTAs could profit by examining the different aspects identified by Koremenos et al. (2001, 37); it would be interesting to see if the many hypotheses they develop are corroborated by these agreements.

Darren Hawkins, David Lake, Daniel Nielson, and Michael Tierney (2006) examine the design of international institutions from a principal-agent viewpoint. They argue that delegation to international institutions can be rational from a domestic political perspective.

> States delegate to IOs [international organizations] in one form or another to bolster state credibility. States delegate to IOs to tie their hands and enhance their credibility

in the international community . . . and with their domestic publics. Some measure of agent autonomy is a prerequisite for states to enhance their credibility, lock in favored policies . . . If agents are directly and wholly controlled by their principals, they cannot be used to create commitments to policies that their principals might prefer in the long run but not in the short run (Hawkins et al. 2006, 342–43).

This argument fits well with ours since it emphasizes how leaders can reassure publics about their intentions through international agreements. We do not consider the degree of agent autonomy or slack in the relationship, but assume that the trade agreement or its members can and do alert the domestic publics to any serious defections by their government. Many PTAs do not have an extensive international organization attached to them, so we are less concerned with the principal-agent relationship. But future research on PTAs could explore this issue.

Our analysis of institutional design concerns the degree of integration a given type of PTA aims to achieve. We argued that more democratic countries and ones with fewer veto players tend to sign deeper agreements and ones with DSMs. States choose whether to enter arrangements that propose more or less integration among members, and their decisions are partly driven by domestic politics. The degree of integration chosen affects the extent to which they can reassure domestic groups. Joining a FTA is much different than joining a CM, and both differ from entering an economic union. Similarly, forming a PTA with a DSM may convey much greater assurance to domestic audiences than one without it, as James Smith (2000) argues.

In some ways this choice about the type of trade agreement could be considered one about the scope of the agreement, in Koremenos et al.'s (2001) terms. It is also notable that the difference in size between two countries affects this decision. In chapter 5, this difference (the log of the ratio of the larger state's GDP to the smaller state's) is often positively related to deeper proposed integration and inclusion of DSMs. That is, as the difference in economic size between members grows, deeper integration and the inclusion of DSMs are more likely. This finding could be interpreted as supporting Koremenos et al.'s (2001) claim that greater actor heterogeneity leads to greater issue scope; more unequally sized actors (i.e., more heterogeneous ones) tend to enter arrangements designed to promote deeper integration. But this finding does not fit well with Smith's (2000) argument that greater economic differences among states lead to a lower likelihood of more legalistic DSMs.

One reason that scholars are concerned about the design of international institutions is that this factor is likely to affect their effectiveness. Poorly designed institutions are not expected to be very effective, although we have not addressed this issue. Economists have debated the impact of PTAs on trade and economic growth for many years. Some PTAs do indeed stimulate trade and perhaps growth, with the EU being the clearest example. But others—especially many PTAs signed soon after World War II—have been less effective from an economic standpoint. Governments, however, have chosen to sign these arrangements at an increasing rate and some have signed many. This would seem to indicate that governments perceive benefits, even if not economic ones, from membership.

Could design differences in these agreements affect their effectiveness? The answer depends on what is meant by effective. If PTAs are providing a visible reassurance mechanism for domestic publics, they may be highly effective even if they have little economic impact. Part of this mechanism involves the increased visibility of governments' compliance with their provisions. Anything that increases public knowledge of the agreement and a government's compliance with it is likely in our argument to increase its reassurance value. Hence, designing trade institutions so they provide greater transparency (through means such as monitoring reports, DSMs, and international courts) should make them more effective in terms of our model of domestic politics. This is why we expect a greater demand for DSMs among more politically competitive countries. The design of international agreements may affect their capacity to induce compliance and generate cooperation (Kono 2007), and this effect may be due to domestic as well as international politics.

Regime Compliance and Domestic Politics

We lack a sufficient understanding of the extent to which states comply with international institutions. Some studies indicate that compliance is extensive (Chayes and Chayes 1995). But others argue that conforming to these institutions reflects the interests of states, irrespective of their institutional obligations (Downs et al. 1996). In the case of trade agreements, we do not know whether states comply frequently or not. The fact that the GATT and the WTO dispute settlement regimes have not been used a great deal suggests that there is a fair degree of compliance since the WTO regime is binding on many states.

Do member-governments comply with PTAs? Related to this question is the longevity of PTAs. If PTAs die quickly, does this imply that they fail to engender compliance? The WTO notes that a significant number of PTAs have dissolved over time. Of the roughly four hundred agreements in the current WTO Regional Trade Agreement database (World Trade Organization 2009), nearly 46 percent are inactive.[4] Does this necessarily mean that many of them are ineffective? Some PTAs were renounced or suspended, such as the South African–Southern Rhodesia agreement or the Arab Cooperation Council, thus suggesting that they failed. However, a much larger number of the agreements disappeared because they were renegotiated into, or replaced by,

---

[4] Recall that our dataset includes both PTAs notified to the GATT/WTO and arrangements formed outside of the multilateral regime.

more integrative agreements. A substantial number of inactive agreements were superseded by more binding, integrative ones. Often a country's accession to a CU or the more integrated arrangement of a currency union, such as the EU, rendered the existing agreement obsolete. The WTO notes how this process worked with the 1995 accession of Austria, Finland, and Sweden to the EC (World Trade Organization 2009). Another example of this change was the transformation of the Caribbean Free Trade Association, the FTA among Caribbean nations, into a common market, the Common Market of the Caribbean. Thus, the death of a PTA does not unequivocally signal lack of compliance; it may even mean greater cooperation in a more extensive agreement.

We do not address compliance directly. We have assumed that compliance is monitored by groups that alert at least some of the domestic public, and that lack of compliance adversely affects a government's longevity in office. Yet we have not directly examined either assumption. Other scholars have, however, provided some evidence that whether or not states comply with international agreements is known by domestic audiences (Dai 2007; McGillivray and Smith 2008). Perhaps most interesting is the argument about human rights advanced by Beth Simmons. She argues that "ratification [of international agreements] stimulates [domestic] groups to form, to organize and to make their views known as a government begins to implement the agreement (or not). Ratification debates give rise to publicity that encourages interested citizens and their advocates to think about, strategize and articulate demands for compliance" (Simmons 2009, 364). This might also be the case for interest groups involved in trade agreements. Our second assumption—that political leaders are punished for noncompliance—is a keystone of the literature on audience costs (Fearon 1994). Michael Tomz (2007) has provided some empirical support for this claim.

Compliance is obviously an important issue in international relations. It is a core aspect of our argument but is not directly addressed in our research. Future research on trade agreements should attempt to address this complex issue.

Open Economy Politics and PTAs

Open economy politics (OEP) refers to an environment where domestic politics is deeply affected by international economic influences (Bates 1997; Lake 2009). It has at least two aspects that are important for this study. First, it often assumes that the preferences of domestic groups for economic policies reflect their standing in the international economy (Rogowski 1989; Frieden 1990; Milner 1997a). Interest group arguments about PTAs make this point most clearly (Milner 1997a; Chase 2005; Manger 2009). Some interesting research also suggests that trade agreements in turn may have an important impact on domestic preferences (Hathaway 1998; Duina 2006), but this is not our focus. Second, OEP hypothesizes that international institutions can provide consequential opportunities and constraints on domestic politics. OEP bears most heavily on our study for this latter reason.

With an open economy, political leaders can turn to international agreements as a way to reassure domestic audiences. The delegation of trade policy to an international institution and its monitoring by foreign and domestic groups constrains leaders. Because international institutions and agreements may be harder to change than national institutions, they provide a stronger mechanism for the public to monitor its leaders. In a world of closed economies, governments would not have the option of choosing such agreements as a reassurance device. Indeed, the more open the economy is, the more such a credibility device is likely to be effective and thus to be used, as we showed in chapter 5. This suggests that history matters. In the early part of our analysis (from the early 1950s until the early 1970s) most economies were not very open and the global economy as a whole had been destroyed by war and depression (James 2001). Turning to the international system, then, to solve domestic problems was probably rarer and less likely than it has been since globalization took off in the 1980s. We expect our argument to be more powerful in an OEP setting.

In sum, we believe that our research provides support for an OEP perspective. International institutions can affect domestic politics, and if leaders understand this, they can create and use such institutions for their own domestic political advantages. Consequently, the demand for international institutions may be related to their benefits for leaders in terms of domestic politics.

PTAs and the World Economy

Scholars have worried about at least two impacts that PTAs could have on the world trading system. First, a number of scholars have expressed concern over the growth of discriminatory trading blocs, particularly, the rise of three regional blocs comprising North America, Europe, and East Asia. In this vein, Robert Gilpin (1987, 397) writes that "[l]oose regional blocs are likely to result [from the decline of U.S. hegemony]. In the 1980s, the world economy is coalescing along [these] three axes. Debt, monetary and trade matters as well as changing security concerns will surely pull the regions of the world economy further apart." The possible splintering of the world economy into three protectionist blocs raises concerns about political-military conflict. The legacy of the interwar period—when the global trading system broke down and countries negotiated discriminatory arrangements with their political-military allies—animates such concerns. As Harold James (2001, 157) points out, "[b]ilateralism in trade developed as a major obstacle to the restoration of a world economy trading on liberal principles in the 1930s. The world was divided into several blocs: the imperial systems of Britain and France, the free trading environment of idealistic Hullian principle, and the barter world of

German trading practice. By the mid-1930s, this was widely recognized as a major problem of the international order." Are we witnessing the same devolution of the global system into a series of regional blocs?

Most scholars seem to think that current trade agreements tend to be more open and less discriminatory than those that marked the era between World Wars I and II. Many contemporary PTAs accept new members and so are not particularly exclusive (Mansfield and Pevehouse forthcoming). Indeed, many of the cases we examine involved countries joining an existing PTA. And current PTAs tend to actually lower trade barriers. As Bernard Hoekman and Michael Kostecki (2001, 366) note, regional trade agreements "may embody many good practices and some go far beyond the WTO in terms of liberalizing markets. . . . The challenge is to pursue multilaterally what the serious [trade agreements] are implementing internally. . . . Indeed, it appears that developments in [PTAs] are frequently reflected in analogous developments on the multilateral front." Furthermore, many of them are also cross-regional so they bind different regions together (Katada and Solis 2008). The more recently formed PTAs, then, seem to be quite different in their impact than earlier ones. They have been more of a force for spreading liberalization and integration into a global economy than for carving out exclusive, discriminatory regional blocs.

The PTAs we studied have also been negotiated and developed within a particular international system. The GATT and then the WTO have existed side-by-side with these trade agreements. They have thus been introduced into a world guided by an established multilateral trading system. PTAs, as long as they follow certain practices, are legal within the GATT/WTO (Hoekman and Kostecki 2001, 352–56). While the monitoring of PTAs was quite weak in the GATT, the WTO has now agreed to a transparency mechanism for notification and operation of PTAs.[5] This new discipline is intended to make the WTO's multilateralism more consistent with spreading preferential agreements and to give the WTO greater say in the development of such agreements. Indeed, if the Doha Round of multilateral trade negotiations fails, the WTO may turn to PTAs as its main mechanism for lowering trade barriers and coordinating economic policies.

As our results in chapter 4 demonstrate, the existence of the WTO and PTAs are mutually compatible. When two countries are in the GATT/WTO, they are more likely to sign a PTA. In addition, having a multilateral trade round in progress seems to encourage PTA formation; and the longer the time since a multilateral trading round has passed, the greater the probability of a PTA forming between two countries. These first two results suggest a positive dynamic

---

[5] See WTO (2006b) available at http://www.wto.org/english/tratop_e/region_e/trans_mecha_e .htm. (Last accessed July 27, 2011.)

between the multilateral trading system and the development of PTAs.[6] The third result implies some substitution between PTAs and the multilateral system. The existence of the GATT/WTO system has made an important difference for the rise of PTAs; their number and terms seem to be positively affected by the multilateral trading regime. Our results do not provide evidence to support the concerns expressed by many that discriminatory regional blocs will arise and undermine the global multilateral trading system (Bhagwati 2008). Instead, there seems to have been a good deal of compatibility between the two so far.

PTAs, however, form a puzzle for standard international trade theory. Neoclassical economic theory would not expect such agreements. Free trade for small countries and optimal tariffs for large ones are the expectations of trade theory. Hence, economists presume that in the absence of such an agreement countries would face an inefficiency that an agreement could resolve. Unilaterally setting trade policies creates inefficiency (Bagwell and Staiger 2002, 2). That is, these agreements arise because of some market failure, the solution to which requires government involvement. Most economists identify this market failure as some form of externality (Maggi and Rodríguez-Clare 1998 and 2007; Bagwell and Staiger 2002). Government intervention in the international trading system thus becomes important to relieve these externalities and improve the welfare of at least some PTA members. Government intervention can itself create costs, and it is not clear that in purely economic welfare terms PTAs provide net benefits to the world trading system. Furthermore, the MFN treatment in the WTO is critical for the solution of the terms-of-trade externality. As Kyle Bagwell and Robert Staiger (2002, 90) argue, "[u]nder MFN the only externality between governments arises through the (single) world price, and governments are not motivated by world price movements when they select politically optimal tariffs. A more surprising finding concerns the necessity of MFN tariffs: politically optimal tariffs are efficient only if they also conform to MFN." But PTAs do not abide by MFN; indeed they are intended to violate it. In this vein, Bagwell and Staiger (2002, 121) conclude that, "[o]n net, the (politically augmented) terms of trade approach suggest that PTAs may pose a threat to the existing multilateral trading system. . . . Such agreements may compromise the effectiveness with which the principles of reciprocity and nondiscrimination (i.e., MFN) can deliver efficient outcomes." Hence, it seems that PTAs may do less to reduce such international externalities than the GATT/WTO and that they may even undermine the WTO's ability to solve these externalities. We

---

[6] In a similar vein, Tang and Wei (2009, 229) claim that WTO accession by developing countries has been driven by their search for economic growth and that the WTO serves as a credible commitment device for leaders in such countries to make binding policy reforms that "serve as a partial substitute for good governance in promoting economic development." Hence, in their view the WTO can serve a similar domestic political purpose as PTAs.

attribute more of the impetus for PTAs to domestic politics than to these international externalities. Under certain conditions, governments can improve their domestic political situation by signing PTAs, and this provides an incentive to join these agreements, even if they do not improve economic outcomes.

What is the future of PTAs in the world economy? The most recent WTO World Trade Report (2011) is devoted to the question of PTAs and their relationship to the multilateral regime. It is subtitled "From Coexistence to Coherence," which expresses the direction in which the WTO hopes this relationship will evolve. The stalling of the WTO's Doha Round, which began in 2001, has been accompanied by a proliferation of PTAs, although whether these developments are causally linked is open to question. The two sets of trade agreements have coexisted without a descent into exclusive, discriminatory trade blocs. The WTO expects that PTAs will continue to grow in number and it aims to provide multilateral discipline on their design and evolution. Many trade agreements now cover more sectors than the WTO does and they regulate more economic policies. Indeed, some observers view these deep PTAs as the main way forward for the WTO (Baldwin 2011). By multilateralizing the provisions in the deepest PTAs, the WTO might be able to move the global trade regime forward. Our argument does not imply any domestic political benefits to forming closed, discriminatory agreements. As such, there is ample reason to expect these agreements to become a more regular part of the WTO. In fact, leaders might reap domestic political benefits if PTAs meet higher standards for transparency, liberalization, and compliance by being subsumed within the WTO. At the same time, leaders have reason to resist such WTO discipline since they also gain from the flexibility that these agreements can provide (Rosendorff and Milner 2001).

PTAs and the International Political Economy: Power and Politics

What kind of political ramifications can we expect from the development of PTAs? There are at least two political concerns raised by scholars about their diffusion. First, some believe that PTAs are simply a vehicle through which large, powerful countries can influence smaller, poor ones (Hirschman 1980 [1945]; McLaren 1997; Gruber 2000). Decades ago, Hirschman (1980 [1945]) noted that trade agreements could be used by countries to promote the dependence of their counterparts; furnishing trade preferences to smaller countries often induced them to join and remain a party to the agreement. Such benefits constitute a source of power for the state extending the preferences to them since it could threaten to withdraw the agreement, thus ending the benefits flowing to the more dependent party. More recently, McLaren (1997) observed that in a world of imperfect competition, signing trade agreements leads countries to alter their domestic production structures to fit with the trading demands of their bigger partners, increasing the costs for a small country of withdrawing from an agreement. Hence, once locked into an agreement, the smaller party would be vulnerable to the demands of the larger country. Lloyd Gruber (2000, 257) puts a new twist on this general proposition by claiming that "[s]ome states may be cooperating, then, not because they regard the new cooperative regime as a good thing, but because they have concluded (correctly) that the alternative—allowing the [other countries] to do it alone—would be even worse." Moreover, as he notes, just because countries rush to join such cooperative agreements does not mean that they see them as "structures of mutual advantage" (Gruber 2000, 257). For all of these reasons, PTAs may be mechanisms of power politics.

Our data cannot directly address this claim. But our results did reveal a tendency for countries to be more likely to sign a PTA as they become more similar in economic size (as measured by GDP).[7] Pairs of countries characterized by a highly asymmetric size distribution are unlikely to form these agreements. Perhaps countries understand the international political ramifications of such agreements and avoid contracting with much larger countries. Governments that are considering a trade agreement may search for similarly sized partners to avoid becoming overly dependent. Turning to countries of roughly the same size may make it easier to negotiate a relatively balanced reciprocal agreement, which would be harder for either side to use as a weapon of power politics.[8] In addition, the fact that these agreements are being signed in a world guided by multilateral trading principles monitored by the GATT/WTO makes it less likely that countries are using them for political leverage. In Gruber's terms, the best alternative to a PTA is the WTO system, and it is much better for weaker countries than no system at all.

We have stressed that governments may be focused more on addressing domestic political problems than on manipulating other countries when they sign such agreements. Obviously, they may prefer to do both at once. But if our argument is correct, it may be harder for countries to use such agreements as a means of international influence. The power derived from international agreements stems from the ability to (threaten to) terminate them and thus deprive a member-country of the associated benefits. But if governments sign these agreements to reassure domestic publics, they cannot simultaneously threaten to end them and gain any domestic benefit. In order for trade agreements to serve as reassurance devices, they cannot easily serve as weapons of power politics. Furthermore, as Hirschman (1980 [1945]) and McLaren (1997)

---

[7] Others have generated similar results (Baier and Bergstrand 2004). And Freund and Ornelas (2010) point out that governments seem to understand the potential drawbacks to PTAs and to avoid those that are worst for them.

[8] We exclude completely nonreciprocal trade agreements from our study, and they may be marked by more of the inequalities emphasized by Hirschman.

note, implementing an agreement may alter domestic political and economic conditions in ways that create new dependencies in *all* countries involved in the agreement and make the exercise of power harder by any member of the PTA.

Second, other scholars have suggested that PTAs represent a mechanism for the spread of neoliberalism and thus for the diffusion of globalization (Duina 2006). Most PTAs, especially those signed since the 1980s, have accompanied the spread of an ideology favoring freer trade and less government intervention in markets.[9] Thus, they can be seen as a means for international policy diffusion (Simmons et al. 2006, 12, 14, and 29). Our results provide some evidence of such diffusion. The more PTAs that countries within a given region are involved in, the more likely a country within the region is to join a PTA with its regional partner. Also, the more a country's top trading partners join PTAs, the greater the likelihood that this state will enter such a grouping. We found less evidence that strong contagion pressures noted by others were present (Baldwin and Jaimovich 2010). These results about diffusion and contagion should be treated guardedly, however, since the specter of endogeneity looms large: trade flows are both shaped by PTAs and affect them.

Overall, our results imply there may be global pressures for policy diffusion through PTAs, and that regionalism and trade competition may be driving some of this diffusion pressure. Scholars disagree on the sources of international policy diffusion. Simmons et al. (2006), for instance, argue that coercion, competition, emulation, or learning could be the sources of diffusion pressures and they note that it is difficult to separately identify such causes. PTAs seem to be part of a diffusion process, but the microfoundations of that process are not obvious. Future research might concentrate on evaluating the different causes of PTA diffusion and identifying the main sources of it. It is interesting to note, however, that while they generally spread the ideology of neoliberalism, PTAs differ substantially in content and hence they do not imply the homogenization of world politics or economics (Duina 2006). PTAs may foster globalization, but they can also enhance regional diversity.

PTAs and Domestic Politics: Supporting or Undermining Democracy and Political Capacity?

Once states enter a PTA, can membership affect their domestic politics? There are two possibly contradictory effects of PTAs on domestic politics. On the one hand, trade agreements may positively affect domestic political institutions. Some have argued that international organizations, including PTAs, can help stabilize democracy (Pevehouse 2005). By giving governments a mechanism for reassuring publics about their intentions, PTAs may help governments

---

[9] This is somewhat ironic since PTAs themselves, as we noted above, imply government intervention in the trading system.

domestically and make domestic institutions more durable and stable. Also, PTAs can help dampen international conflict, induce direct foreign investment, and help promote human rights (Mansfield and Pevehouse 2000; Büthe and Milner 2008; Hafner-Burton 2009). All of these effects are likely to have beneficial domestic consequences. Others even claim that PTAs enhance the quality of democracy since they reduce the power of special interests in politics, which accords well with our model (Keohane et al. 2009).

On the other hand, PTAs may exert negative effects on domestic politics and political institutions. Like other international institutions, they take decision-making power away from national governments. This can lead the public to perceive that its government is less democratic than is actually the case and can erode the capacity of domestic political institutions. It also creates political space for supranational institutions. Complex legal systems, bureaucracies, and transnational societal and interest group organizations have grown around various PTAs, such as NAFTA, the EU, and Mercosur (Duina 2006). These actors may render national governments less effective, either as democracies or as governing institutions. PTAs could thus end up having adverse domestic effects. Which of these two outcomes PTAs exert on domestic politics should be the subject of future research.

Trade agreements are an important element of international politics. They have proliferated over the past few decades and virtually every country signed at least one. We argue that the decision to enter a PTA owes much to domestic politics. Clearly there are other sources of trade agreements as well. But the domestic political factors we have uncovered have been vastly neglected. Moreover, the linkages between domestic politics and international institutions, like PTAs, have been underappreciated. Political leaders are highly attuned to their domestic political situation; they take few actions without considering the consequences for domestic politics and their longevity in office. Combining an understanding of their domestic political calculations and their foreign policy behavior may better illuminate the sources of their actions. This book has attempted to bring together a specific set of claims about domestic politics and foreign policy choices. Our rationalist theory of cooperation in international trade highlights the opportunities and constraints that open economy politics creates for political leaders. Globalization and democratization, two major trends in world politics, have made the interaction between domestic politics and international relations more complex and important.

Bibliography

ACAN-EFE (2006). "Ottón Solís Conversa con Empresarios sobre TLC y Reforma Fiscal." *La Nación.* February 10, 2006.

Accominotti, Olivier, and Marc Flandreau (2008). "Bilateral Treaties and the Most-Favored Nation Clause: The Myth of Trade Liberalization in the Nineteenth Century." *World Politics* 60(2): 147–88.

Acemoglu, Daron, Simon Johnson, and James Robinson (2001). "The Colonial Origins of Comparative Development: An Empirical Investigation." *American Economic Review* 91(5): 1369–401.

Africa, Cherrel, Etannabi Alemika, Michael Bratton, Amon Chaligha, Massa Coulibaly, Mamadou Dansokho, Derek Davids, Reis Deolinda, Annie Dzenga, Thuso Green, E. Gyimah-Boadi, Christiaan Keulder, Stanley Khaila, Mogoodi Lekorwe, Carolyn Logan, Robert Mattes, Mpho Molomo, Chileshe Mulenga, Suzie Muwanga, Joao Pereira, Deolinda Reis, Fransico Rodrigues, Joseph Semboja, Robert Sentamu, Masipula Sithole, and Maxton Tsoka (2003/2004). Afrobarometer: Round II 16-Country Merged Dataset, 2003–2004. Ann Arbor, MI. Inter-University Consortium for Political and Social Research (ICPSR).

Aghion, Philippe, Pol Antràs, and Elhanan Helpman (2007). "Negotiating Free Trade." *Journal of International Economics* 73(1): 1–30.

Alesina, Alberto, and Alan Drazen (1991). "Why are Stabilizations Delayed?" *American Economic Review* 81(5): 1170–88.

Anderson, Kym, and Richard Blackhurst, eds. (1993). *Regional Integration and the Global Trading System.* London (UK). Harvester Wheatsheaf.

Angrist, Joshua D., and Joern-Steffen Pischke (2009). *Mostly Harmless Econometrics: An Empiricist's Companion.* Princeton, NJ. Princeton University Press.

Associated Press (1998). "India, Sri Lanka to Establish Free-Trade Area." *Associated Press Archive.* December 28, 1998.

Bagwell, Kyle, and Petros C. Mavroidis, eds. (2011). *Preferential Trade Agreements: A Law and Economics Analysis.* New York. Cambridge University Press.

Bagwell, Kyle, and Robert W. Staiger (1999). "An Economic Theory of GATT." *American Economic Review* 89(1): 215–48.

—— (2001). "Domestic Policies, National Sovereignty, and International Economic Institutions." *Quarterly Journal of Economics* 116(2): 519–62.

—— (2002). *The Economics of the World Trading System.* Cambridge, MA. MIT Press.

—— (2010). "The World Trade Organization: Theory and Practice." *Annual Review of Economics* 2(1): 223–56.

Baier, Scott L., and Jeffrey H. Bergstrand (2004). "Economic Determinants of Free Trade Agreements." *Journal of International Economics* 64(1): 29–63.

—— (2007). "Do Free Trade Agreements Actually Increase Members' International Trade?" *Journal of International Economics* 71(1): 72–95.

Bailey, Michael A., Judith Goldstein, and Barry R. Weingast (1997). "The Institutional Roots of American Trade Policy: Politics, Coalitions, and International Trade." *World Politics* 49(3): 309–38.

Baker, Andy (2008). *The Market and the Masses in Latin America: Policy Reform and Consumption in Liberalizing Economies.* New York. Cambridge University Press.

Baldwin, David A. (1985). *Economic Statecraft.* Princeton, NJ. Princeton University Press.

Baldwin, Richard (1995). "A Domino Theory of Regionalism." In *Expanding Membership of the European Union.* Richard Baldwin, Pertti Haaparanta, and Jaakko Kiander, eds. New York. Cambridge University Press: 25–53.

——— (2008). "Big-Think Regionalism: A Critical Survey." *NBER Working Paper No. 14056.* Cambridge, MA. National Bureau of Economic Research.

——— (2011). "21st Century Regionalism: Filling the Gap between 21st Century Trade and 20th Century Trade Rules." *CTEI Working Paper No. 2010-31.* Geneva (Switzerland). The Graduate Institute.

Baldwin, Richard, and Dany Jaimovich (2010). "Are Free Trade Agreements Contagious?" *NBER Working Paper 16084.* Cambridge, MA. National Bureau of Economic Research.

Baldwin, Richard, and Anthony J. Venables (1995). "Regional Economic Integration." In *Handbook of International Economics.* Gene M. Grossman and Kenneth Rogoff, eds. San Diego, CA. Elsevier Science. Vol. 3: 1597–644.

Baldwin, Robert E. (1993). "Adapting the GATT to a More Regionalized World: A Political Economy Perspective." In *Regional Integration and the Global Trading System.* Kym Anderson and Richard Blackhurst, eds. London (UK). Harvester Wheatsheaf: 387–407.

Baltagi, Badi H., Peter Egger, and Michael Pfaffermayr (2008). "Estimating Regional Trade Agreement Effects on FDI in an Interdependent World." *Journal of Econometrics* 145(1–2): 194–208.

Barro, Robert J. (1996). "Democracy and Growth." *Journal of Economic Growth* 1(1): 1–28.

Barro, Robert J., and David B. Gordon (1983). "Rules, Discretion and Reputation in a Model of Monetary Policy." *Journal of Monetary Economics* 12(1): 101–21.

Bates, Robert H. (1997). *Open-Economy Politics: The Political Economy of the World Coffee Trade.* Princeton, NJ. Princeton University Press.

Bauer, Raymond A., Ithiel de Sola Pool, and Lewis A. Dexter (1972). *American Business and Public Policy: The Politics of Foreign Trade.* Chicago. Aldine-Atherton.

Bearak, Barry (2011). "Police Officers in Swaziland Squash Rally for Democracy." *New York Times.* April 13, 2011: A5.

Bearce, David H. (2003). "Grasping the Commercial Institutional Peace." *International Studies Quarterly* 47(3): 347–70.

Beck, Nathaniel, and Jonathan N. Katz (2001). "Throwing Out the Baby with the Bath Water: A Comment on Green, Kim, and Yoon." *International Organization* 55(2): 487–95.

Beck, Nathaniel, Jonathan N. Katz, and Richard Tucker (1998). "Taking Time Seriously: Time-Series-Cross-Section Analysis with a Binary Dependent Variable." *American Journal of Political Science* 42(4): 1260–88.

Beck, Thorsten, George Clarke, Alberto Groff, Philip Keefer, and Patrick Walsh (2001). "New Tools in Comparative Political Economy: The Database of Political Institutions." *World Bank Economic Review* 15(1): 165–76.

—— (2005). "Database of Political Institutions v.3." http://www.worldbank.org/wbi/governance/pubs/wps2283.htm. (Last accessed September 23, 2008.)

Bennett, D. Scott, and Allan Stam (2000). "EUGene: A Conceptual Manual." *International Interactions* 26(2): 179–204.

Besley, Timothy, and Ian Preston (2007). "Electoral Bias and Policy Choice: Theory and Evidence." *Quarterly Journal of Economics* 122(4): 1473–510.

Bhagwati, Jagdish (1968). "Trade Liberalization Among LCDs, Trade Theory, and GATT Rules." In *Value, Capital, and Growth: Essays in Honour of Sir John Hicks*. J. N. Wolfe, ed. Edinburgh (UK). University of Edinburgh Press: 21–43.

—— (1991). *The World Trading System at Risk*. Princeton, NJ. Princeton University Press.

—— (1993). "Regionalism and Multilateralism: An Overview." In *New Dimensions in Regional Intergration*. Jaime de Melo and Arvind Panagariya, eds. New York. Cambridge University Press: 22–51.

—— (2008). *Termites in the Trading System: How Preferential Agreements Undermine Free Trade*. New York. Oxford University Press.

Bhagwati, Jagdish, and Arvind Panagariya (1996a). *The Economics of Preferential Trade Agreements*. Washington, DC. AEI Press.

—— (1996b). "Preferential Trading Areas and Multilateralism–Strangers, Friends, or Foes?" In *The Economics of Preferential Trade Agreements*. Jagdish Bhagwati and Arvind Panagariya, eds. Washington, DC. AEI Press: 1–78.

Bhattacharjee, Subhomoy (2000). "Nod to Free Trade Deal with Lanka Passes Off Quietly." *Business Standard*. July 13, 2000: 2.

Bollen, Kenneth A. (1980). "Issues in the Comparative Measurement of Political Democracy." *American Sociological Review* 45(3): 370–90.

Bong, Youngshik, and Heon-Joo Jung (2005). "The South Korea-Chile Free Trade Agreement: Implications for Regional Economic Integration in East Asia." *International Journal of Korean Studies* 9(1): 143–65.

Boockmann, Bernhard (2001). "The Ratification of ILO Conventions: A Hazard Rate Analysis." *Economics and Politics* 13(3): 281–309.

Box-Steffensmeier, Janet M., and Bradford S. Jones (2004). *Event History Modeling: A Guide for Social Scientists*. New York. Cambridge University Press.

Brander, James A. (1991). "Election Polls, Free Trade, and the Stock Market: Evidence from the 1988 Canadian General Election." *Canadian Journal of Economics* 24(4): 827–43.

Bueno de Mesquita, Bruce, Alastair Smith, Randolph M. Siverson, and James Morrow (2003). *The Logic of Political Survival*. Cambridge, MA. MIT Press.

Büthe, Tim, and Helen V. Milner (2008). "The Politics of Foreign Direct Investment into Developing Countries: Increasing FDI through International Trade Agreements?" *American Journal of Political Science* 52(4): 741–62.

Buzan, Barry (1984). "Economic Structure and International Security: The Limits of the Liberal Case." *International Organization* 38(4): 597–64.

Cameron, David R. (1978). "The Expansion of the Public Economy: A Comparative Analysis." *American Political Science Review* 72(4): 1243–61.

Cassing, James H., and Arye L. Hillman (1986). "Shifting Comparative Advantage and Senescent Industry Collapse." *American Economic Review* 76(3): 516–23.

Castle, Stephen (2010). "Europe and South Korea Agree to Lift Trade Barriers in 2011." *New York Times.* September 17, 2010: B8.

Chang, Won, and L. Alan Winters (2002). "How Regional Blocs Affect Excluded Countries: The Price Effects of MERCOSUR." *American Economic Review* 92(4): 889–904.

Chase, Kerry A. (2003). "Economic Interests and Regional Trading Arrangements: The Case of NAFTA." *International Organization* 57(1): 137–74.

—— (2005). *Trading Blocs: States, Firms, and Regions in the World Economy.* Ann Arbor, MI. University of Michigan Press.

Chau, Nancy H., and Ravi S. M. Kanbur (2001). "The Adoption of International Labor Standards Conventions: Who, What, and Why?" *Brookings Trade Forum, 2001.* Washington, D.C. Brookings Institution: 113–56.

Chaudoin, Stephen (2012). "Information Transmission and Dispute Settlement in International Institutions" (unpublished manuscript). Princeton University.

Chayes, Abram, and Antonia Handler Chayes (1995). *The New Sovereignty: Compliance with International Regulatory Agreements.* Cambridge, MA. Harvard University Press.

Cleves, Mario A., William W. Gould, and Roberto G. Gutierrez (2004). *An Introduction to Survival Analysis Using Stata.* College Station, TX. Stata Press.

Cloete, Kim (2011). "Swaziland at Crossroads." *Moneyweb.co.za.* April 13, 2011.

Cohen, Benjamin J. (1997). "The Political Economy of Currency Regions." In *The Political Economy of Regionalism.* Edward D. Mansfield and Helen V. Milner, eds. New York. Columbia University Press: 50–76.

Collett, David (2003). *Modelling Survival Data in Medical Research.* Boca Raton, FL. Chapman & Hall.

Condliffe, John B. (1940). *The Reconstruction of World Trade.* New York. W.W. Norton.

Conkey, Christopher (2009). "U.S. Moves to Patch Mexico Rift." *Wall Street Journal.* March 21, 2009: A3.

Cooper, Charles A., and Benton F. Massell (1965a). "A New Look at Customs Union Theory." *Economic Journal* 75(3): 742–47.

—— (1965b). "Toward a General Theory of Customs Unions for Developing Countries." *Journal of Political Economy* 73(5): 461–76.

Correlates of War Project (2003a). "Militarized Interstate Disputes (v3.10)." Murray Research Archive. http://hdl.handle.net/1902.1/10168. (Last accessed July 25, 2011.)

—— (2003b). "Alliances (v3.03)." Murray Research Archive. http://hdl.handle.net/1902.1/10172. (Last accessed July 25, 2011.)

Cramton, Peter C. (1992). "Strategic Delay in Bargaining with Two-Sided Uncertainty." *Review of Economic Studies* 59(1): 205–25.

Crawford, Jo-Ann, and Roberto V. Fiorentino (2005). "The Changing Landscape of Regional Trade Agreements." *WTO Discussion Paper No. 8.* Geneva (Switzerland). World Trade Organization.

Dahl, Robert A. (1971). *Polyarchy: Participation and Opposition.* New Haven, CT. Yale University Press.

Dai, Xinyuan (2007). *International Institutions and National Policies.* New York. Cambridge University Press.

Daubler, Thomas (2008). "Veto Players and Welfare State Change: What Delays Social Entitlement Bills?" *Journal of Social Policy* 37(4): 683–706.

de la Cruz, Vladimir (2006). "¿Se decidió electoralmente el TLC?" *La Nación*. November 26, 2006.

De la Rocha, Manuel (2003). "The Cotonou Agreement and its Implications for the Regional Trade Agenda in Eastern and Southern Africa." *World Bank Policy Research Working Paper No. 3090*. Washington, DC. World Bank.

de Melo, Jaime, and Arvind Panagariya (1993a). "Introduction." In *New Dimensions in Regional Integration*. Jaime de Melo and Arvind Panagariya, eds. New York. Cambridge University Press: 3–21.

———— eds. (1993b). *New Dimensions in Regional Integration*. New York. Cambridge University Press.

de Melo, Jaime, Arvind Panagariya, and Dani Rodrik (1993). "The New Regionalism: A Country Prespective." In *New Dimensions in Regional Integration*. Jaime de Melo and Arvind Panagariya, eds. New York. Cambridge University Press: 159–93.

Deutsch, Karl W., Sidney A. Burrell, Robert A. Kann, Maurice Lee, Jr., Martin Lichterman, Raymond E. Lindgren, Francis L. Lowenheim, and Richard W. Van Wagen (1957). *Political Community and the North Atlantic Area: International Organization in the Light of Historical Experience*. Princeton, NJ. Princeton University Press.

Dludlu, John (1999). "SADC Unions Oppose Free Trade." *Business Day*. May 13, 1999.

Doran, Charles F. (1999). "Introduction: After NAFTA." In *A New North America: Cooperation and Enhanced Interdependence*. Charles F. Doran and Alvin P. Drischler, eds. Westport, CT. Praeger Publishers: xi–xv.

Downs, George W., and David M. Rocke (1995). *Optimal Imperfection? Domestic Uncertainty and Institutions in International Relations*. Princeton, NJ. Princeton University Press.

Downs, George W., David M. Rocke, and Peter N. Barsoom (1996). "Is the Good News about Compliance Good News about Cooperation?" *International Organization* 50(3): 379–406.

Doyle, Michael W. (1983a). "Kant, Liberal Legacies, and Foreign Affairs, Part 1." *Philosophy and Public Affairs* 12(3): 205–35.

———— (1983b). "Kant, Liberal Legacies, and Foreign Affairs, Part 2." *Philosophy and Public Affairs* 12(4): 323–53.

Drazen, Allan (1996). "The Political Economy of Delayed Reform." *Journal of Economic Policy Reform* 1(1): 25–46.

Duina, Francesco (2006). "Varieties of Regional Integration: The EU, NAFTA and Mercosur." *Journal of European Integration* 28(3): 247–75.

Dutt, Pushan, and Devashish Mitra (2005). "Political Ideology and Endogenous Trade Policy: An Empirical Investigation." *Review of Economics and Statistics* 87(1): 59–72.

Economist Intelligence Unit (2011). "Mexico/USA: Truck Repair." *EIU – Business Latin America*. January 24, 2011: Section 6 of 17.

Eichengreen, Barry, and Jeffrey A. Frankel (1995). "Economic Regionalism: Evidence from Two 20th Century Episodes." *North American Journal of Economics and Finance* 6(2): 89–106.

Eichengreen, Barry, and David Leblang (2008). "Democracy and Globalization." *Economics and Politics* 20(3): 289–334.

Eicher, Theo, and Christian Henn (2009). "In Search of WTO Trade Effects: Preferential Trade Agreements Promote Trade Strongly, But Unevenly." Washington, DC. International Monetary Fund.

Elman, Colin, and Miriam Fendius Elman (2003). "Lessons from Lakatos." In *Progress in International Relations Theory: Appraising the Field*. Colin Elman and Miriam Fendius Elman, eds. Cambridge, MA. MIT Press: 21–68.

Erasmus, Janine (2008). "SADC Free Trade Area Launched." http://www.mediaclubsouth africa.com/index.php?option=com_content&view=article&id=633:sadc-free-trade -area-180808&catid=45:economy_news&Itemid=55. (Last accessed October 6, 2010.)

Ethier, Wilfred J. (1998). "Multilateral Roads to Liberalization." In *International Trade Policy and the Pacific Rim*. John Piggott and Alan Woodland, eds. New York. St. Martin's: 131–52.

Evans, H. David (1999). *SADC: The Cost of Non-Integration*. Harare (Zimbabwe). SAPES.

Fair, Ray (1978). "The Effect of Economic Events on Votes for the President." *Review of Economics and Statistics* 60(2): 159–73.

—— (2009). "Presidential and Congressional Vote-Share Equations." *American Journal of Political Science* 53(1): 55–72.

Fearon, James D. (1994). "Domestic Political Audiences and the Escalation of International Disputes." *American Political Science Review* 88(3): 577–92.

—— (1995). "Rationalist Explanations for War." *International Organization* 49(3): 379–414.

—— (1999). "Electoral Accountability and the Control of Politicians: Selecting Good Types versus Sanctioning Poor Performances." In *Democracy, Accountability, and Representation*. Adam Przeworski, Susan C. Stokes and Bernard Manin, eds. New York. Cambridge University Press: 55–97.

Ferejohn, John (1986). "Incumbent Performance and Electoral Control." *Public Choice* 50 (1/3 – Carnegie Papers on Political Economy, Volume 6: Proceedings on the Carnegie Conference on Political Economy): 5–25.

Fernández, Raquel, and Jonathan Portes (1998). "Returns to Regionalism: An Analysis of Nontraditional Gains from Regional Trade Agreements." *World Bank Economic Review* 12(2): 197–220.

Finger, J. Michael (1993). "GATT's Influence on Regional Arrangements." In *New Dimensions in Regional Integration*. Jaime de Melo and Arvind Panagariya, eds. New York. Cambridge University Press: 128–48.

Fiorentino, Roberto V., Luis Verdeja, and Christelle Toqueboeuf (2007). "The Changing Landscape of Regional Trade Agreements: 2006 Update." *WTO Discussion Paper No. 12*. Geneva (Switzerland). World Trade Organization.

Fiorina, Morris P. (1981). *Retrospective Voting in American National Elections*. New Haven, CT. Yale University Press.

Fishlow, Albert, and Stephan Haggard (1992). *The United States and the Regionalization of the World Economy*. Paris (France). OECD Development Center Research Project on Globalization and Regionalization.

Frankel, Jeffrey A., and Shang-Jin Wei (1998). "Regionalization of World Trade and Currencies: Economics and Politics." In *The Regionalization of the World Economy*. Jeffrey A. Frankel, ed. Chicago. University of Chicago Press: 189–226.

Fredriksson, Per G., and Noel Gaston (2000). "Ratification of the 1992 Climate Change Convention: What Determines Legislative Delay?" *Public Choice* 104(3): 345–68.

Freund, Caroline (2000a). "Multilateralism and the Endogenous Formation of Preferential Trade Agreements." *Journal of International Economics* 52(2): 359–76

—— (2000b). "Different Paths to Free Trade: The Gains from Regionalism." *Quarterly Journal of Economics* 115(4): 1317–41.

—— (2011). "Third-Country Effects of Regional Trade Agreements." In *Preferential Trade Agreements: A Law and Economics Analysis*. Kyle W. Bagwell and Petros C. Mavroidis, eds. New York. Cambridge University Press: 40–59.

Freund, Caroline, and Emanuel Ornelas (2010). "Regional Trade Agreements." *Annual Review of Economics* 2(1): 139–66.

Frieden, Jeffry A. (1990). *Debt, Development, and Democracy*. Princeton, NJ. Princeton University Press.

Friedman, Milton (1953). *Essays in Positive Economics*. Chicago. University of Chicago Press.

Gandhi, Jennifer (2008). *Political Institutions under Dictatorship*. New York. Cambridge University Press.

Gandhi, Jennifer, and Adam Przeworski (2006). "Cooperation, Cooptation, and Rebellion under Dictatorships." *Economics and Politics* 18(1): 1–26.

—— (2007). "Authoritarian Institutions and the Survival of Autocrats." *Comparative Political Studies* 40(11): 1279–301.

Gardini, Gian Luca (2005). "Two Critical Passages on the Road to Mercosur." *Cambridge Review of International Affairs* 18(3): 405–20.

—— (2007). "Who Invented Mercosur?" *Diplomacy and Statecraft* 18(4): 805–30.

—— (2010). *The Origins of Mercosur: Democracy and Regionalization in South America*. New York. Palgrave Macmillan.

Garrett, Geoffrey, and Barry Weingast (1993). "Ideas, Interests, and Institutions: Constructing the European Community's Internal Market." In *Ideas and Foreign Policy: Beliefs, Institutions, and Political Change*. Judith Goldstein and Robert O. Keohane, eds. Ithaca, NY. Cornell University Press: 173–206.

Gasiorowski, Mark (1996). "An Overview of the Political Regime Change Dataset." *Comparative Political Studies* 29(4): 469–83.

Gastil, Raymond D. (1980 and 1990). *Freedom in the World: Political Rights and Civil Liberties*. New York. Freedom House.

Gaubatz, Kurt Taylor (1996). "Democratic States and Commitment in International Relations." *International Organization* 50(1): 109–39.

Gawande, Kishore, Pravin Krishna, and Marcelo Olarreaga (2009). "What Governments Maximize and Why: The View from Trade." *International Organization* 63(3): 491–532.

Geddes, Barbara (2003). *Paradigms and Sandcastles: Theory Building and Research Design in Comparative Politics*. Ann Arbor, MI. University of Michigan Press.

—— (2004). "Authoritarian Breakdown" (unpublished manuscript). UCLA.

George, Aurelia (1991/1992). "The Politics of Interest Representation in the Japanese Diet: The Case of Agriculture." *Pacific Affairs* 64(4): 506–28.

Ghosn, Faten, and Scott Bennett (2003). "Codebook for the Dyadic Militarized Interstate Incident Data, Version 3.10." http://correlatesofwar.org. (Last accessed July 25, 2011.)

Ghosn, Faten, Glenn Palmer, and Stuart Bremer (2004). "The MID3 Data Set, 1993–2001: Procedures, Coding Rules, and Description." *Conflict Management and Peace Science* 21(2): 133-54

Gibb, Richard (2007). "Regional Integration in Post-Apartheid Southern Africa." *Tijdschrift voor economische en sociale geografie* 98(4): 421–35.

Gilligan, Michael J. (1997). *Empowering Exporters: Reciprocity, Delegation, and Collective Action in American Trade Policy.* Ann Arbor, MI. University of Michigan Press.

Gilpin, Robert (1975). *U.S. Power and the Multinational Corporation: The Political Economy of Foreign Direct Investment.* New York. Basic Books.

—— (1981). *War and Change in World Politics.* New York. Cambridge University Press.

—— (1987). *The Political Economy of International Relations.* Princeton, NJ. Princeton University Press.

Gleditsch, Kristian Skrede (2002). "Expanded Trade and GDP Data." *Journal of Conflict Resolution* 46(5): 712–24.

Gleditsch, Nils Petter, Peter Wallensteen, Mikael Eriksson, Margareta Sollenberg, and Havard Strand (2002). "Armed Conflict 1946–2001: A New Dataset." *Journal of Peace Research* 39(5): 615–37.

Goemans, Henk E., Kristian Skrede Gleditsch, and Giacomo Chiozza (2009). "Introducing Archigos: A Dataset of Political Leaders." *Journal of Peace Research* 46(2): 269–83.

Goldstein, Judith (1993). *Ideas, Interests and American Trade Policy.* Ithaca, NY. Cornell University Press.

—— (1996). "International Law and Domestic Institutions." *International Organization* 50(4): 541–64.

Goldstein, Judith, Miles Kahler, Robert O. Keohane, and Anne-Marie Slaughter, eds. (2001). *Legalization and World Politics.* Cambridge, MA. MIT Press.

Goldstein, Judith, Douglas Rivers, and Michael Tomz (2007). "Institutions in International Relations: Understanding the Effects of the GATT and the WTO on World Trade." *International Organization* 61(1): 37–67.

Golub, Jonathan (1999). "In the Shadow of the Vote? Decision Making in the European Community." *International Organization* 53(4): 733–64.

—— (2007). "Survival Analysis and European Union Decision-Making." *European Union Politics* 8(2): 155–79.

—— (2008). "Survival Analysis." In *The Oxford Handbook of Political Methodology.* Janet M. Box-Steffensmeier, Henry E. Brady and David Collier, eds. New York. Oxford University Press: 530–46.

Gowa, Joanne S. (1994). *Allies, Adversaries, and International Trade.* Princeton, NJ. Princeton University Press.

Gowa, Joanne S., and Soo Yeon Kim (2005). "An Exclusive Country Club: The Effects of the GATT on Trade, 1950–94." *World Politics* 57(4): 453–78.

Gowa, Joanne S., and Edward D. Mansfield (1993). "Power Politics and International Trade." *American Political Science Review* 87(2): 408–20.

Green, Donald P., Soo Yeon Kim, and David H. Yoon (2001). "Dirty Pool." *International Organization* 55(2): 441–68.

Greene, William H. (2003). *Econometric Analysis.* Upper Saddle River, NJ. Prentice-Hall.

Grossman, Gene M., and Elhanan Helpman (1994). "Protection for Sale." *American Economic Review* 84(4): 833–50.

—— (1995). "The Politics of Free Trade Agreements." *American Economic Review* 85(4): 667–90.

—— (2002). *Interest Groups and Trade Policy.* Princeton, NJ. Princeton University Press.

Gruber, Lloyd (2000). *Ruling the World: Power Politics and the Rise of Supranational Institutions.* Princeton, NJ. Princeton University Press.

Gunning, Jan Willem (2001). "Trade Blocs: Relevant for Africa?" *Journal of African Economics* 10(3): 311–35.

Gunter, Frank R. (1989). "Customs Union Theory: Retrospect and Prospect." In *Economic Aspects of Regional Trading Agreements*. David Greenaway, Thomas Hyclak, and Robert J. Thornton, eds. New York. Harvester Wheatsheaf: 1–30.

Gurr, Ted Robert, Keith Jaggers, and Will H. Moore (1989). *Polity II: Political Structures and Regime Change, 1800–1986*. Ann Arbor, MI. Inter-University Consortium for Political and Social Research.

Haas, Ernst B. (1958). *The Uniting of Europe*. Palo Alto, CA. Stanford University Press.

—— (1964). *Beyond the Nation State: Functionalism and International Organization*. Palo Alto, CA. Stanford University Press.

Habib, Adam, and Vishnu Padayachee (2000). "Economic Policy and Power Relations in South Africa's Transition to Democracy." *World Development* 28(2): 245–63.

Hafner-Burton, Emilie M. (2005). "Trading Human Rights: How Preferential Trade Agreements Influence Government Repression." *International Organization* 59(3): 593–627.

—— (2009). *Forced to be Good: Why Trade Agreements Boost Human Rights*. Ithaca, NY. Cornell University Press.

Haggard, Stephan (1997). "Regionalism in Asia and the Americas." In *The Political Economy of Regionalism*. Edward D. Mansfield and Helen V. Milner, eds. New York. Columbia University Press: 20–49.

Hale, Thomas (2009). "The de Facto Preferential Trade Agreement in East Asia" (unpublished manuscript). Princeton University.

Hallerberg, Mark (2002). "Veto Players and Monetary Commitment Technologies." *International Organization* 56(4): 775–802.

Hathaway, Oona (1998). "Positive Feedback." *International Organization* 52(3): 575–612.

Hawkins, Darren, David A. Lake, Daniel Nielson, and Michael Tierney, eds. (2006). *Delegation and Agency in International Organizations*. New York. Cambridge University Press.

Hayes, Jarrod (2008). Structural Indeterminacy? The Effect of Japanese Electoral Reform on Economic Foreign Policy. Presented at the annual meeting of the International Studies Association, San Francisco, CA.

Henisz, Witold J. (2000). "The Institutional Environment for Multinational Investment." *Journal of Law, Economics, and Organization* 16(2): 334–64.

—— (2002). "The Institutional Environment for Infrastructure Investment." *Industrial and Corporate Change* 11(2): 355–89.

Henisz, Witold J., and Edward D. Mansfield (2006). "Votes and Vetoes: The Political Determinants of Commercial Openness." *International Studies Quarterly* 50(1): 189–212.

Hentz, James J. (2005). "South Africa and the Political Economy of Regional Cooperation in Southern Africa." *Journal of Modern African Studies* 43(1): 21–51.

Herrmann, Richard K., Philip E. Tetlock, and Matthew N. Diascro (2001). "How Americans Think about Trade: Reconciling Conflicts among Money, Power, and Principles." *International Studies Quarterly* 45(2): 191–218.

Hicks, Raymond, Helen V. Milner, and Dustin Tingley (2008). Globalization and Domestic Politics: Sources of Preferences of CAFTA-DR in Costa Rica. Presented at the annual meeting of the International Political Economy Society, Philadelphia, PA.

Hillman, Arye L. (1982). "Declining Industries and Political-Support Protectionist Motives." *American Economic Review* 72(5): 1180–90.

Hirschman, Albert O. (1980 [1945]). *National Power and the Structure of Foreign Trade.* Berkeley, CA. University of California Press.

Hirst, Monica (1988). "El Programa de Integración Argentina-Brasil: de la Formulación a la Implementación." *FLACSO Document no. 67.* Buenos Aires (Argentina). Facultad Latinoamericana de Ciencias Sociales.

Hiscox, Michael J. (2002). *International Trade and Political Conflict: Commerce, Coalitions, and Mobility.* Princeton, NJ. Princeton University Press.

Hitt, Greg, Christopher Conkey, and Jose De Cordoba (2009). "Mexico Strikes Back in Trade Spat." *Wall Street Journal.* March 17, 2009: A1.

Hocking, Brian, and Steven McGuire, eds. (1999). *Trade Politics.* London (UK). Routledge.

Hoekman, Bernard, and Michel Kostecki (2001). *The Political Economy of the World Trading System.* New York. Oxford University Press.

Holzman, Franklyn D. (1976). *International Trade Under Communism: Politics and Economics.* New York. Basic Books.

Horn, Henrik, Petros C. Mavroidis, and Andre Sapir (2010). "Beyond the WTO? An Anatomy of EU and US Preferential Trade Agreements." *World Economy* 33(11): 1565–88.

Hufbauer, Gary C., and Jeffrey Schott (2009). "Fitting Asia-Pacific Agreements into the WTO System." In *Multilateralizing Regionalism: Challenges for the Global Trading System.* Richard E. Baldwin and Patrick Low, eds. New York. Cambridge University Press: 554–636.

Huntington, Samuel P. (1991). *The Third Wave: Democratization in the Late Twentieth Century.* Norman, OK. Oklahoma University Press.

Hussein, Zarir (1999). "Storm Brewing in Indian Tea Industry over Imports from Neighbours." *Agence France-Presse.* February 19, 1999.

Hyde, Susan, and Nikolay Marinov (2010). "National Elections Across Democracy and Autocracy: Which Elections Can Be Lost?" (unpublished manuscript). New Haven, CT. Yale University.

Inside U.S. Trade (2011). "DeFazio Withholds Judgment On Trucks Proposal, But Wants A Solution." 29(2): 5–6.

International Monetary Fund (2010). *Direction of Trade Statistics.* Washington, DC. International Monetary Fund.

—— (various years and cd-rom). *International Financial Statistics.* Washington, DC. International Monetary Fund.

Irwin, Douglas A. (1993). "Multilateral and Bilateral Trade Policies in the World Trading System: An Historical Perspective." In *New Dimensions in Regional Integration.* Jaime de Melo and Arvind Panagariya, eds. New York. Cambridge University Press: 90–127.

—— (1996). "Industry or Class Cleavages over Trade Policy." In *The Political Economy of Trade Policy.* Robert C. Feenstra, Gene M. Grossman, and Douglas A. Irwin, eds. Cambridge, MA. MIT Press: 53–75.

ISSP Research Group (1995). International Social Survey Programme (ISSP): National Identity I. Cologne (Germany), GESIS Data Archive.

—— (2003). International Social Survey Programme (ISSP): National Identity II. Cologne (Germany), GESIS Data Archive.

Jaggers, Keith, and Ted Robert Gurr (1995). "Tracking Democracy's Third Wave with the Polity III Data." *Journal of Peace Research* 32(4): 469–82.

Jalan, Prateek (1999). "The Indian Parliamentary Elections of 1998." *Electoral Studies* 18(1): 124–27.

James, Harold (2001). *The End of Globalization: Lessons from the Great Depression.* Cambridge, MA. Harvard University Press.

Jayasinghe, Amal (1999a). "India Backtracks on Trade Accord with Sri Lanka." *Agence France-Presse.* March 2, 1999.

—— (1999b). "Free Trade Treaty Totters as India - Sri Lanka Talks Deadlock." *Agence France-Presse.* April 11, 1999.

Jervis, Robert (1978). "Cooperation under the Security Dilemma." *World Politics* 30(2): 167–214.

—— (1997). *System Effects: Complexity in Political and Social Life.* Princeton, NJ. Princeton University Press.

Johnson, Harry (1965). *The World Economy at the Crossroads.* Oxford (UK). Clarendon Press.

Jones, Daniel M., Stuart A Bremer, and David Singer (1996). "Militarized Interstate Dispute, 1816–1992: Rationale, Coding Rules, and Empirical Patterns." *Conflict Management and Peace Science* 15(2): 163–213.

Jones, Mark P. (1997). "Evaluating Argentina's Presidential Democracy: 1983–1995." In *Presidentialism and Democracy in Latin America.* Scott Mainwaring and Matthew S. Shugart, eds. New York. Cambridge University Press: 259–99.

Kaltenthaler, Karl, and Frank O. Mora (2002). "Explaining Latin American Economic Integration: the Case of Mercosur." *Review of International Political Economy* 9(1): 72–97.

Katada, Saori N., and Mireya Solis, eds. (2008). *Cross Regional Trade Agreements: Understanding Permeated Regionalism in East Asia.* Berlin (Germany). Springer.

Katzenstein, Peter J., ed. (1978). *Between Power and Plenty: Foreign Economic Policies of Advanced Industrial States.* Madison, WI. University of Wisconsin Press.

Keefer, Philip (2004). "What Does Political Economy Tell Us about Economic Development – and Vice Versa?" *Annual Review of Political Science* 7(1): 247–72.

Keefer, Philip, and David Stasavage (2003). "The Limits of Delegation: Veto Players, Central Bank Independence, and the Credibility of Monetary Policy." *American Political Science Review* 97(3): 407–23.

Kenwood, A. G., and A. L. Lougheed (1971). *The Growth of the International Economy 1820–1960.* London (UK). George Allen & Unwin.

Keohane, Robert O. (1984). *After Hegemony: Cooperation and Discord in the World Political Economy.* Princeton, NJ. Princeton University Press.

Keohane, Robert O., Stephen Macedo, and Andrew Moravcsik (2009). "Democracy-Enhancing Multilateralism." *International Organization* 63(1): 1–31.

Keynes, John Maynard (1919). *The Economic Consequences of the Peace.* London (UK). Macmillan.

Khandelwal, Padamja (2003). "COMESA and SADC: Prospects and Challenges for Regional Trade Integration." *IMF Working Paper 04/227.* Washington, DC. International Monetary Fund.

Kiewiet, D. Roderick (1983). *Macroeconomics & Micropolitics: The Electoral Effects of Economic Issues.* Chicago. University of Chicago Press.

Kim, Hong Nack (2000). "The 2000 Parliamentary Election in South Korea." *Asian Survey* 40(6): 894–913.

Kindleberger, Charles P. (1973). *The World in Depression*. Berkeley. University of California Press.

—— (1975). "The Rise of Free Trade in Western Europe." *Journal of Economic History* 35(1): 20–55.

King, Gary (1989). *Unifying Political Methodology: The Likelihood Theory of Statistical Inference*. New York. Cambridge University Press.

King, Gary, James Honaker, Anne Joseph, and Kenneth Scheve (2001). "Analyzing Incomplete Political Science Data: An Alternative Algorithm for Multiple Imputation." *American Political Science Review* 95(1): 49–69.

King, Gary, and Langche Zeng (2001). "Logistic Regression in Rare Events Data." *Political Analysis* 9(2): 137–63.

King, Neil, Jr. (2002). "Errant Shot? So far, Steel Tariffs do Little of what President Envisioned." *Wall Street Journal*. September 13, 2002: A1.

König, Thomas (2007). "Divergence or Convergence? From Ever-Growing to Ever-Slowing European Legislative Decision Making." *European Journal of Political Research* 46(3): 417–44.

—— (2008). "Analysing the Process of EU Legislative Decision-Making: To Make a Long Story Short." *European Union Politics* 9(1): 145–65.

Kono, Daniel Y. (2006). "Optimal Obfuscation: Democracy and Trade Policy Transparency." *American Political Science Review* 100(3): 369–84.

—— (2007). "Making Anarchy Work: International Legal Institutions and Trade Cooperation." *Journal of Politics* 69(3): 746–59.

Koremenos, Barbara, Charles Lipson, and Duncan Snidal (2001). "Rational Designs: Explaining the Form of International Institutions." *International Organization* 55(4): 1–32.

—— eds. (2004). *The Rational Design of International Institutions*. Cambridge (UK). Cambridge University Press.

Kornai, Janos (1992). *The Socialist System: The Political Economy of Communism*. Princeton, NJ. Princeton University Press.

Kramer, Gerald H. (1971). "Short-Term Fluctuations in U.S. Voting Behavior, 1896–1964." *American Political Science Review* 65(1): 131–43.

Krasner, Stephen D. (1976). "State Power and the Structure of International Trade." *World Politics* 28(3): 317–47.

—— ed. (1983). *International Regimes*. Ithaca, NY. Cornell University Press.

Krishna, Pravin (1998). "Regionalism and Multilateralism: A Political Economy Approach." *Quarterly Journal of Economics* 113(1): 227–52.

Krueger, Anne O. (1999). "Are Preferential Trading Arrangements Trade-Liberalizing or Protectionist?" *Journal of Economic Perspectives* 13(4): 105–24.

Krugman, Paul R. (1991). "The Move to Free Trade Zones." In *Policy Implications of Trade and Currency Zones*. Federal Reserve Bank of Kansas City, ed. Kansas City, MO. Federal Reserve Bank: 7–41.

—— (1993). "Regionalism versus Multilateralism: Analytical Notes." In *New Dimensions in Regional Integration*. Jaime de Melo and Arvind Panagariya, eds. New York. Cambridge University Press: 58–79.

Kurian, George T. (1992). *Encyclopedia of the Third World*. New York. Facts on File.

Kydland, Finn E., and Edward C. Prescott (1977). "Rules Rather than Discretion: The Inconsistency of Optimal Plans." *Journal of Political Economy* 85(3): 473–91.

Ladewig, Jeffrey W. (2006). "Domestic Influences on International Trade Policy: Factor Mobility in the United States, 1963 to 1992." *International Organization* 60(1): 69–103.

Lagos, Marta (1995–98). Latinobarometro. Santiago (Chile), Latinobarometro Corporation.

—— (2000–08). Latinobarometro. Santiago (Chile), Latinobarometro Corporation.

Lakatos, Imre (1974). "Falsification and the Methodology of Scientific Research Programmes." In *Criticism and the Growth of Knowledge: Proceedings of the International Colloquium in the Philosophy of Science, 1965.* Imre Lakatos and Alan Musgrave, eds. Cambridge (UK). Cambridge University Press. Vol. 4: 91–196.

Lakatos, Imre, ed. (1978). *The Methodology of Scientific Research Programmes.* Philosophical Papers Vol. 1. Cambridge (UK). Cambridge University Press.

Lake, David A. (1988). *Power, Protectionism, and Free Trade: International Sources of U.S. Commercial Strategy.* Ithaca, NY. Cornell University Press.

—— (1992). "Powerful Pacifists: Democratic States and War." *American Political Science Review* 86(1): 24–37.

—— (2009). "Open Economy Politics: A Critical Review." *Review of International Organizations* 4(3): 219–44.

Lampe, Markus (2009). "Effects of Bilateralism and the MFN Clause on International Trade: Evidence for the Cobden-Chevalier Network, 1860–1875." *Journal of Economic History* 69(4): 1012–40.

Lane, Philip R. (1999). "What Determines the Nominal Exchange Rate? Some Cross-Sectional Evidence." *Canadian Journal of Economics* 32(1): 118–38.

Lawrence, Robert Z. (1996). *Regionalism, Multilateralism, and Deeper Integration.* Washington, DC. Brookings Institution Press.

Lazer, David (1999). "The Free Trade Epidemic of the 1860s and Other Outbreaks of Economic Discrimination." *World Politics* 51(4): 447–83.

Lee, Seungjoo, and Chung-in Moon (2008). "South Korea's Regional Economic Cooperation Policy: The Evolution of an Adaptive Strategy." In *Northeast Asia: Ripe for Integration?* Vinod K. Aggarwal, Min Gyo Koo, Seungjoo Lee, and Chung-in Moon, eds. Berlin (Germany). Springer: 37–61.

Leeds, Brett Ashley (1999). "Domestic Political Institutions, Credible Commitments, and International Cooperation." *American Journal of Political Science* 43(4): 979–1002.

Leeds, Brett Ashley, Jeffrey Ritter, Sara Mitchell, and Andrew Long (2002). "Alliance Treaty Obligations and Provisions, 1815–1944." *International Interactions* 28(3): 237–60.

Leiras, Marcelo, and Hernan Soltz (2006). "The Political Economy of International Trade Policy in Argentina." In *Domestic Determinants of National Trade Strategies: A Comparative Analysis of MERCOSUR Countries, Mexico and Chile.* Roberto Bouzas, ed. Paris (France). Chaire Mercosur de Sciences Po: 45–84.

Lesbirel, S. Hayden (1987). "The Political Economy of Project Delay." *Policy Sciences* 20(2): 153–71.

Lewis-Beck, Michael S. (1988). *Economics and Elections: The Major Western Democracies.* Ann Arbor, MI. University of Michigan Press.

Lewis, David, Kabelo Reed, and Ethel Teljeur (2004). "South Africa: Economic Policy-Making and Implementation in Africa: A Study of Strategic Trade and Selective

Industrial Policies." In *The Politics of Trade and Industrial Policy in Africa: Force Consensus?* Charles Soludo, Osita Ogbu, and Ha-Joon Change, eds. Ottawa. International Development Research Centre: 151–78.

Lewis, Jeffrey D. (2002). "Promoting Growth and Employment in South Africa." *South African Journal of Economics* 70(4): 338–58.

Lewis, Jeffrey D., Sherman Robinson, and Karen Thierfelder (1999). "After the Negotiations: Assessing the Impact of Free Trade Agreements in Southern Africa." *IFPRI, TMD Discussion Paper No. 46.* Washington, DC. International Food Policy Research Institute.

Lieberthal, Kenneth (2004). *Governing China: From Revolution through Reform.* New York. W. W. Norton.

Limão, Nuno (2005). "Trade Policy, Cross-Border Externalities and Lobbies: Do Linked Agreements Enforce More Cooperative Outcomes?" *Journal of International Economics* 67(1): 175–99.

Lindberg, Leon N. (1963). *The Political Dynamics of European Economic Integration.* Palo Alto, CA. Stanford University Press.

Lohmann, Susanne (2003). "Why Do Institutions Matter? An Audience-Cost Theory of Institutional Commitment." *Governance* 16(1): 95–110.

Machlup, Fritz (1977). *A History of Thought on Economic Integration.* New York. Columbia University Press.

Maddala, G. S. (1983). *Limited-Dependent and Qualitative Variables in Econometrics.* New York. Cambridge University Press.

Magee, Christopher S. P. (2008). "New Measures of Trade Creation and Trade Diversion." *Journal of International Economics* 75(2): 349–62.

Magee, Stephen P., William A. Brock, and Leslie Young (1989). *Black Hole Tariffs and Endogenous Policy Theory.* Cambridge (UK). Cambridge University Press.

Maggi, Giovanni (1999). "The Role of Multilateral Institutions in International Trade." *American Economic Review* 89(1): 190–214.

Maggi, Giovanni, and Andrés Rodríguez-Clare (1998). "The Value of Trade Agreements in the Presence of Political Pressures." *Journal of Political Economy* 106(3): 574–601.

——— (2007). "A Political-Economy Theory of Trade Agreements." *American Economic Review* 97(4): 1374–406.

Mainwaring, Scott (1997). "Multipartism, Robust Federalism, and Presidentialism in Brazil." In *Presidentialism and Democracy in Latin America.* Scott Mainwaring and Matthew S. Shugart, eds. New York. Cambridge University Press: 55–109.

Manger, Mark (2005). "Competition and Bilateralism in Trade Policy: The Case of Japan's Free Trade Agreements." *Review of International Political Economy* 12(5): 804–28.

——— (2009). *Investing in Protection: The Politics of Preferential Trade Agreements between North and South.* New York. Cambridge University Press.

Manow, Philip, and Simone Burkhart (2008). "Delay as a Political Technique under Divided Government? Empirical Evidence from Germany, 1976–2005." *German Politics* 17(3): 353–66.

Mansfield, Edward D. (1993). "Effects of International Politics on Regionalism in International Trade." In *Regional Integration and the Global Trading System.* Kym Anderson and Richard Blackhurst, eds. New York. Harvester Wheatsheaf: 199–217.

——— (1998). "The Proliferation of Preferential Trading Arrangements." *Journal of Conflict Resolution* 42(5): 523–43.

Mansfield, Edward D., and Marc L. Busch (1995). "The Political Economy of Nontariff Barriers: A Cross-National Analysis." *International Organization* 49(4): 723–49.

Mansfield, Edward D., and Helen V. Milner (1999). "The New Wave of Regionalism." *International Organization* 53(3): 589–627.

Mansfield, Edward D., Helen V. Milner, and Jon C. Pevehouse (2007). "Vetoing Co-Operation: The Impact of Veto Players on Preferential Trading Arrangements." *British Journal of Political Science* 37(3): 403–32.

——— (2008). "Democracy, Veto Players and the Depth of Regional Integration." *World Economy* 31(1): 67–96.

Mansfield, Edward D., Helen V. Milner, and B. Peter Rosendorff (2000). "Free to Trade: Democracies, Autocracies and International Trade." *American Political Science Review* 94(2): 305–21.

——— (2002). "Why Democracies Cooperate More: Electoral Control and International Trade Agreements." *International Organization* 56(3): 477–513.

Mansfield, Edward D., and Jon C. Pevehouse (2000). "Trade Blocs, Trade Flows, and International Conflict." *International Organization* 54(4): 775–808.

——— (forthcoming). "The Expansion of Preferential Trading Arrangements." *International Studies Quarterly*.

Mansfield, Edward D., Jon C. Pevehouse, and David H. Bearce (1999). "Preferential Trading Arrangements and Military Disputes." *Security Studies* 9(1–2): 92–118.

Mansfield, Edward D., and Eric Reinhardt (2003). "Multilateral Determinants of Regionalism: The Effects of GATT/WTO on the Formation of Preferential Trading Arrangements." *International Organization* 57(4): 829–62.

Mansfield, Edward D., and Jack Snyder (2005). *Electing to Fight: Why Emerging Democracies Go to War.* Cambridge, MA. MIT Press.

Mansfield, Edward D., and Etel Solingen (2010). "Regionalism." *Annual Review of Political Science* 13(1): 145–63.

Manzetti, Luigi (1993). "The Political Economy of Mercosur." *Journal of Interamerican Studies and World Affairs* 35(4): 101–41.

Marshall, Monty, and Keith Jaggers (2005). "Polity IV Project: Political Regime Characteristics and Transitions, 1800–2007." Integrated Network for Societal Conflict Research (INSCR) Program, Center International Development and Conflict Management (CIDCM), University of Maryland. http://www.systemicpeace.org/polity/polity4.htm. (Last accessed May 1, 2009.)

Martin, Lanny W., and Georg Vanberg (2003). "Wasting Time? The Impact of Ideology and Size on Delay in Coalition Formation." *British Journal of Political Science* 33(2): 323–32.

Martin, Lisa L. (1992). *Coercive Cooperation: Explaining Multilateral Economic Sanctions.* Princeton, NJ. Princeton University Press.

——— (2000). *Democratic Commitments: Legislatures and International Cooperation.* Princeton, NJ. Princeton University Press.

Mattli, Walter (1999). *The Logic of Regional Integration: Europe and Beyond.* New York. Cambridge University Press.

McCalman, Phillip (2002). "Multi-Lateral Trade Negotiations and the Most Favored Nation Clause." *Journal of International Economics* 57(1): 151–76.

McGillivray, Fiona, and Alastair Smith (2004). "The Impact of Leadership Turnover on Trading Relations Between States." *International Organization* 58(3): 567–600.

—— (2008). *Punishing the Prince: A Theory of Interstate Relations, Political Institutions, and Leader Change.* Princeton, NJ. Princeton University Press.

McKeown, Timothy J. (1991). "A Liberal Trading Order? The Long-Run Pattern of Imports to the Advanced Capitalist States." *International Studies Quarterly* 35(2): 151–72.

McLaren, John (1997). "Size, Sunk Costs, and Judge Bowker's Objection to Free Trade." *American Economic Review* 87(3): 400–20.

Mettes, Robert, and Annie Chikwanha (2002). Afrobarometer: Round II Survey of South Africa, 2002. Ann Arbor, MI. Inter-University Consortium for Political and Social Research (ICPSR).

Michalopoulos, Constantine (2000). "The Role of Special and Differential Treatment for Developing Countries in GATT and the World Trade Organization." *World Bank Policy Research Working Paper No. 2388.* Washington, DC. World Bank.

Milner, Helen V. (1988). *Resisting Protectionism: Global Industries and the Politics of International Trade.* Princeton, NJ. Princeton University Press.

—— (1992). "International Theories of Cooperation Among Nations: Strengths and Weaknesses." *World Politics* 44(3): 466–96.

—— (1997a). *Interests, Institutions, and Information: Domestic Politics and International Relations.* Princeton, NJ. Princeton University Press.

—— (1997b). "Industries, Governments, and the Creation of Regional Trade Blocs." In *The Political Economy of Regionalism.* Edward D. Mansfield and Helen V. Milner, eds. New York. Columbia University Press: 77–106.

Milner, Helen V., and B. Peter Rosendorff (1997). "Democratic Politics and International Trade Negotiations: Elections and Divided Government as Constraints on Trade Liberalization." *Journal of Conflict Resolution* 41(1): 117–46.

Milner, Helen V., and Benjamin Judkins (2004). "Partisanship, Trade Policy and Globalization: Is There a Left-Right Party Divide on Trade Policy?" *International Studies Quarterly* 48(1): 95–119.

Milner, Helen V., and Keiko Kubota (2005). "Why the Move to Free Trade? Democracy and Trade Policy in the Developing Countries." *International Organization* 59(1): 107–43.

Milner, Helen V., and Bumba Mukherjee (2009). "Democratization and Economic Globalization." *Annual Review of Political Science* 12(1): 163–81.

Mitra, Devashish (2002). "Endogenous Political Organization and the Value of Trade Agreements." *Journal of International Economics* 57(2): 473–85.

Mitrany, David (1943). *A Working Peace System: An Argument for the Functional Development of International Organization.* London (UK). Royal Institute of International Affairs.

Moravcsik, Andrew (1998). *The Choice for Europe: Social Purpose and State Power from Messina to Maastricht.* Ithaca, NY. Cornell University Press.

Mulgan, Aurelia G. (2005). "Where Tradition Meets Change: Japan's Agricultural Politics in Transition." *Journal of Japanese Studies* 31(2): 261–98.

Nattrass, Nicoli (1994). "Politics and Economics in ANC Economic Policy." *African Affairs* 93(372): 343–59.

Neumayer, Eric (2002). "Does Trade Openness Promote Multilateral Environmental Cooperation?" *World Economy* 25(6): 815–32.

North, Douglass C., and Barry R. Weingast (1989). "Constitutions and Commitment: The Evolution of Institutions Governing Public Choice in Seventeenth-Century England." *Journal of Economic History* 49(4): 803–32.

Nye, John V. (1991). "Changing French Trade Conditions, National Welfare, and the 1860 Anglo-French Treaty of Commerce." *Explorations in Economic History* 28(4): 460–77.

Nye, Joseph S. (1971). *Peace in Parts: Integration and Conflict in Regional Organization.* Boston. Little, Brown.

——— (1988). "Neorealism and Neoliberalism." *World Politics* 40(2): 235–51.

Obstfeld, Maurice, and Kenneth Rogoff (1995). "The Intertemporal Approach to the Current Account." In *Handbook of International Economics.* Gene M. Grossman and Kenneth Rogoff, eds. San Diego, CA. Elsevier Science. Vol. 3: 1731–99.

Oelsner, Andrea (2003). "Two Sides of the Same Coin: Mutual Perceptions and Security Community in the Case of Argentina and Brazil." In *Comparative Regional Integration: Theoretical Perspectives.* Finn Laursen, ed. Burlington, VT. Ashgate Publishing Company: 185–206.

Olson, Mancur (1965). *The Logic of Collective Action.* Cambridge, MA. Harvard University Press.

Organisation for Economic Co-operation and Development (2001). *International Development Statistics.* Paris (France). OECD.

Organski, A.F.K., and Jacek Kugler (1980). *The War Ledger.* Chicago. University of Chicago Press.

Ornelas, Emanuel (2005). "Rent Destruction and the Political Viability of Free Trade Agreements." *Quarterly Journal of Economics* 120(4): 1475–506.

Ossa, Ralph (2011). "A 'New Trade' Theory of GATT/WTO Negotiations." *Journal of Political Economy* 119(1): 122–52.

Oye, Kenneth A. (1992). *Economic Discrimination and Political Exchange: World Political Economy in the 1930s and 1980s.* Princeton, NJ. Princeton University Press.

Özden, Çaglar, and Eric Reinhardt (2005). "The Perversity of Preferences: GSP and Developing Country Trade Policies, 1976–2000." *Journal of Development Economics* 78(1): 1–21.

Pahre, Robert (2008). *Politics and Trade Cooperation in the Nineteenth Century: The "Agreeable Customs" of 1815–1914.* New York. Cambridge University Press.

Panagariya, Arvind (2000). "Preferential Trade Liberalization: The Traditional Theory and New Developments." *Journal of Economic Literature* 38(2): 287–331.

Panagariya, Arvind, and Ronald Findlay (1996). "A Political-Economy Analysis of Free Trade Areas and Customs Unions." In *The Political Economy of Trade Reform.* Robert C. Feenstra, Gene M. Grossman, and Douglas A. Irwin, eds. Cambridge, MA. MIT Press: 265–88.

Park, Mi (2009). "Framing Free Trade Agreements: The Politics of Nationalism in the Anti-Neoliberal Globalization Movement in South Korea." *Globalizations* 6(4): 451–66.

Park, Seungjoo, and Chung-in Koo (2008). "Forming a Cross-Regional Partnership: The South Korea-Chile FTA and Its Implications." In *Cross Regional Trade Agreements: Understanding Permeated Regionalism in East Asia.* Saori N. Katada and Mireya Solis, eds. Berlin (Germany). Springer: 27–46.

Pekkanen, Saadia M., Mireya Solis, and Saori N. Katada (2007). "Trading Gains for Control: International Trade Forums and Japanese Economic Diplomacy." *International Studies Quarterly* 51(4): 945–70.

Perales, Jose R. (2003). "A Supply-Side Theory of International Economic Institutions for the Mercosur." In *Comparative Regional Integration: Theoretical Perspectives.* Finn Laursen, ed. Burlington, VT. Ashgate Publishing Company: 75–101.

Perroni, Carlo, and John Whalley (1996). "How Severe is Global Retaliation Risk under Increasing Regionalism?" *American Economic Review* 86(2): 57–61.

—— (2000). "The New Regionalism: Trade Liberalization or Insurance?" *Canadian Journal of Economics* 33(1): 1–24.

Pevehouse, Jon C. (2005). *Democracy from Above: Regional Organizations and Democratization*. Cambridge (UK). Cambridge University Press.

—— (2007). "Domestic Politics and the Design of International Cooperation" (*unpublished manuscript*). University of Chicago.

Pew Research Center for the People and the Press (2002). Pew/PSRAI Poll # 2002-44NAT: Global Attitudes Survey. Washington, DC.

—— (2003). Pew/PSRA Poll # 2003-21NAT: United Nations/Iraq/Democracy/Islam/United States/Middle East/Political Leaders/SARS. Washington, DC.

—— (2007). Pew Global Attitudes Project: Spring 2007 Survey – Survey of 47 Publics. Washington, DC.

—— (2008). Pew Research Center Poll: Global Attitudes Project 2008. Washington, DC.

Poast, Paul (2010). "(Mis)Using Dyadic Data to Analyze Multilateral Events." *Political Analysis* 18(4): 403–25.

Pollard, Sidney (1974). *European Economic Integration 1815–1970*. London (UK). Thames and Hudson.

Pollins, Brian M. (1996). "Global Political Order, Economic Change, and Armed Conflict: Coevolving Systems and the Use of Force." *American Political Science Review* 90(1): 103–17.

Pomfret, Richard (1988). *Unequal Trade: The Economics of Discriminatory International Trade Policies*. Oxford (UK). Basil Blackwell.

—— (2007). "Is Regionalism an Increasing Feature of the World Economy?" *World Economy* 30(6): 923–47.

Powell, G. Bingham (2000). *Elections as Instruments of Democracy: Majoritarian and Proportional Visions*. New Haven, CT. Yale University Press.

Powell, Robert (1999). *Bargaining in the Shadow of Power*. Princeton, NJ. Princeton University Press.

Prusa, Thomas J., and Robert Teh (2011). "Contingent Protection in Regional Trade Agreements." In *Preferential Trade Agreements: A Law and Economics Analysis*. Kyle Bagwell and Petros C. Mavroidis, eds. New York. Cambridge University Press: 60–100.

Przeworski, Adam, Michael Alvarez, Jose A. Cheibub, and Fernando Limongi (2000). *Democracy and Development: Political Institutions and Well-Being in the World, 1950–1990*. New York. Cambridge University Press.

Putnam, Robert D. (1988). "Diplomacy and Domestic Politics: The Logic of Two-Level Games." *International Organization* 42(3): 427–60.

Ravenhill, John (2003). "The New Bilateralism in the Asia Pacific." *Third World Quarterly* 24(2): 299–317.

Reif, Karlheinz, and Anna Melich (1988). Euro-Barometer 30: Immigrants and Out-Groups in Western Europe, October–November 1988. Ann Arbor, MI. Inter-University Consortium for Political and Social Research (ICPSR).

Reiter, Dan, and Allan C. Stam (2002). *Democracies at War*. Princeton, NJ. Princeton University Press.

Reuters (1998). "India, Sri Lanka Move Closer to Free Trade Pact." *Reuters*. December 18, 1998.

—— (1999a). "India State Opposes Plantation Import from S.Lanka." *Reuters*. February 13, 1999.

—— (1999b). "India, Sri Lanka Free Trade Deal Hits Snag." *Reuters*. March 3, 1999.

—— (2000). "India, S. Lanka Finalise Tea, Garment Trade Plans." *Reuters*. April 19, 2000.

Richardson, Martin (1993). "Endogenous Protection and Trade Diversion." *Journal of International Economics* 34(3–4): 309–24.

—— (1994). "Why a Free Trade Area? The Tariff Also Rises." *Economics and Politics* 6(1): 79–96.

Rodrik, Dani (1998). "Why Do More Open Economies Have Bigger Governments?" *Journal of Political Economy* 106(5): 997–1032.

Rogowski, Ronald (1987). "Political Cleavages and Changing Exposure to Trade." *American Political Science Review* 81(4): 1121–37.

—— (1989). *Commerce and Coalitions: How Trade Affects Domestic Political Alignments*. Princeton, NJ. Princeton University Press.

Rogowski, Ronald, and Mark Kayser (2002). "Majoritarian Electoral Systems and Consumer Power: Price-Level Evidence from OECD Countries." *American Journal of Political Science* 46(3): 526–39.

Romalis, John (2007). "NAFTA's and CUSFTA's Impact on International Trade." *Review of Economics and Statistics* 89(3): 416–35.

Rose, Andrew K. (2004). "Do We Really Know that the WTO Increases Trade?" *American Economic Review* 94(1): 98–114.

Rosendorff, B. Peter, and Helen V. Milner (2001). "The Optimal Design of International Trade Institutions: Uncertainty and Escape." *International Organization* 55(4): 829–57.

Russett, Bruce (1993). *Grasping the Democratic Peace: Principles for a Post–Cold War World*. Princeton, NJ. Princeton University Press.

Russett, Bruce, and John R. Oneal (2001). *Triangulating Peace: Democracy, Interdependence, and International Organizations*. New York. W. W. Norton.

SADC Barometer (2003). *Trading for Development?* Braamfontein (South Africa). South African Institute of International Affairs.

Sandholtz, Wayne, and Alec Stone-Sweet, eds. (1998). *European Integration and Supranational Governance*. New York. Oxford University Press.

Schattschneider, Elmer E. (1935). *Politics, Pressures and the Tariff*. New York. Prentice Hall.

Schelling, Thomas C. (1960). *The Strategy of Conflict*. Cambridge, MA. Harvard University Press.

Scheve, Kenneth F., and Matthew J. Slaughter (2001). "What Determines Individual Trade-Policy Preferences?" *Journal of International Economics* 54(2): 267–92.

Schiff, Maurice, and L. Alan Winters (1998). "Regional Integration as Diplomacy." *World Bank Economic Review* 12(2): 271–95.

Schonhardt-Bailey, Cheryl (1998). "Parties and Interests in the 'Marriage of Iron and Rye.'" *British Journal of Political Science* 28(2): 291–332.

—— (2006). *From the Corn Laws to Free Trade: Interests, Ideas, and Institutions in Historical Perspective*. Cambridge, MA. MIT Press.

Schultz, Kenneth A. (2001). *Democracy and Coercive Diplomacy*. Cambridge (UK). Cambridge University Press.

Schulz, Heiner, and Thomas König (2000). "Institutional Reform and Decision-Making Efficiency in the European Union." *American Journal of Political Science* 44(4): 653–66.

Schumpeter, Joseph A. (1976 [1942]). *Capitalism, Socialism, and Democracy*. New York. Harper Colophon.

Serra, Jaime, Guillermo Aguilar, José Córdoba, Gene Grossman, Carla Hills, John Jackson, Julius Katz, Pedro Noyola, and Michael Wilson (1997). *Reflections on Regionalism*. Washington, DC. Brookings Institution.

Sharpe, Samantha (1998). "Clotex Warns against Free Trade Area." *Business Day*. November 6, 1998.

Shepsle, Kenneth A. (1979). "Institutional Arrangements and Equilibria in Multidimensional Voting Models." *American Journal of Political Science* 23(1): 27–59.

——— (1989). "Studying Institutions: Some Lessons From the Rational Choice Approach." *Journal of Theoretical Politics* 1(2): 131–47.

Shih, Victor C. (2008). *Factions and Finance in China*. New York. Cambridge University Press.

Shirk, Susan L. (1993). *The Political Logic of Economic Reform in China*. Berkeley. University of California Press.

——— (2007). *China: Fragile Superpower*. New York. Oxford University Press.

Signorino, Curtis S., and Jeffrey M. Ritter (1999). "Tau-b or Not Tau-b: Measuring the Similarity of Foreign Policy Positions." *International Studies Quarterly* 43(1): 115–44.

Simmons, Beth A. (2009). *Mobilizing for Human Rights: International Law in Domestic Politics*. New York. Cambridge University Press.

Simmons, Beth A., Frank Dobbin, and Geoffrey Garrett (2006). "Introduction: The International Diffusion of Liberalism." *International Organization* 60(4): 781–810.

Simmons, Beth A., and Zachary Elkins (2004). "The Globalization of Liberalization: Policy Diffusion in the International Political Economy." *American Political Science Review* 98(1): 171–89.

Smith, James M. (2000). "The Politics of Dispute Settlement Design: Explaining the Legalism in Regional Trade Pacts." *International Organization* 54(1): 137–80.

Snyder, James M. Jr., and Michael M. Ting (2008). "Interest Groups and the Electoral Control of Politicians." *Journal of Public Economics* 92(3–4): 482–500.

Solingen, Etel (2008). "The Genesis, Design and Effects of Regional Institutions: Lessons from East Asia and the Middle East." *International Studies Quarterly* 52(2): 261–94.

Solis, Mireya (2003). "Japan's New Regionalism: The Politics of Free Trade Talks with Mexico." *Journal of East Asian Studies* 3(3): 377–404.

Staiger, Robert W., and Guido Tabellini (1999). "Do GATT Rules Help Governments Make Domestic Commitments?" *Economics and Politics* 11(2): 109–44.

Stone-Sweet, Alec, Wayne Sandholtz, and Neil Fligstein, eds. (2001). *The Institutionalization of Europe*. New York. Oxford University Press.

Summers, Lawrence H. (1991). "Regionalism and the World Trading System." In *Policy Implications of Trade and Currency Zones*. The Federal Reserve Bank of Kansas City, ed. Kansas City, MO. Federal Reserve Bank: 295–301.

Tang, Man-Keung, and Shang-Jin Wei (2009). "The Value of Making Commitments Externally: Evidence from WTO Accessions." *Journal of International Economics* 78(2): 216–29.

Tavares, José (2004). "Does Right or Left Matter? Cabinets, Credibility and Fiscal Adjustments." *Journal of Public Economics* 88(12): 2447–68.

Taylor, John B. (1983). "'Rules, Discretion and Reputation in a Model of Monetary Policy' by Robert J. Barro and David B. Gordon." *Journal of Monetary Economics* 12(1): 123–25.

Thies, Michael F. (2002). "The General Election in Japan, June 2000." *Electoral Studies* 21(1): 147–54.

Tieku, Thomas Kwasi (2004). "Explaining the Clash and Accomodation of Interests of Major Actors in the Creation of the African Union." *African Affairs* 103(411): 249–67.

Tomz, Michael (2007). "Domestic Audience Costs in International Relations: An Experimental Approach." *International Organization* 61(4): 821–40.

Tornell, Aaron (1991). "On the Ineffectiveness of Made-to-Measure Protectionist Programs." In *International Trade and Trade Policy*. Elhanan Helpmann and Assaf Razin, eds. Cambridge, MA. MIT Press: 66–79.

Tornell, Aaron, and Gerardo Esquivel (1997). "The Political Economy of Mexico's Entry into NAFTA." In *Regionalism versus Multilateral Trade Arrangements*. Takatoshi Ito and Anne O. Krueger, eds. Chicago. University of Chicago Press. Vol. 6: 25–56.

Tsebelis, George (1995). "Decision Making in Political Systems: Veto Players in Presidentialism, Parliamentarism, Multicameralism and Multipartyism." *British Journal of Political Science* 25(3): 289–325.

——— (2002). *Veto Players: How Political Institutions Work*. Princeton, NJ. Princeton University Press.

U.S. Central Intelligence Agency (2010). "The World Factbook." https://www.cia.gov/library/publications/the-world-factbook/index.html. (Last accessed June 30, 2010.)

U.S. Department of State (2010). "Background Notes." http://www.state.gov/r/pa/ei/bgn/. (Last accessed July 1, 2010.)

UCDP/PRIO (2009). "Armed Conflict Dataset v4-2008" Uppsala Conflict Data Program / International Peace Research Institute. http://www.prio.no/CSCW/Datasets/Armed-Conflict/UCDP-PRIO/Old-Versions/4-2007/. (Last accessed July 15, 2011.)

Van Long, Ngo, and Neil Vousden (1991). "Protectionist Responses and Declining Industries." *Journal of International Economics* 30(1–2): 87–103.

Vanden, Harry E., and Gary Prevost, eds. (2002). *Politics of Latin America: The Power Game*. New York. Oxford University Press.

Viner, Jacob (1950). *The Customs Union Issue*. New York. Carnegie Endowment for International Peace.

von Stein, Jana (2008). "The International Law and Politics of Climate Change: Ratification of the United Nations Framework Convention and the Kyoto Protocol." *Journal of Conflict Resolution* 52(2): 243–68.

Waltz, Kenneth N. (1979). *Theory of International Politics*. Reading, MA. Addison-Wesley.

Weart, Spencer R. (1998). *Never at War: Why Democracies Will Not Fight One Another*. New Haven, CT. Yale University Press.

Weeks, Jessica L. (2008). "Autocratic Audience Costs: Regime Type and Signaling Resolve." *International Organization* 62(1): 35–64.

Weerakoon, Dushni (2007). "Regional Economic Cooperation Under SAARC." In *India and South Asia: Economic Developments in the Age of Globalization*. Anjum Siddiqui, ed. Armonk, NY. M. E. Sharpe: 234–51.

Westhoff, Frank H., Beth V. Yarbrough, and Robert M. Yarbrough (1994). "Preferential Trade Agreements and the GATT: Can Bilateralism and Multilateralism Coexist?" *Kyklos* 47(2): 179–95.

Whalley, John (1993). "Regional Trade Agreements in North America: CUSTA and NAFTA." In *New Dimensions in Regional Integration*. Jaime de Melo and Arvind Panagariya, eds. Cambridge (UK). Cambridge University Press: 352–87.

——— (1998). "Why Do Countries Seek Regional Trade Agreements?" In *The Regionalism of the World Economy*. Jeffrey Frankel, ed. Chicago. University of Chicago Press: 63–89.

Williamson, Elizabeth (2011). "U.S., Mexico Agree to Settle Truck Feud." *Wall Street Journal*. March 4, 2011.

Winestock, Geoff, and Neil King Jr. (2002). "EU Aims at White House in Retaliation to Steel Tariffs—Product List Targets States Valuable to Republicans In Bid for House Control." *Wall Street Journal*. March 22, 2002: A2.

Wohlforth, William C. (1999). "The Stability of a Unipolar World." *International Security* 24(1): 5–41.

World Bank (2004). *Global Economic Prospects 2005: Trade, Regionalism and Development*. World Bank Global Economic Prospects Report, Washington, DC. The International Bank for Reconstruction and Development and The World Bank.

World Bank (2011). "World Development Indicators." World Bank. http://data.worldbank .org/data-catalog/world-development-indicators. (Last accessed February 9, 2011.)

World Trade Institute (2009). *TIDS Database*. Bern (Switzerland). University of Bern; World Trade Institute.

World Trade Organization (1995). *Regionalism and the World Trading System*. Geneva (Switzerland). WTO.

——— (2005). "International Trade Statistics 2005—Appendix tables" *International Trade Statistics*. WTO. http://www.wto.org/english/res_e/statis_e/its2005_e/appendix _e/a01.xls. (Last accessed July 26, 2011.)

——— (2006a). "Members and Observers." Understanding the WTO: The Organization. http://www.wto.org/english/thewto_e/whatis_e/tif_e/org6_e.htm. (Last accessed October 19, 2006.)

——— (2006b). "Transparency Mechanism for Regional Trade Agreements." http://www. wto.org/english/tratop_e/region_e/trans_mecha_e.htm. (Last accessed July 26, 2011.)

——— (2008). *World Trade Report 2008*. Geneva (Switzerland). WTO.

——— (2009). "Regional Trade Agreements – Information System (RTA-IS)." World Trade Organization – Regional Trade Agreements Section. http://rtais.wto.org/UI/ PublicMaintainRTAHome.aspx. (Last accessed June 24, 2009.)

——— (2011). *World Trade Report 2011*. Geneva (Switzerland). WTO.

Wright, Joseph (2008). "Do Authoritarian Institutions Constrain? How Legislatures Affect Economic Growth and Investment." *American Journal of Political Science* 52(2): 322–43.

Yarbrough, Beth V., and Robert M. Yarbrough (1992). *Cooperation and Governance in International Trade: The Strategic Organizational Approach*. Princeton, NJ. Princeton University Press.

——— (1997). "Dispute Settlement in International Trade: Regionalism and Procedural Coordination." In *The Political Economy of Regionalism*. Edward D. Mansfield and Helen V. Milner, eds. New York. Columbia University Press: 134–63.

Yoshimatsu, Hidetaka (2006). "The Politics of Japan's Free Trade Agreement." *Journal of Contemporary Asia* 36(4): 479–99.

Index

Accominotti, Olivier, and Marc Flandreau, 10
Act of Buenos Aires, 51
adjustment costs, 66, 137
adverse selection, 27
Africa, 1, 12, 31, 110
African Economic Community (AEC), 46,
    46n10, 48, 150
African National Congress (ANC), 46, 47,
    48, 49
Afrobarometer, 50
agriculture, 1, 59–60, 61, 62
Akaike Information Criterion (AIC), 147
Alfonsín, Raúl, 51–53, 55
alliances, 76–77, 111, 112–13, 157, 162
Alliance Treaty Obligations and Provisions
    (ATOP), 101, 104, 107, 111
Anglo-French Treaty of Commerce (1860),
    10, 11, 41
apartheid, 46, 47, 50
Arab Cooperation Council, 169
Arab Maghreb Union, 111
Argentina, 1, 50–55
Armenia, 150
Asia, 1, 58, 61, 110
Asia-Pacific region, 74
Association of Southeast Asian Nations
    (ASEAN), 5, 61, 133
Association of Southeast Asian Nations
    (ASEAN) plus three, 155
Australia, 111
Austria, 10, 11, 170
autocracies, 11, 22, 50; audience costs in, 134;
    and Brazil and Argentina, 51; and deeper
    integration agreements, 139; and dispute
    settlement mechanisms, 18, 139, 143; and
    elections, 15, 42; and exposure to trade,
    123, 130; governance structures of, 133–34;
    incentives of, 24, 44–45; informal ratifica-
    tion in, 57; information in, 44; and interest
    groups, 16, 42; and leaders, 15, 133; and
    likelihood of entering agreements, 4, 15, 16,
    18, 28, 45, 108, 132–37; measurement of,
    97–98; militarist, 133, 153; military/single-
    party, 134; personalistic, 133–34, 136, 153;

personalistic-military, 134; and political
    competition, 16, 45, 65, 69, 123, 132–37,
    145n15, 152, 153, 159; and protectionism, 2;
    reassurance of public by, 41–42; and rents,
    2; and shallow integration, 45; single-party,
    133, 134, 136–37, 153; single-party-military-
    personalistic, 134; single-party-
    personalistic, 134; and trade dependence,
    65, 153; and veto players, 17, 56, 57

Bagwell, Kyle, and Robert Staiger, 8, 24, 39n7,
    173
Baier, Scott L., and Jeffrey H. Bergstrand, 40
Baldwin, Richard, 8n6
Baldwin, Richard, and Dany Jaimovich, 103
Baltagi, Badi, et al., 9
bargaining costs, 24–25
Bauer, Raymond, Ithiel de Sola Pool, and
    Lewis Dexter, 166
Beck, Thorsten, et al., 99, 113
Belgium, 11
Benin, 150
Berlin Wall, collapse of, 76, 91, 102, 110, 111,
    143n13
Bhagwati, Jagdish, 8n6
Bharatiya Janata Party (BJP), 62, 63
bilateral agreements, 10, 74, 138
bilateral influences, 161
bilateral investment treaties (BITs), 159n1, 161
bilateral trade, 171–72
Bong, Youngshik, and Heon-Joo Jung, 59–60
Brazil, 1, 50–55
bribery, of veto players, 17, 56, 58, 95
Brunei, 61
Bueno de Mesquita, Bruce, et al., 124–25
Buenos Aires Act, 53
Bulgaria, 11
bureaucracy, 59, 60
Bush, George W., 34
businesses, 46n11, 48, 49, 52, 54, 60–61
Büthe, Tim, and Helen Milner, 9

Calderón, Felipe, 34
Canada, 1, 3, 31, 32, 96, 171